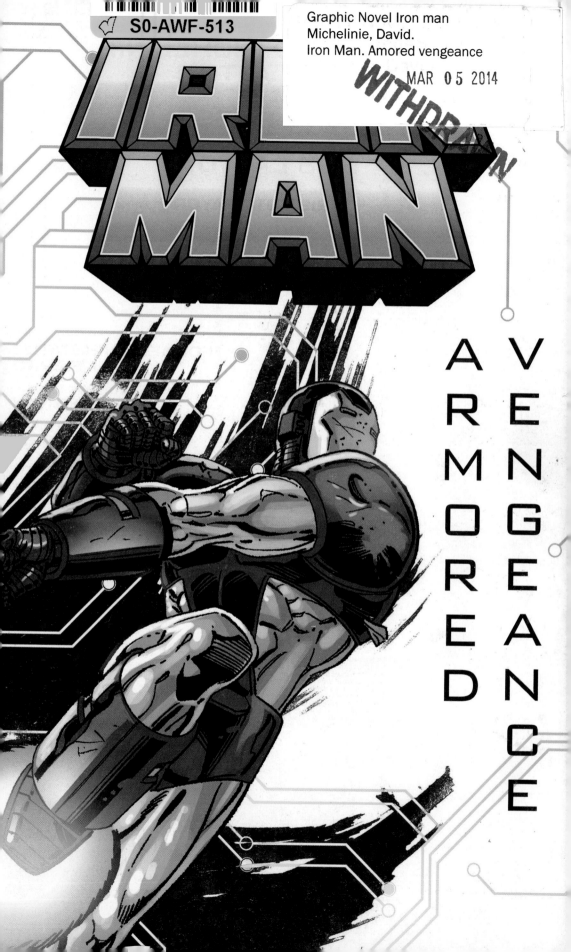

IRON MAN

ARMORED VENGEANCE

PLOT
DAVID MICHELINIE
BOB LAYTON

BREAKDOWN ART
DAVE ROSS

FINISHES
BOB LAYTON

COLORS
CHRIS SOTOMAYOR

LETTERS
DAVE LANPHEAR

COVER ART
DAVE ROSS, TOM PALMER
& CHRIS SOTOMAYOR

ASSISTANT EDITORS
MICHAEL CHRISTATOS
A.J. FIERRO

ASSOCIATE EDITOR
TOM BRENNAN

EDITOR
JUSTIN GABRIE

COLLECTION EDITOR & DESIGN
CORY LEVINE
ASSISTANT EDITORS
ALEX STARBUCK
NELSON RIBEIRO
EDITORS, SPECIAL PROJECTS
JENNIFER GRÜNWALD
MARK D. BEAZLEY
SENIOR EDITOR,
SPECIAL PROJECTS
JEFF YOUNGQUIST
SVP OF PRINT & DIGITAL
PUBLISHING SALES
DAVID GABRIEL

EDITOR IN CHIEF
AXEL ALONSO
CHIEF CREATIVE OFFICER
JOE QUESADA
PUBLISHER
DAN BUCKLEY
EXECUTIVE PRODUCER
ALAN FINE

IRON MAN: ARMORED VENGEANCE. Contains material originally published in magazine form as IRON MAN #258.1-258.4. First printing 2013. ISBN# 978-0-7851-5164-7. Published by MARVEL WORLDWIDE, INC., a subsidiary of MARVEL ENTERTAINMENT, LLC. OFFICE OF PUBLICATION: 135 West 50th Street, New York, NY 10020. Copyright © 2013 Marvel Characters, Inc. All rights reserved. All characters featured in this issue and the distinctive names and likenesses thereof, and all related indicia are trademarks of Marvel Characters, Inc. No similarity between any of the names, characters, persons, and/or institutions in this magazine with those of any living or dead person or institution is intended, and any such similarity which may exist is purely coincidental. **Printed in the U.S.A.** ALAN FINE, EVP - Office of the President, Marvel Worldwide, Inc. and EVP & CMO Marvel Characters B.V.; DAN BUCKLEY, Publisher & President - Print, Animation & Digital Divisions; JOE QUESADA, Chief Creative Officer; TOM BREVOORT, SVP of Publishing; DAVID BOGART, SVP of Operations & Procurement, Publishing; C.B. CEBULSKI, SVP of Creator & Content Development; DAVID GABRIEL, SVP of Print & Digital Publishing Sales; JIM O'KEEFE, VP of Operations & Logistics; DAN CARR, Executive Director of Publishing Technology; SUSAN CRESPI, Editorial Operations Manager; ALEX MORALES, Publishing Operations Manager; STAN LEE, Chairman Emeritus. For information regarding advertising in Marvel Comics or on Marvel.com, please contact Niza Disla, Director of Marvel Partnerships, at ndisla@ marvel.com. For Marvel subscription inquiries, please call 800-217-9158. **Manufactured between 8/16/2013 and 9/23/2013 by R.R. DONNELLEY, INC., SALEM, VA, USA.**

10 9 8 7 6 5 4 3 2 1

_258.1

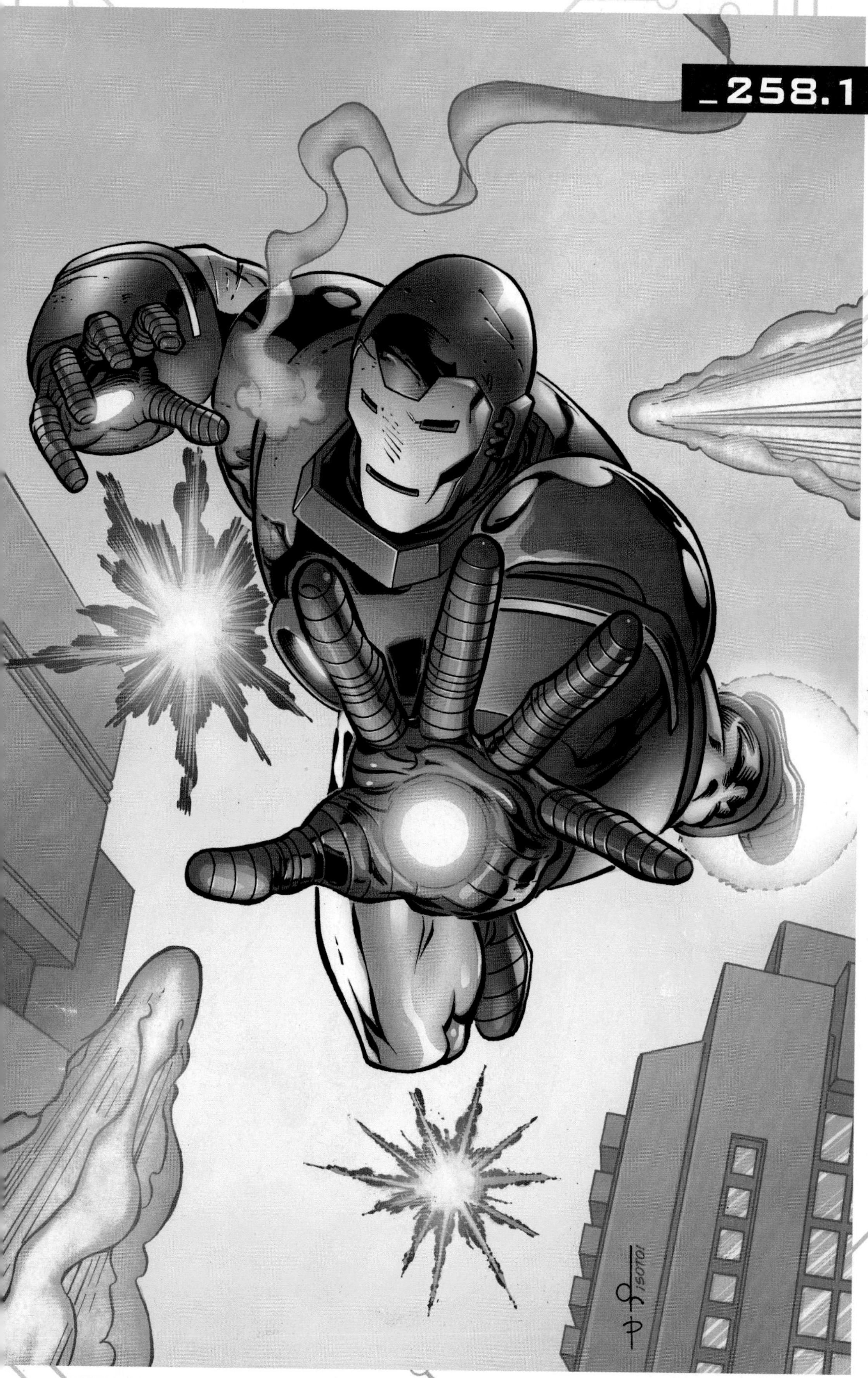

_258.1
VARIANT BY BOB LAYTON
& MARIE JAVINS

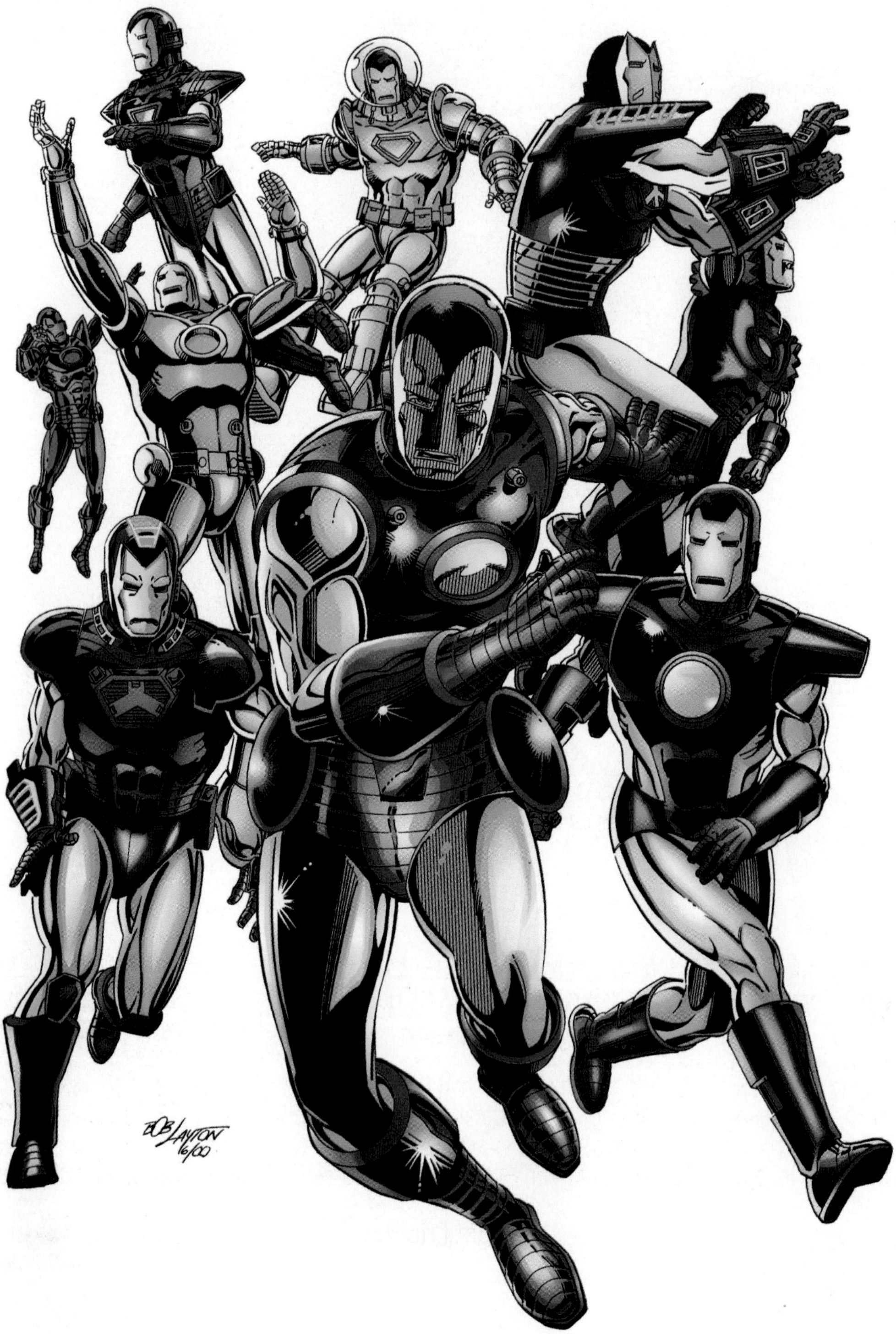
BOB LAYTON
6/00

Billionaire industrialist Tony Stark suffered a severe chest injury during a kidnapping in which his captors attempted to force him to build a weapon of mass destruction. He instead created a powered suit of armor to save his life and escape captivity. He later turned to that suit to protect the world as the invincible...

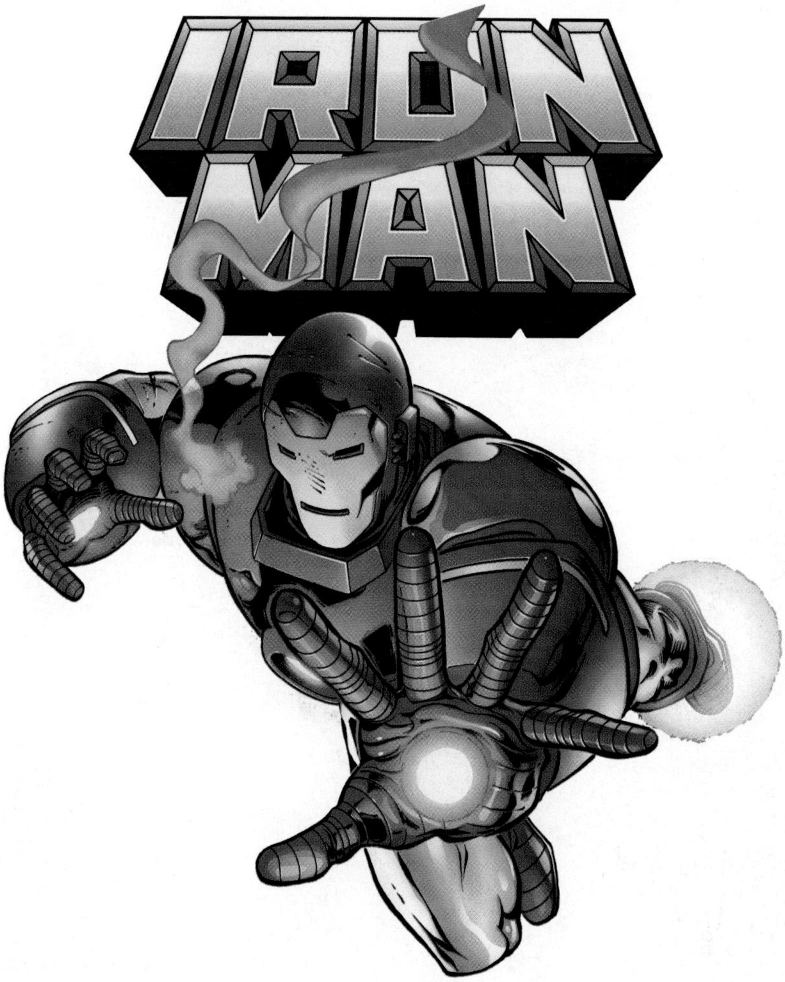
IRON MAN

DATELINE July 1990! The economies of Eastern Germany and Western Germany begin merging during the German reunification! Martina Navratilova wins the 1990 Wimbledon Championships – Women singles division! And feisty publishing powerhouse Marvel Comics publishes IRON MAN #258, part one of the Armor Wars II story by John Byrne and John Romita Jr. While a terrific story in its own right, Armor Wars II was a follow-up to the seminal Armor Wars tale, written by David Michelinie and Bob Layton. Those two legendary creators, who have left an indelible mark on Marvel History and that of Iron Man in particular, have never had a chance to revisit the world of Armor Wars.

Until now.

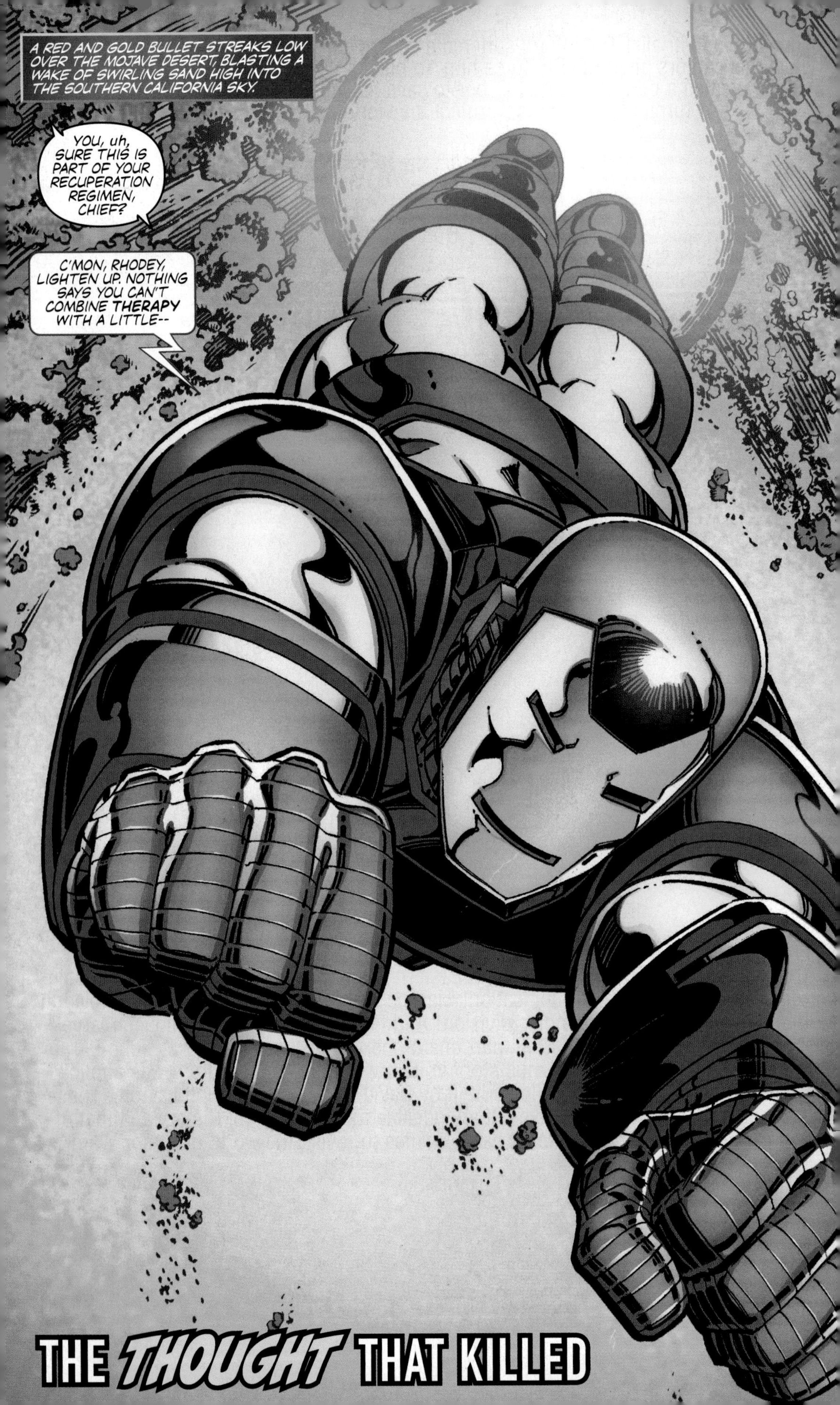

A RED AND GOLD BULLET STREAKS LOW OVER THE MOJAVE DESERT, BLASTING A WAKE OF SWIRLING SAND HIGH INTO THE SOUTHERN CALIFORNIA SKY.
YOU, uh, SURE THIS IS PART OF YOUR RECUPERATION REGIMEN, CHIEF?
C'MON, RHODEY, LIGHTEN UP. NOTHING SAYS YOU CAN'T COMBINE THERAPY WITH A LITTLE--
THE THOUGHT THAT KILLED

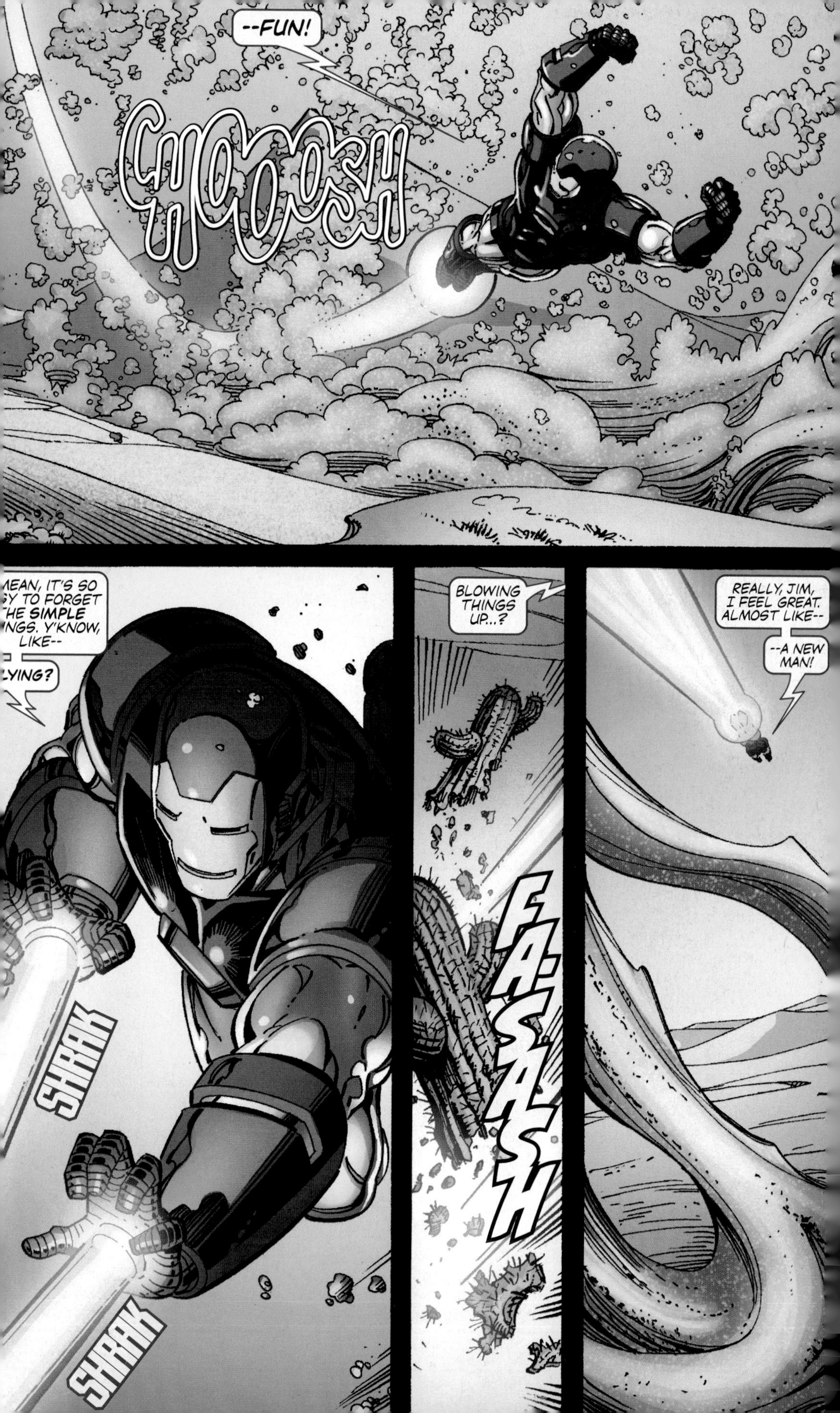
--FUN!
CHOOOSH
MEAN, IT'S SO
GY TO FORGET
THE SIMPLE
NGS. Y'KNOW,
LIKE--
LYING?
SHRAK
SHRAK
BLOWING
THINGS
UP...?
FA-SASH
REALLY, JIM,
I FEEL GREAT.
ALMOST LIKE--
--A NEW
MAN!

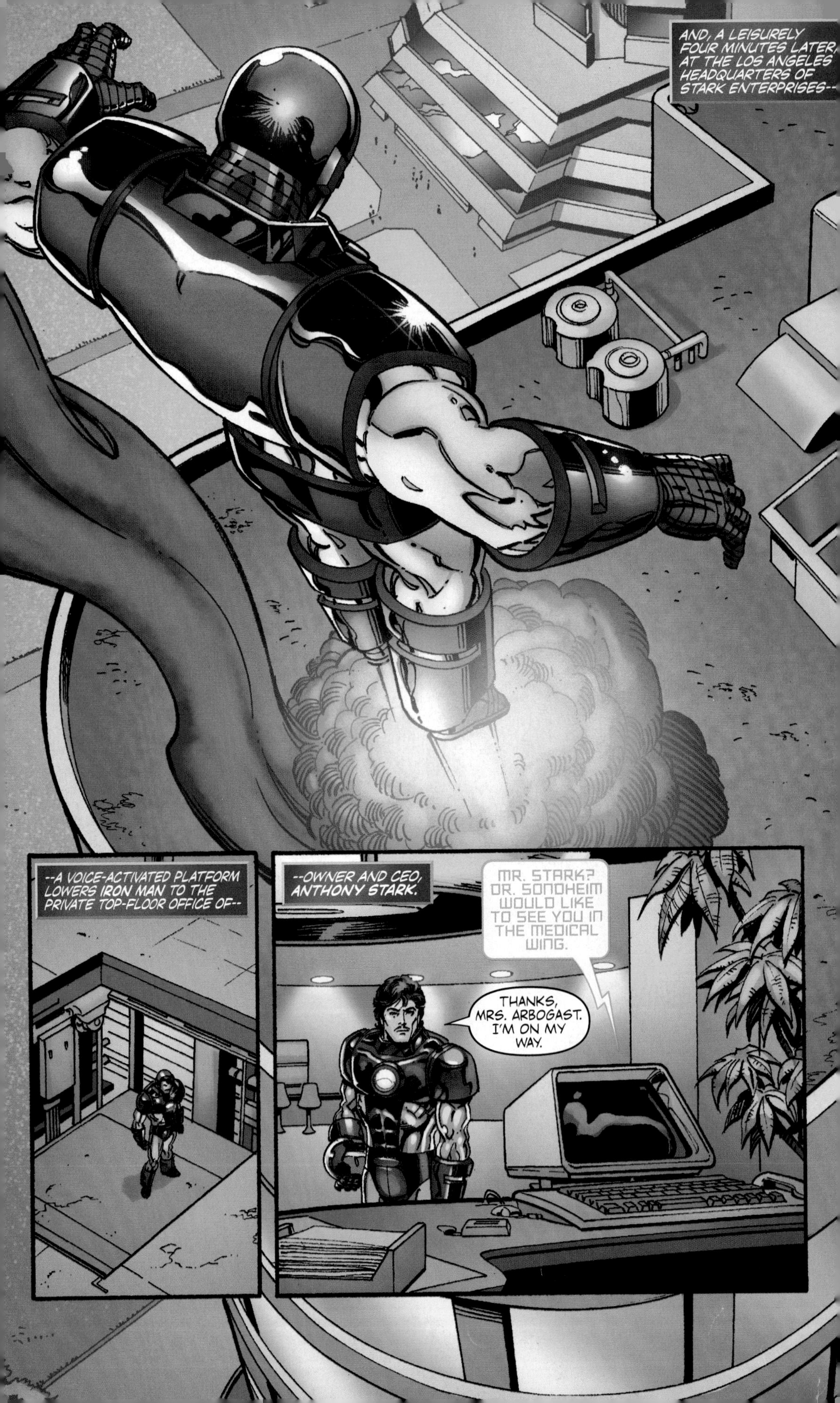
AND, A LEISURELY FOUR MINUTES LATER, AT THE LOS ANGELES HEADQUARTERS OF STARK ENTERPRISES--
--A VOICE-ACTIVATED PLATFORM LOWERS IRON MAN TO THE PRIVATE TOP-FLOOR OFFICE OF--
--OWNER AND CEO, ANTHONY STARK.
MR. STARK? DR. SONDHEIM WOULD LIKE TO SEE YOU IN THE MEDICAL WING.
THANKS, MRS. ARBOGAST. I'M ON MY WAY.

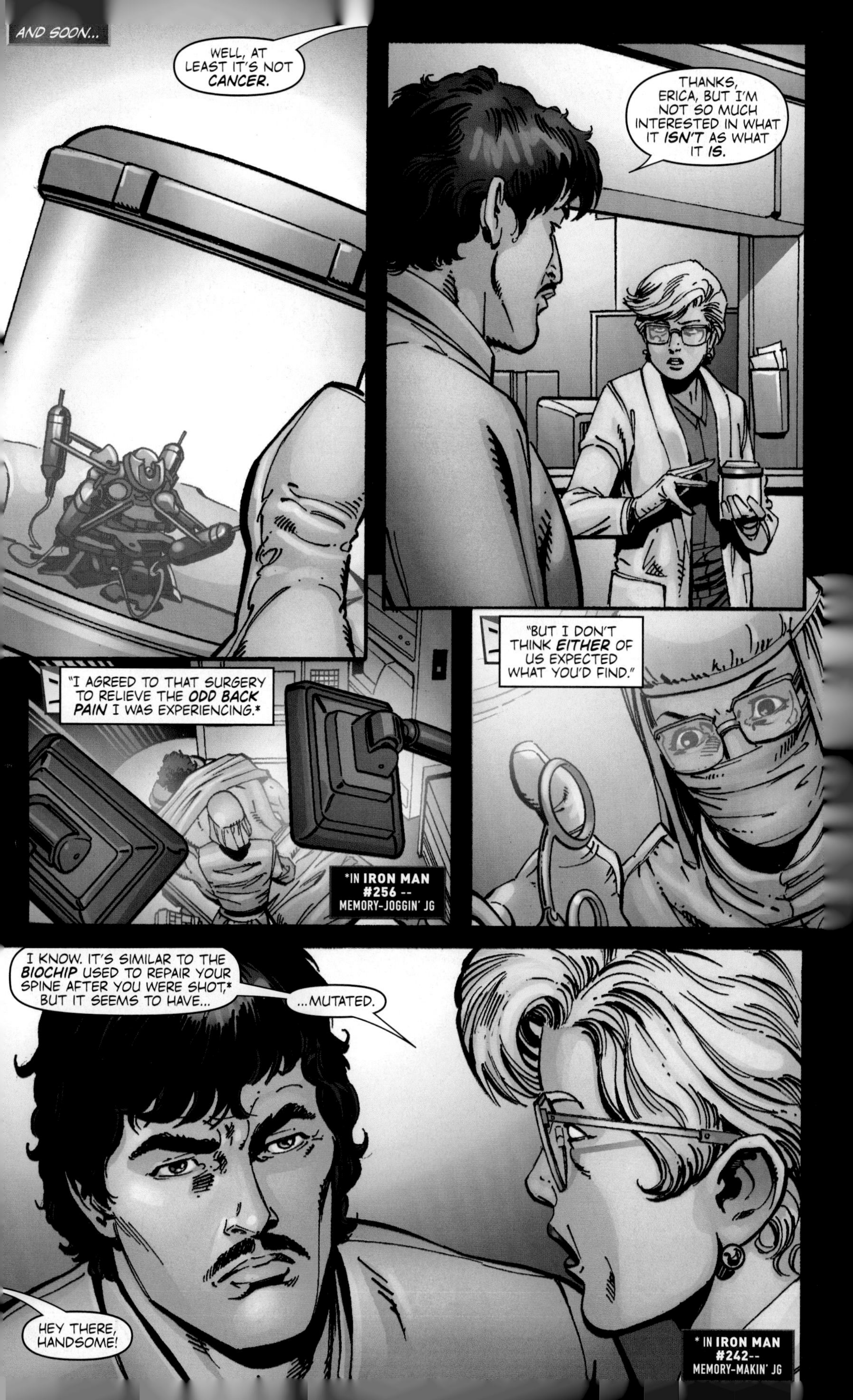
AND SOON...
WELL, AT LEAST IT'S NOT CANCER.
THANKS, ERICA, BUT I'M NOT SO MUCH INTERESTED IN WHAT IT ISN'T AS WHAT IT IS.
"I AGREED TO THAT SURGERY TO RELIEVE THE ODD BACK PAIN I WAS EXPERIENCING.*
*IN IRON MAN #256 -- MEMORY-JOGGIN' JG
"BUT I DON'T THINK EITHER OF US EXPECTED WHAT YOU'D FIND."
I KNOW. IT'S SIMILAR TO THE BIOCHIP USED TO REPAIR YOUR SPINE AFTER YOU WERE SHOT,* BUT IT SEEMS TO HAVE...
...MUTATED.
HEY THERE, HANDSOME!
* IN IRON MAN #242-- MEMORY-MAKIN' JG

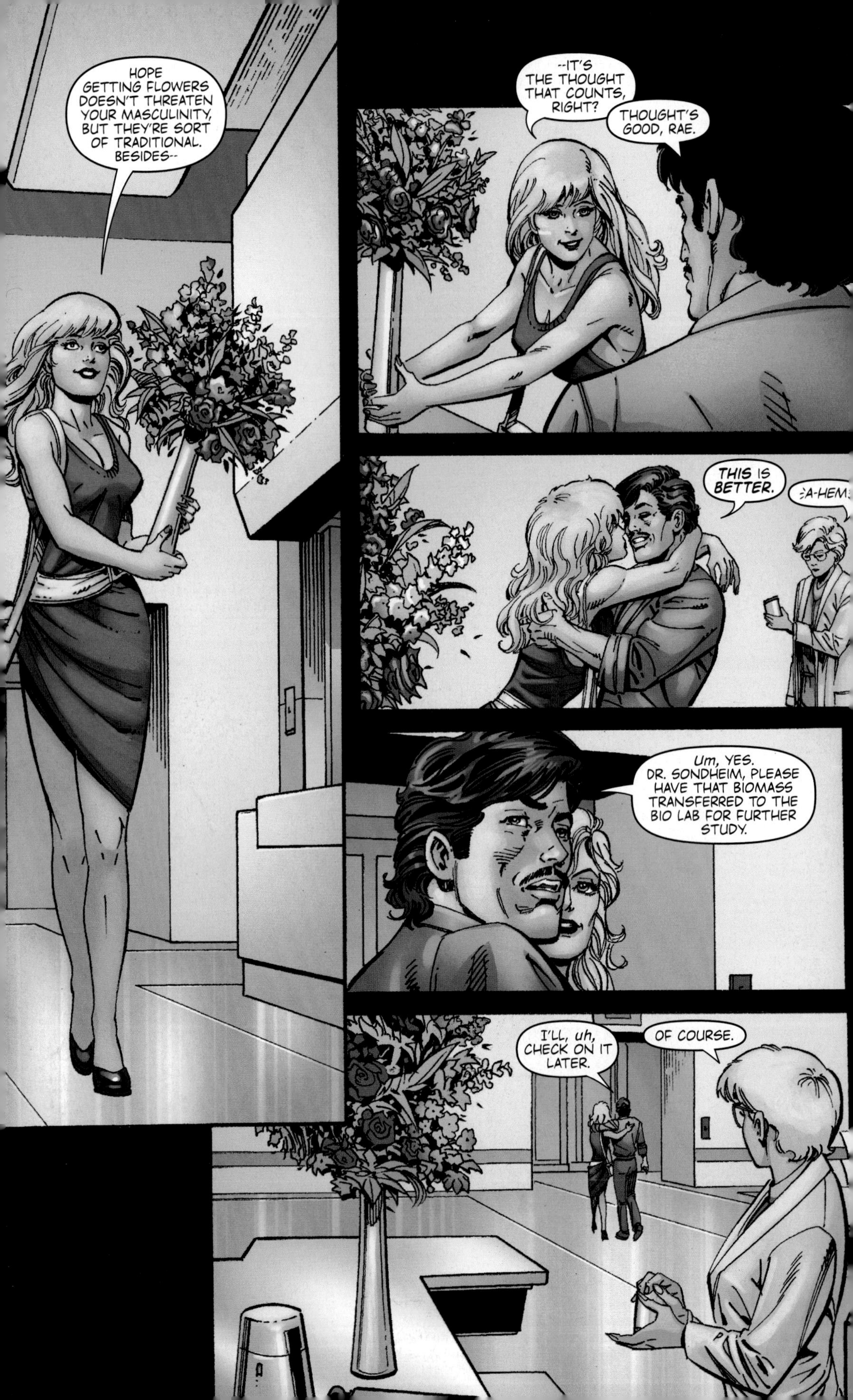
HOPE GETTING FLOWERS DOESN'T THREATEN YOUR MASCULINITY, BUT THEY'RE SORT OF TRADITIONAL. BESIDES--
--IT'S THE THOUGHT THAT COUNTS, RIGHT?
THOUGHT'S GOOD, RAE.
THIS IS BETTER.
A-HEM
Um, YES. DR. SONDHEIM, PLEASE HAVE THAT BIOMASS TRANSFERRED TO THE BIO LAB FOR FURTHER STUDY.
I'LL, uh, CHECK ON IT LATER.
OF COURSE.

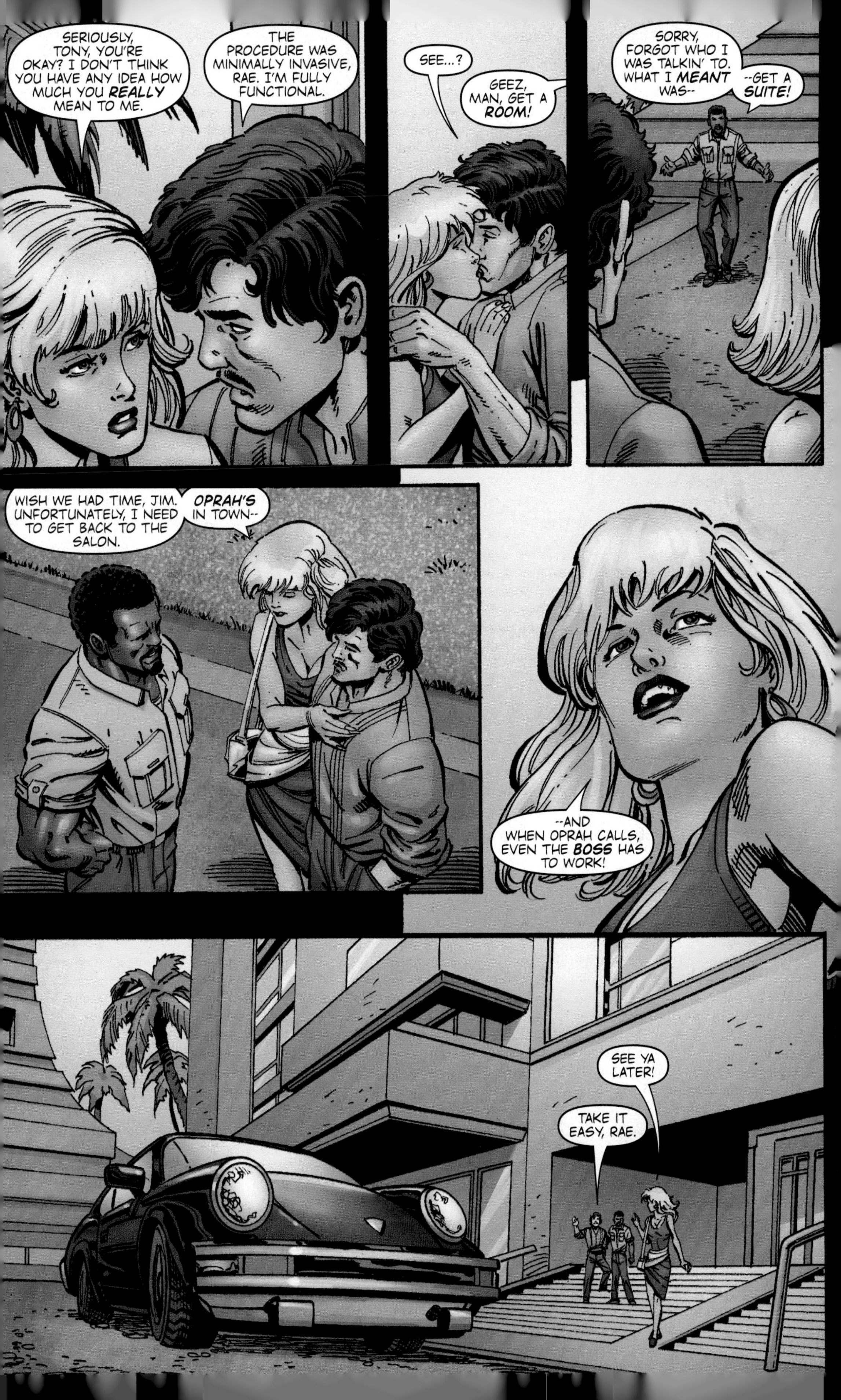
SERIOUSLY, TONY, YOU'RE OKAY? I DON'T THINK YOU HAVE ANY IDEA HOW MUCH YOU **REALLY** MEAN TO ME.
THE PROCEDURE WAS MINIMALLY INVASIVE, RAE. I'M FULLY FUNCTIONAL.
SEE...?
GEEZ, MAN, GET A **ROOM!**
SORRY, FORGOT WHO I WAS TALKIN' TO. WHAT I **MEANT** WAS--
--GET A **SUITE!**
WISH WE HAD TIME, JIM. UNFORTUNATELY, I NEED TO GET BACK TO THE SALON.
OPRAH'S IN TOWN--
--AND WHEN OPRAH CALLS, EVEN THE **BOSS** HAS TO WORK!
SEE YA LATER!
TAKE IT EASY, RAE.

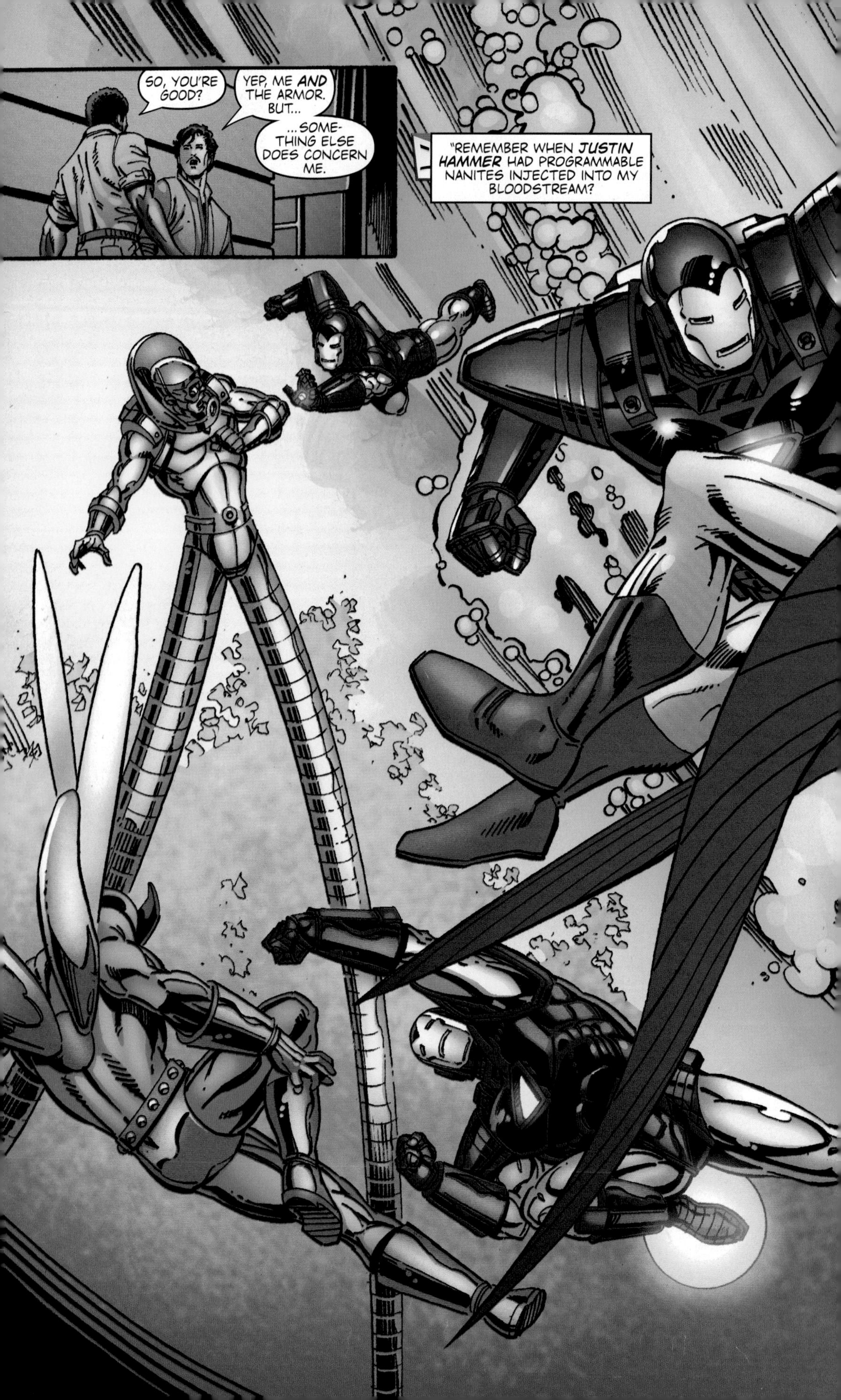

SO, YOU'RE GOOD?
YEP, ME AND THE ARMOR. BUT...
...SOMETHING ELSE DOES CONCERN ME.
"REMEMBER WHEN JUSTIN HAMMER HAD PROGRAMMABLE NANITES INJECTED INTO MY BLOODSTREAM?

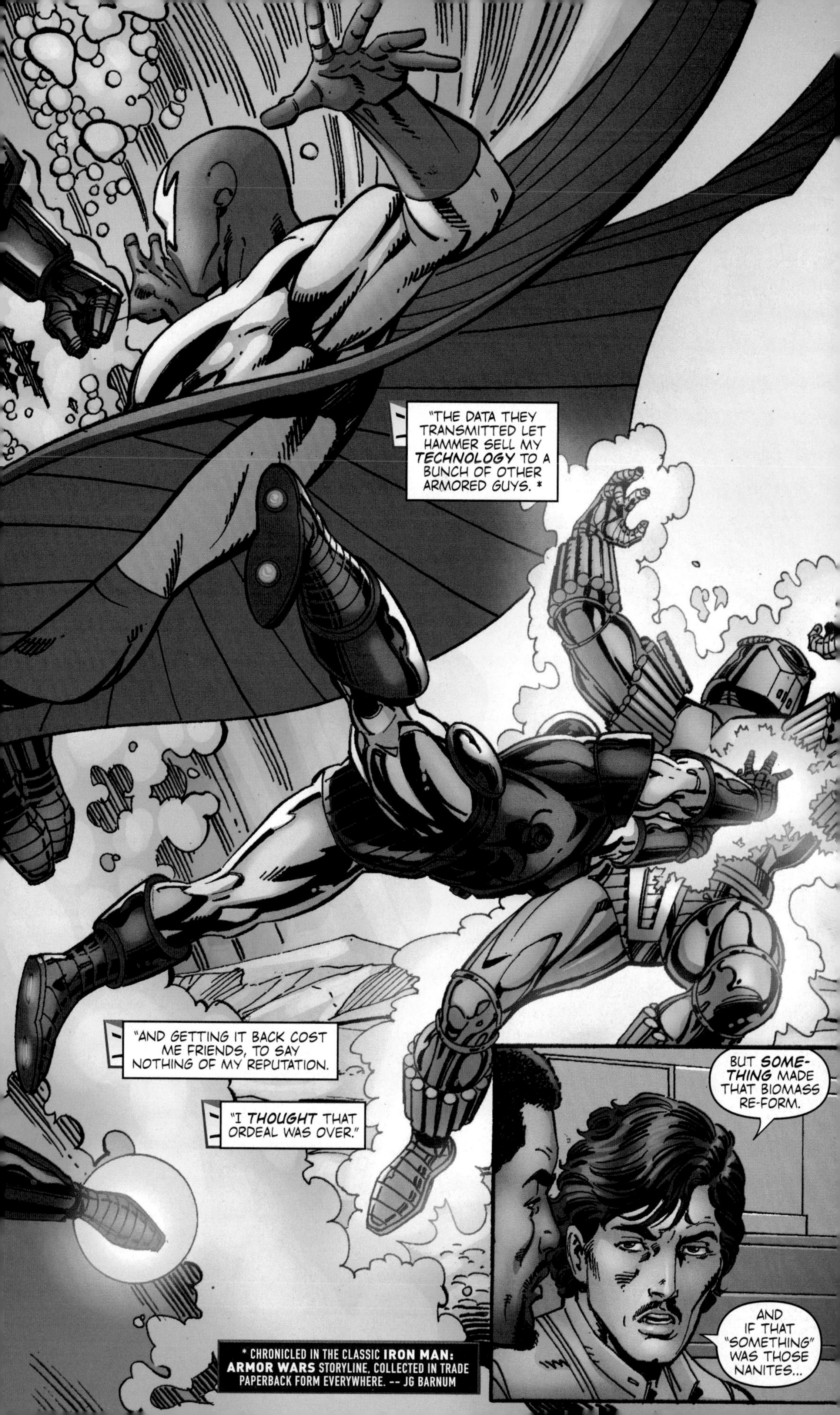

"THE DATA THEY TRANSMITTED LET HAMMER SELL MY TECHNOLOGY TO A BUNCH OF OTHER ARMORED GUYS. *
"AND GETTING IT BACK COST ME FRIENDS, TO SAY NOTHING OF MY REPUTATION.
"I THOUGHT THAT ORDEAL WAS OVER."
BUT SOME-THING MADE THAT BIOMASS RE-FORM.
AND IF THAT "SOMETHING" WAS THOSE NANITES...
* CHRONICLED IN THE CLASSIC IRON MAN: ARMOR WARS STORYLINE, COLLECTED IN TRADE PAPERBACK FORM EVERYWHERE. -- JG BARNUM

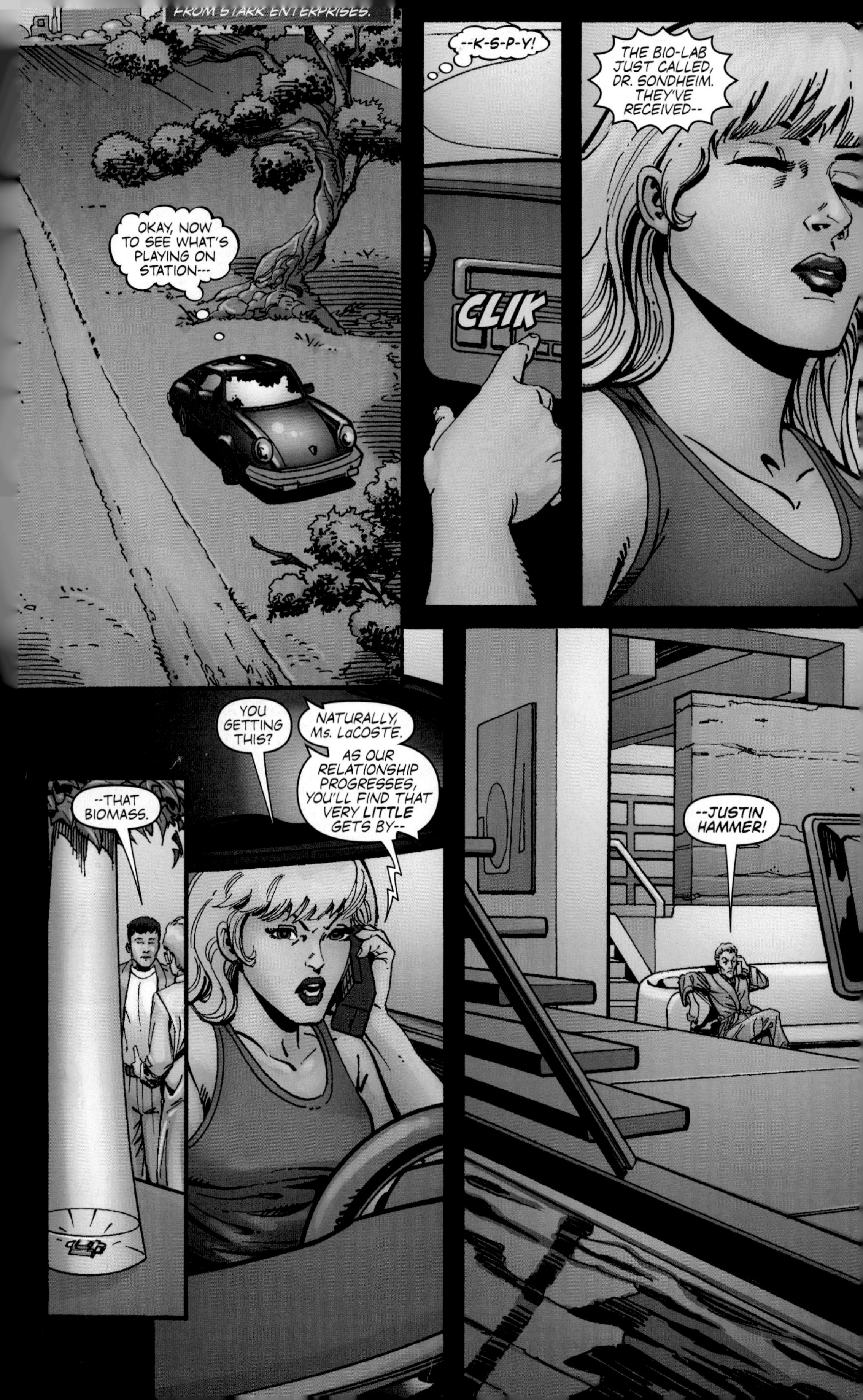
FROM STARK ENTERPRISES.
OKAY, NOW TO SEE WHAT'S PLAYING ON STATION---
--K-S-P-Y!
CLIK
THE BIO-LAB JUST CALLED, DR. SONDHEIM. THEY'VE RECEIVED--
--THAT BIOMASS.
YOU GETTING THIS?
NATURALLY, Ms. LaCOSTE.
AS OUR RELATIONSHIP PROGRESSES, YOU'LL FIND THAT VERY LITTLE GETS BY--
--JUSTIN HAMMER!

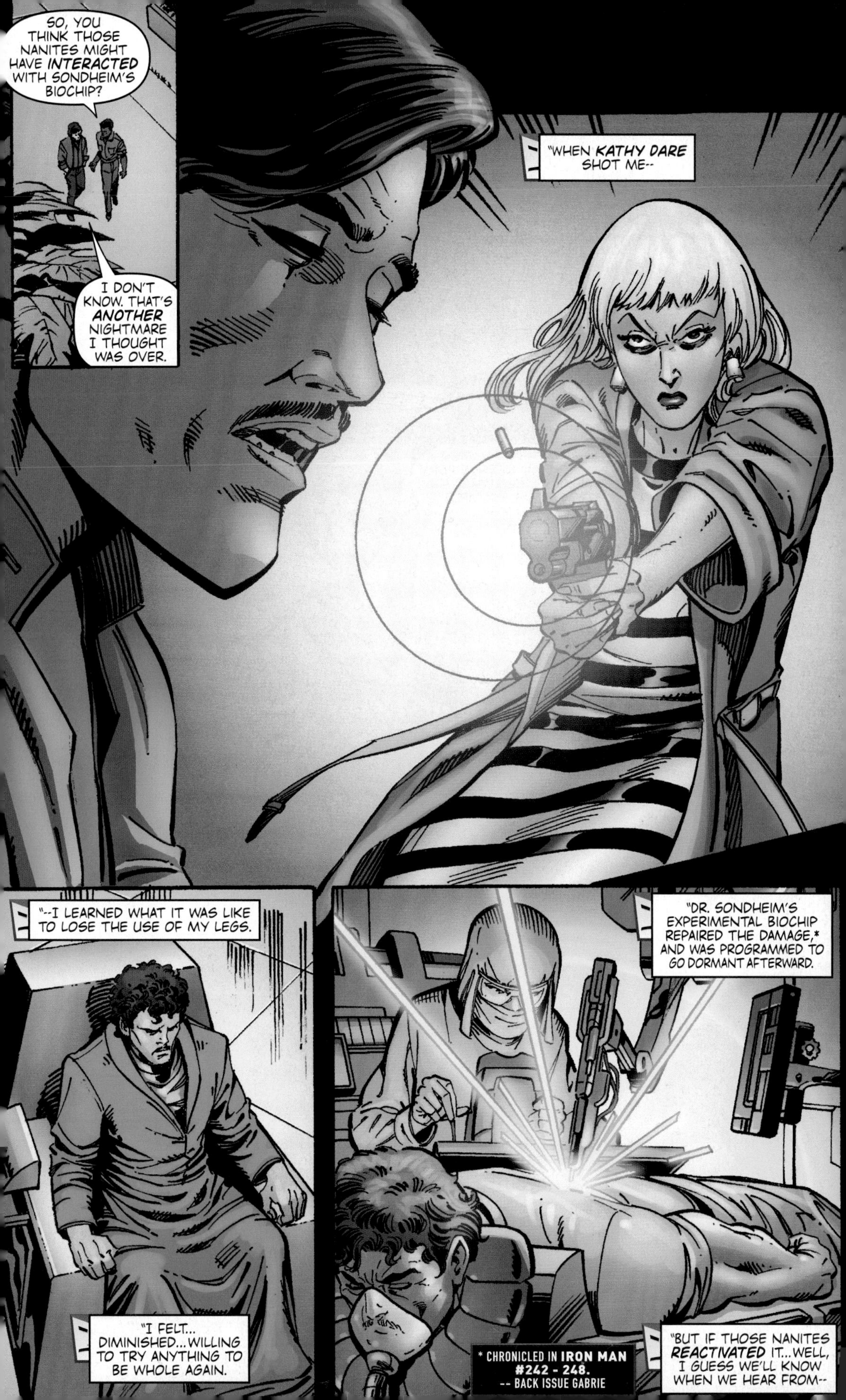
SO, YOU THINK THOSE NANITES MIGHT HAVE INTERACTED WITH SONDHEIM'S BIOCHIP?
I DON'T KNOW. THAT'S ANOTHER NIGHTMARE I THOUGHT WAS OVER.
"WHEN KATHY DARE SHOT ME--
"--I LEARNED WHAT IT WAS LIKE TO LOSE THE USE OF MY LEGS.
"I FELT... DIMINISHED...WILLING TO TRY ANYTHING TO BE WHOLE AGAIN.
"DR. SONDHEIM'S EXPERIMENTAL BIOCHIP REPAIRED THE DAMAGE,* AND WAS PROGRAMMED TO GO DORMANT AFTERWARD.
* CHRONICLED IN IRON MAN #242 - 248. -- BACK ISSUE GABRIE
"BUT IF THOSE NANITES REACTIVATED IT...WELL, I GUESS WE'LL KNOW WHEN WE HEAR FROM--

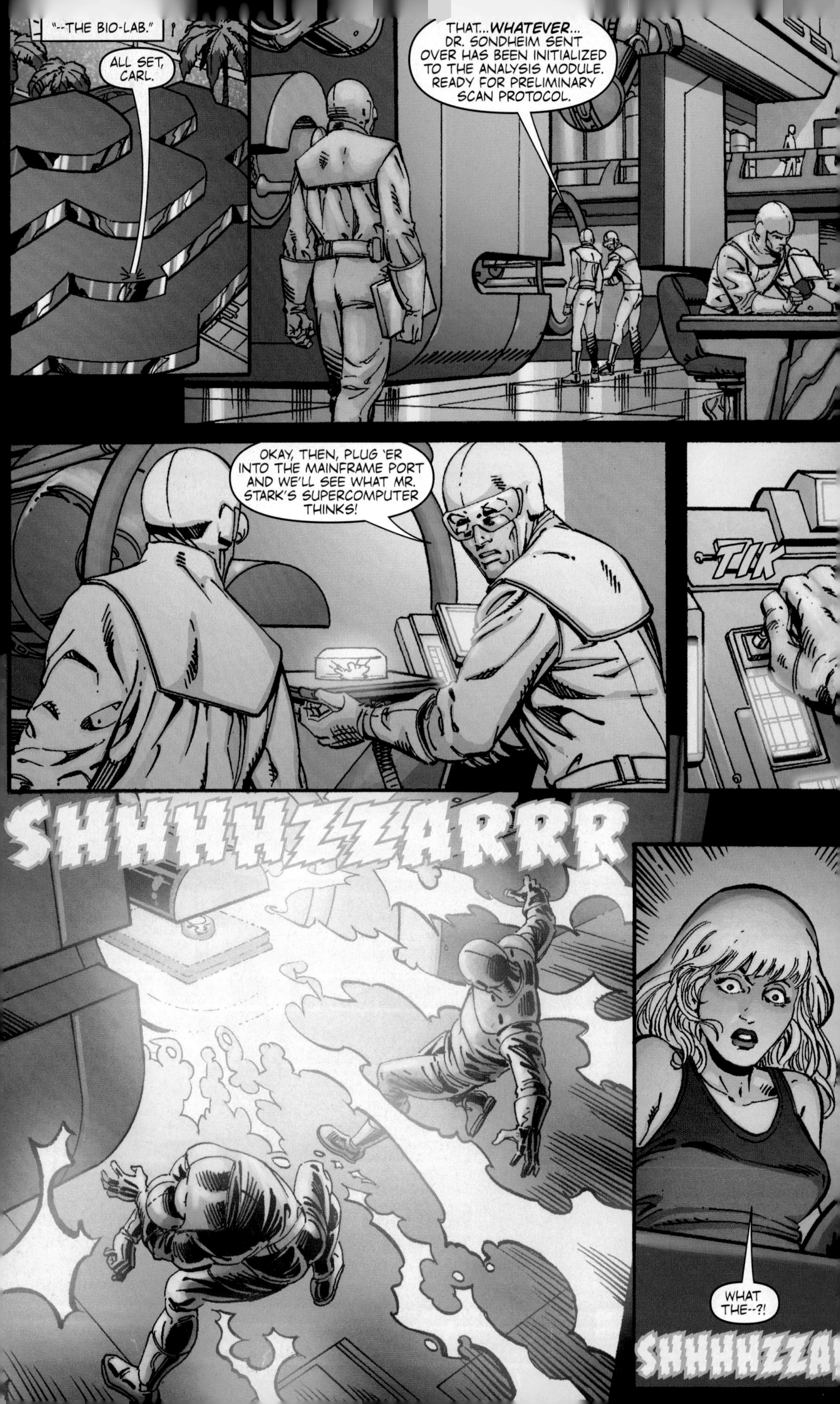

"--THE BIO-LAB."
ALL SET, CARL.
THAT...*WHATEVER*... DR. SONDHEIM SENT OVER HAS BEEN INITIALIZED TO THE ANALYSIS MODULE. READY FOR PRELIMINARY SCAN PROTOCOL.
OKAY, THEN, PLUG 'ER INTO THE MAINFRAME PORT AND WE'LL SEE WHAT MR. STARK'S SUPERCOMPUTER THINKS!
TIK
SHHHZZARRR
WHAT THE--?!
SHHHHZZA

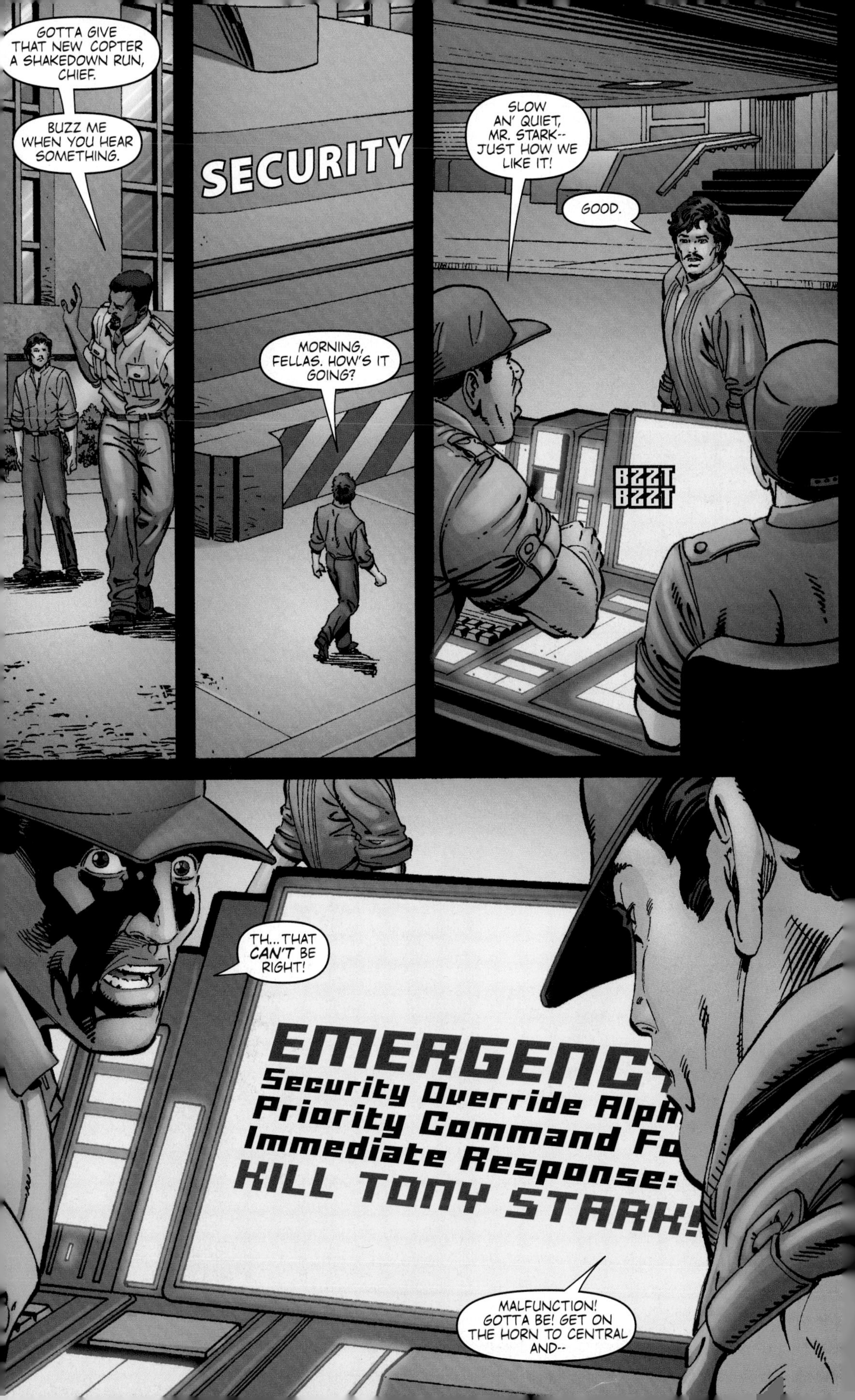
GOTTA GIVE THAT NEW COPTER A SHAKEDOWN RUN, CHIEF.
BUZZ ME WHEN YOU HEAR SOMETHING.
SECURITY
MORNING, FELLAS. HOW'S IT GOING?
SLOW AN' QUIET, MR. STARK-- JUST HOW WE LIKE IT!
GOOD.
BZZT BZZT
TH...THAT CAN'T BE RIGHT!
EMERGENC
Security Override Alph
Priority Command Fo
Immediate Response:
KILL TONY STARK!
MALFUNCTION! GOTTA BE! GET ON THE HORN TO CENTRAL AND--

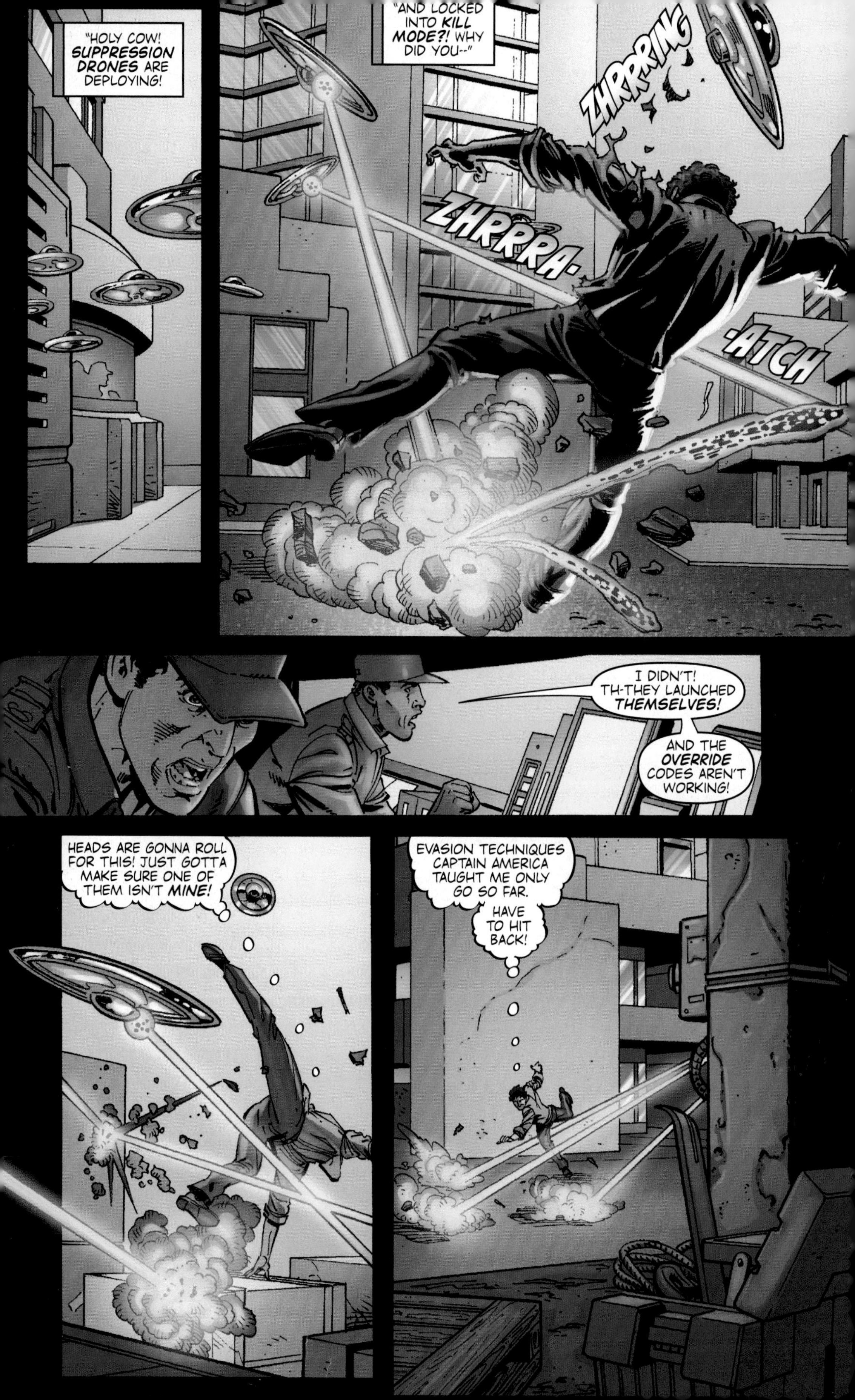
"HOLY COW! SUPPRESSION DRONES ARE DEPLOYING!
"AND LOCKED INTO KILL MODE?! WHY DID YOU--"
ZHRRRING
ZHRRRA-
-ATCH
I DIDN'T! TH-THEY LAUNCHED THEMSELVES!
AND THE OVERRIDE CODES AREN'T WORKING!
HEADS ARE GONNA ROLL FOR THIS! JUST GOTTA MAKE SURE ONE OF THEM ISN'T MINE!
EVASION TECHNIQUES CAPTAIN AMERICA TAUGHT ME ONLY GO SO FAR.
HAVE TO HIT BACK!

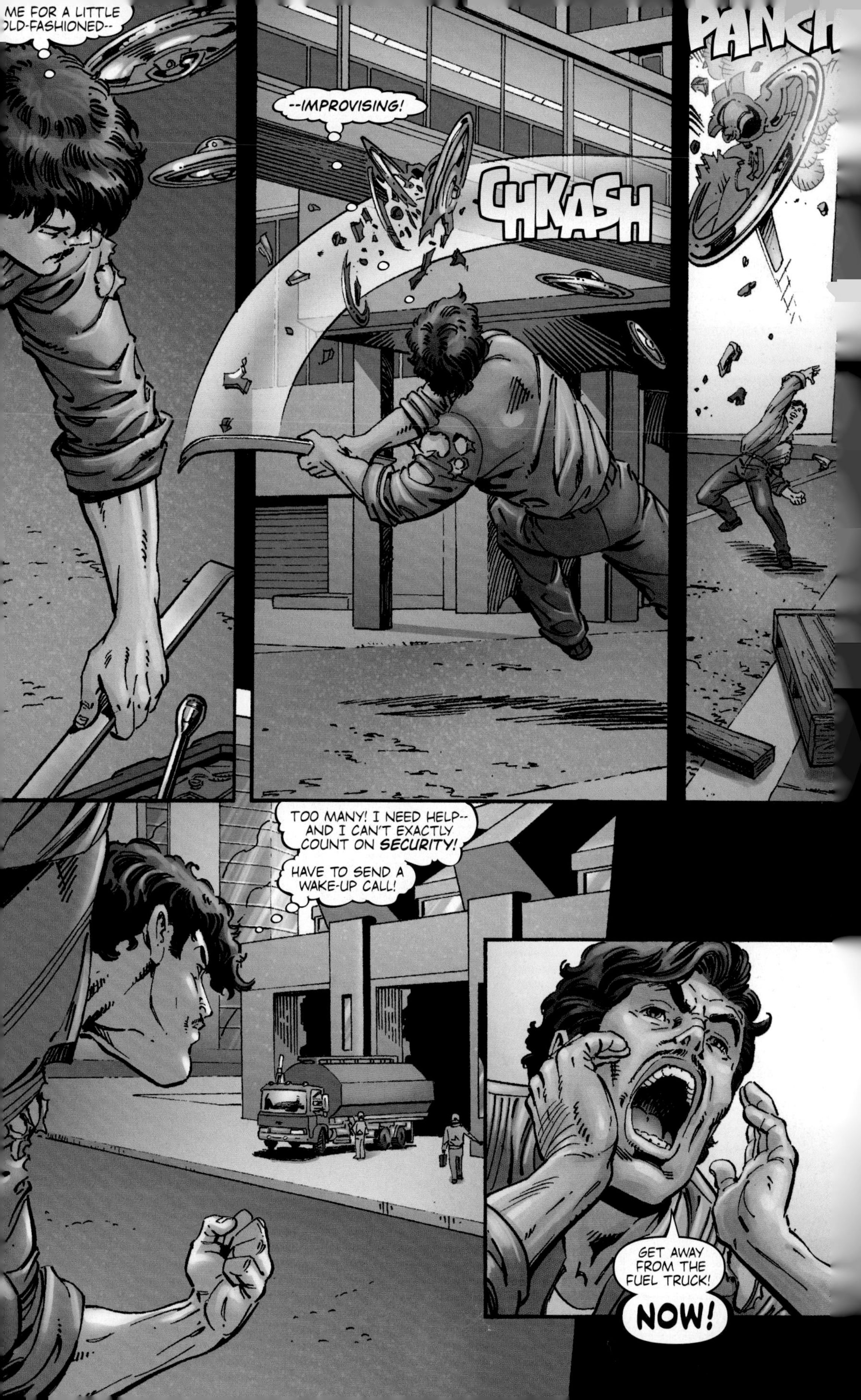

ME FOR A LITTLE
OLD-FASHIONED--
--IMPROVISING!
CHKASH
PANCH
TOO MANY! I NEED HELP-- AND I CAN'T EXACTLY COUNT ON SECURITY!
HAVE TO SEND A WAKE-UP CALL!
GET AWAY FROM THE FUEL TRUCK!
NOW!

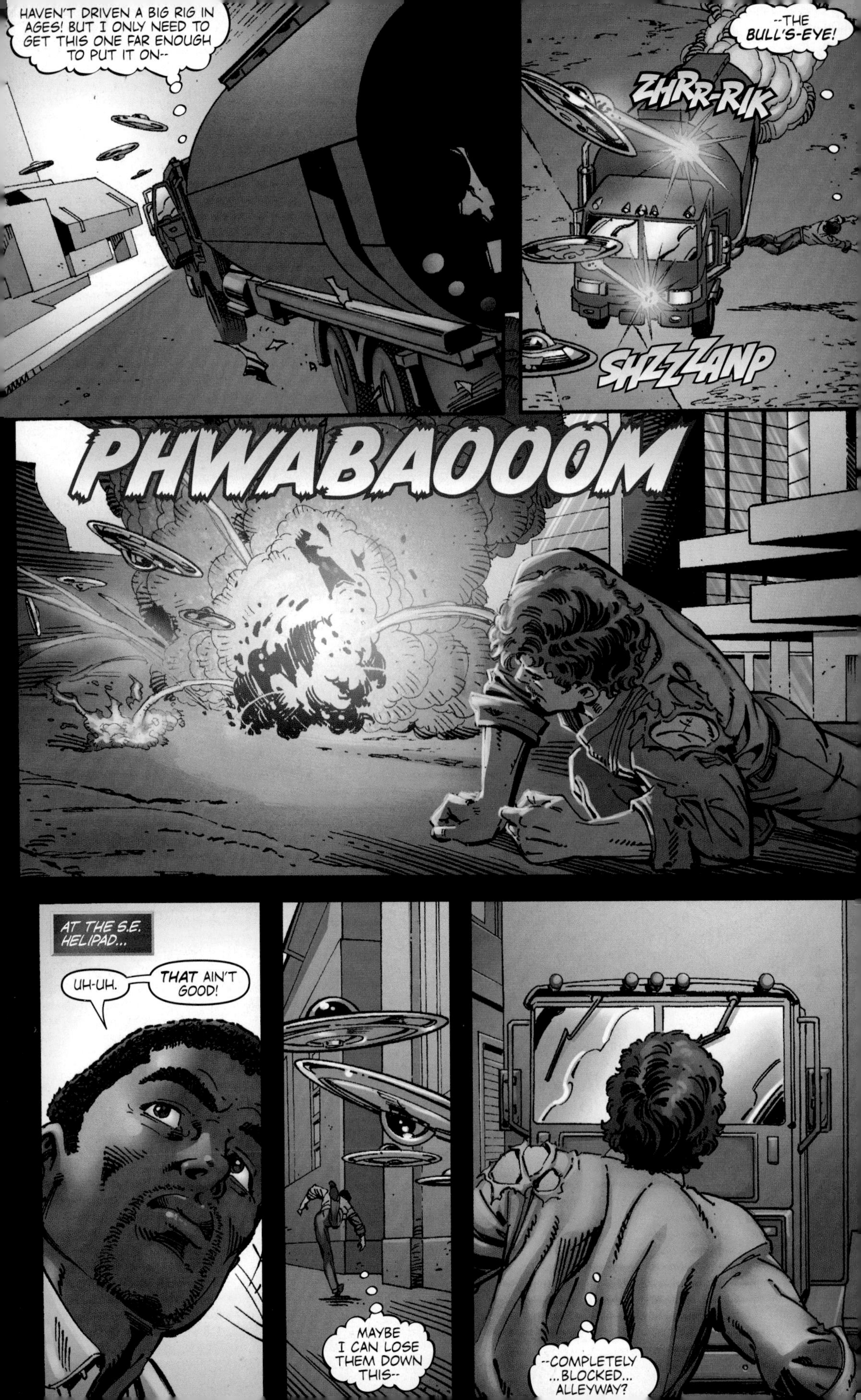

HAVEN'T DRIVEN A BIG RIG IN AGES! BUT I ONLY NEED TO GET THIS ONE FAR ENOUGH TO PUT IT ON--
--THE BULL'S-EYE!
ZHRR-RIK
SHZZZANP
PHWABAOOOM
AT THE S.E. HELIPAD...
UH-UH.
THAT AIN'T GOOD!
MAYBE I CAN LOSE THEM DOWN THIS--
--COMPLETELY ...BLOCKED... ALLEYWAY?

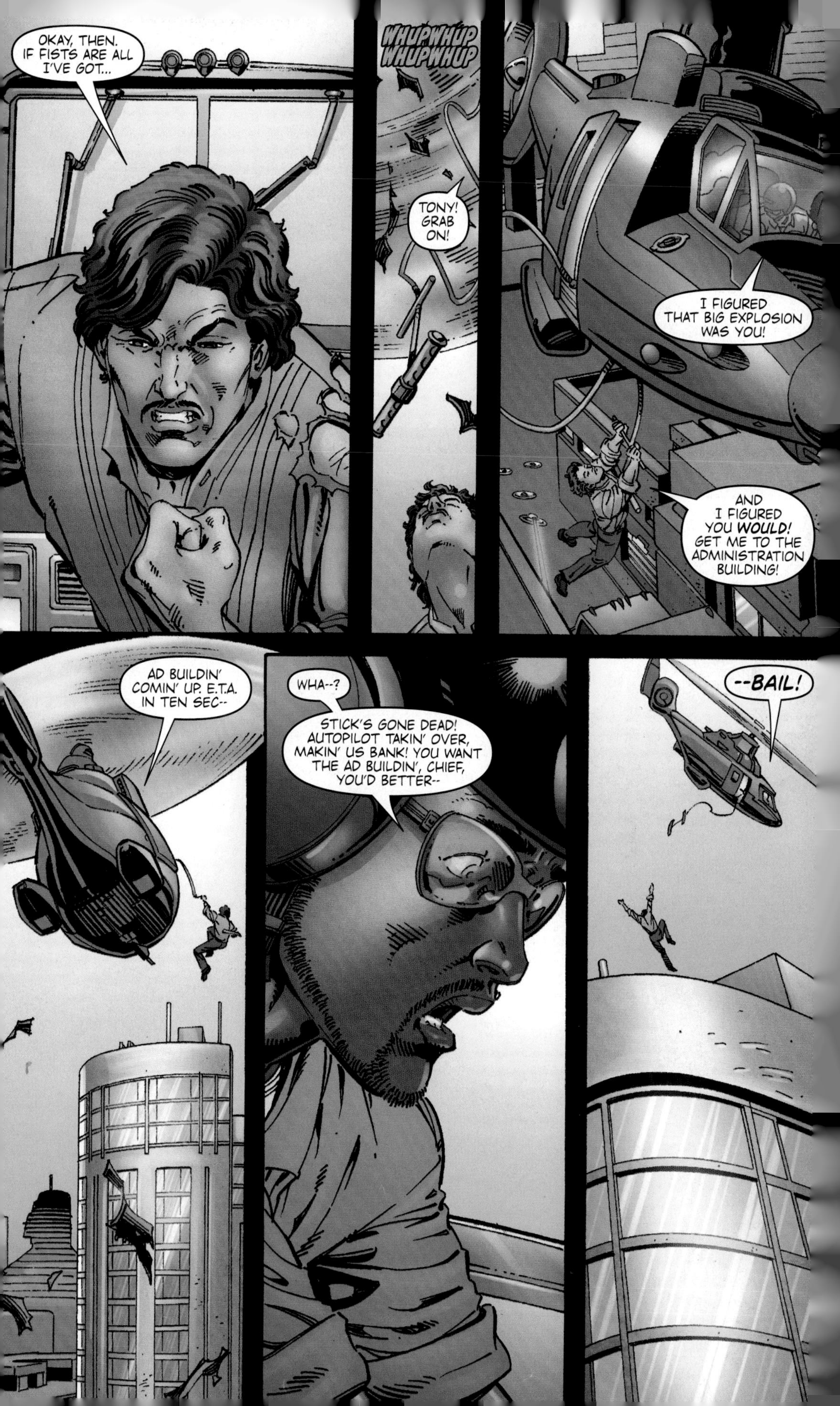
OKAY, THEN. IF FISTS ARE ALL I'VE GOT...
WHUPWHUP WHUPWHUP
TONY! GRAB ON!
I FIGURED THAT BIG EXPLOSION WAS YOU!
AND I FIGURED YOU WOULD! GET ME TO THE ADMINISTRATION BUILDING!
AD BUILDIN' COMIN' UP. E.T.A. IN TEN SEC--
WHA--?
STICK'S GONE DEAD! AUTOPILOT TAKIN' OVER, MAKIN' US BANK! YOU WANT THE AD BUILDIN', CHIEF, YOU'D BETTER--
--BAIL!

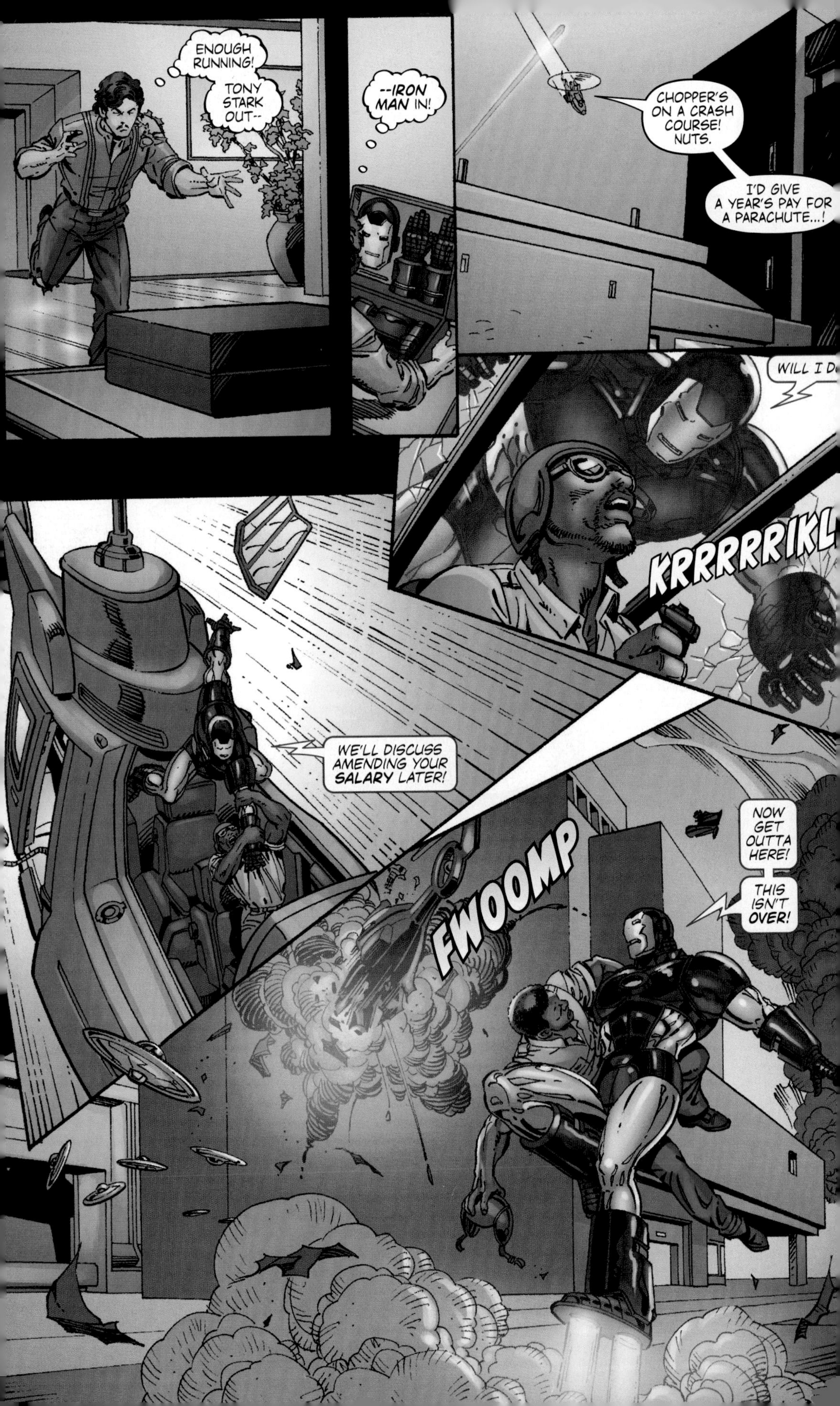
ENOUGH RUNNING!
TONY STARK OUT--
--IRON MAN IN!
CHOPPER'S ON A CRASH COURSE! NUTS.
I'D GIVE A YEAR'S PAY FOR A PARACHUTE...!
WILL I D
KRRRRRIKL
WE'LL DISCUSS AMENDING YOUR SALARY LATER!
FWOOMP
NOW GET OUTTA HERE!
THIS ISN'T OVER!

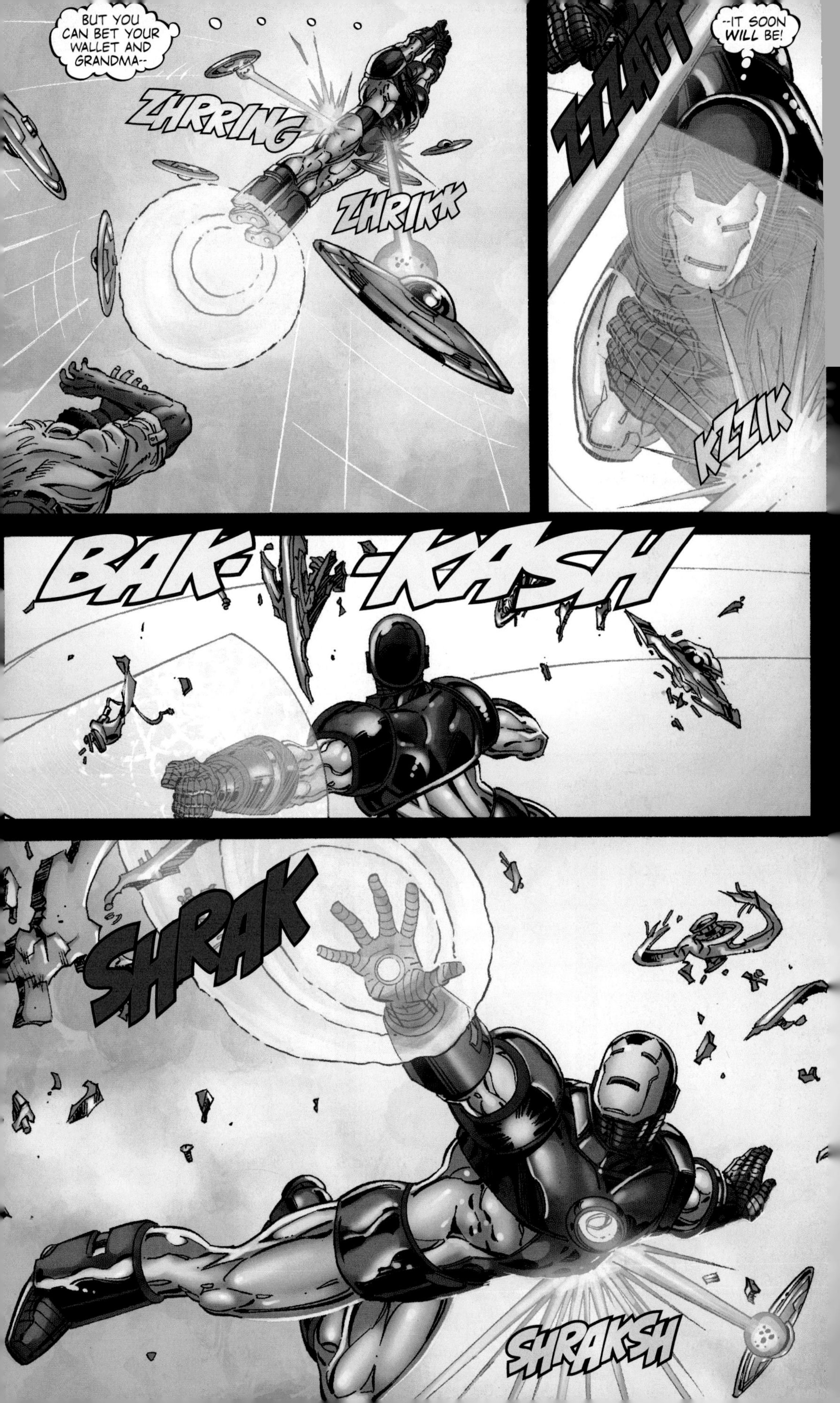
BUT YOU CAN BET YOUR WALLET AND GRANDMA--
ZHRRING
ZHRIKK
ZZZATT
--IT SOON WILL BE!
KZZIK
BAK-KASH
SHRAK
SHRAKSH

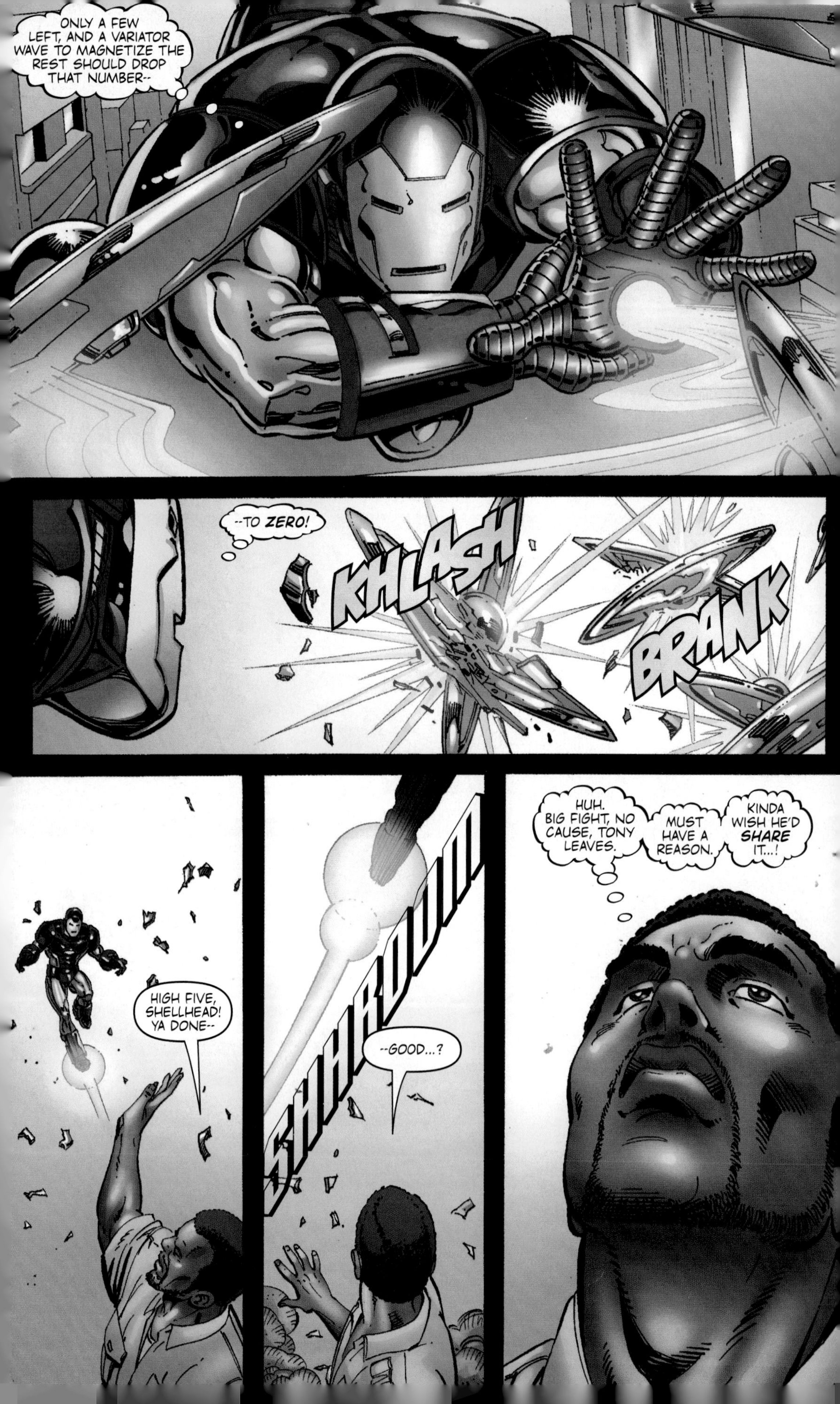
ONLY A FEW LEFT, AND A VARIATOR WAVE TO MAGNETIZE THE REST SHOULD DROP THAT NUMBER--
--TO ZERO!
KHLASH
BRANK
HIGH FIVE, SHELLHEAD! YA DONE--
SHHROOM
--GOOD...?
HUH. BIG FIGHT, NO CAUSE, TONY LEAVES.
MUST HAVE A REASON.
KINDA WISH HE'D SHARE IT...!

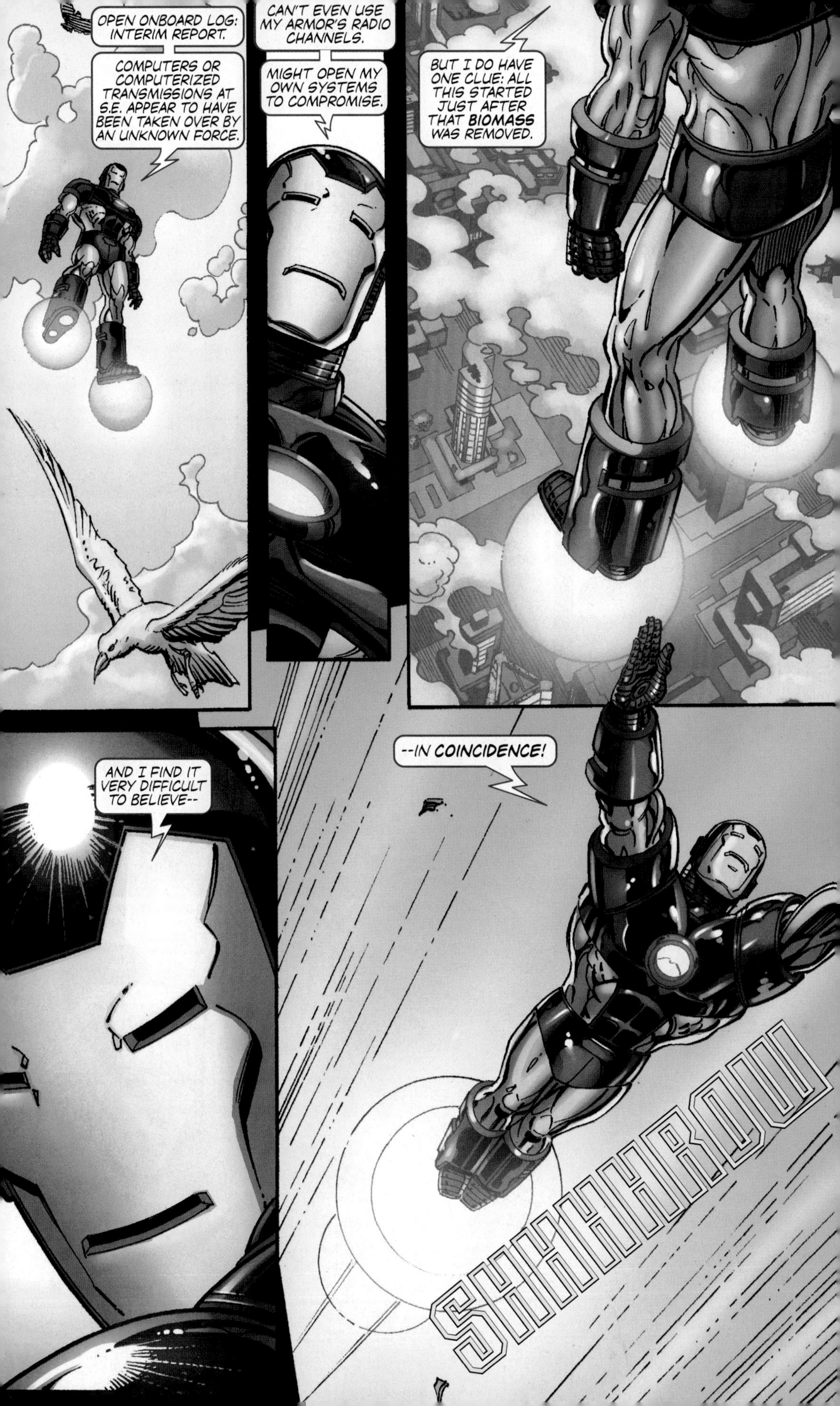
OPEN ONBOARD LOG: INTERIM REPORT.
COMPUTERS OR COMPUTERIZED TRANSMISSIONS AT S.E. APPEAR TO HAVE BEEN TAKEN OVER BY AN UNKNOWN FORCE.
CAN'T EVEN USE MY ARMOR'S RADIO CHANNELS.
MIGHT OPEN MY OWN SYSTEMS TO COMPROMISE.
BUT I DO HAVE ONE CLUE: ALL THIS STARTED JUST AFTER THAT BIOMASS WAS REMOVED.
AND I FIND IT VERY DIFFICULT TO BELIEVE--
--IN COINCIDENCE!
SHHHHROOW

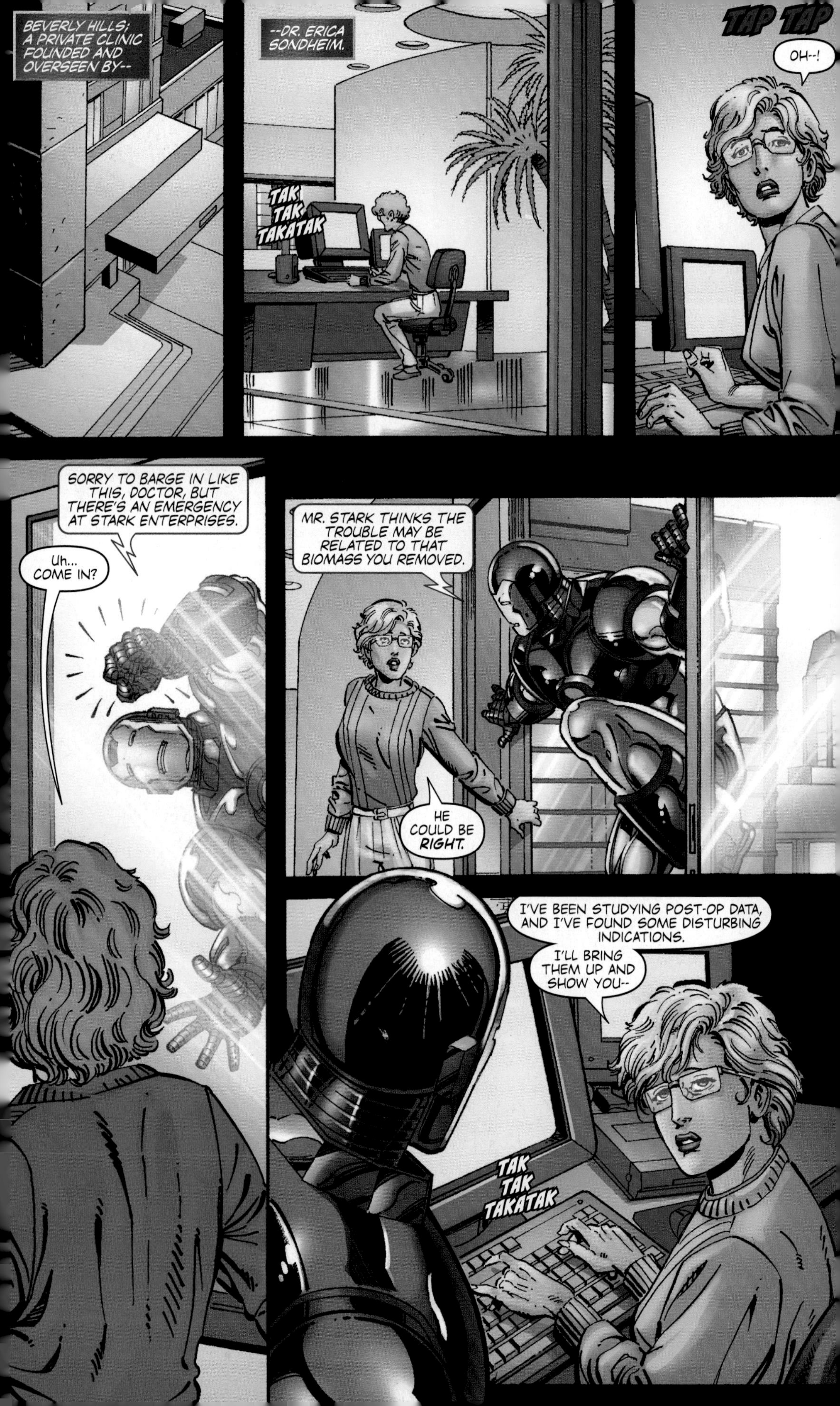

BEVERLY HILLS; A PRIVATE CLINIC FOUNDED AND OVERSEEN BY--
--DR. ERICA SONDHEIM.
TAK TAK TAKATAK
TAP TAP
OH--!
SORRY TO BARGE IN LIKE THIS, DOCTOR, BUT THERE'S AN EMERGENCY AT STARK ENTERPRISES.
Uh... COME IN?
MR. STARK THINKS THE TROUBLE MAY BE RELATED TO THAT BIOMASS YOU REMOVED.
HE COULD BE RIGHT.
I'VE BEEN STUDYING POST-OP DATA, AND I'VE FOUND SOME DISTURBING INDICATIONS.
I'LL BRING THEM UP AND SHOW YOU--
TAK TAK TAKATAK

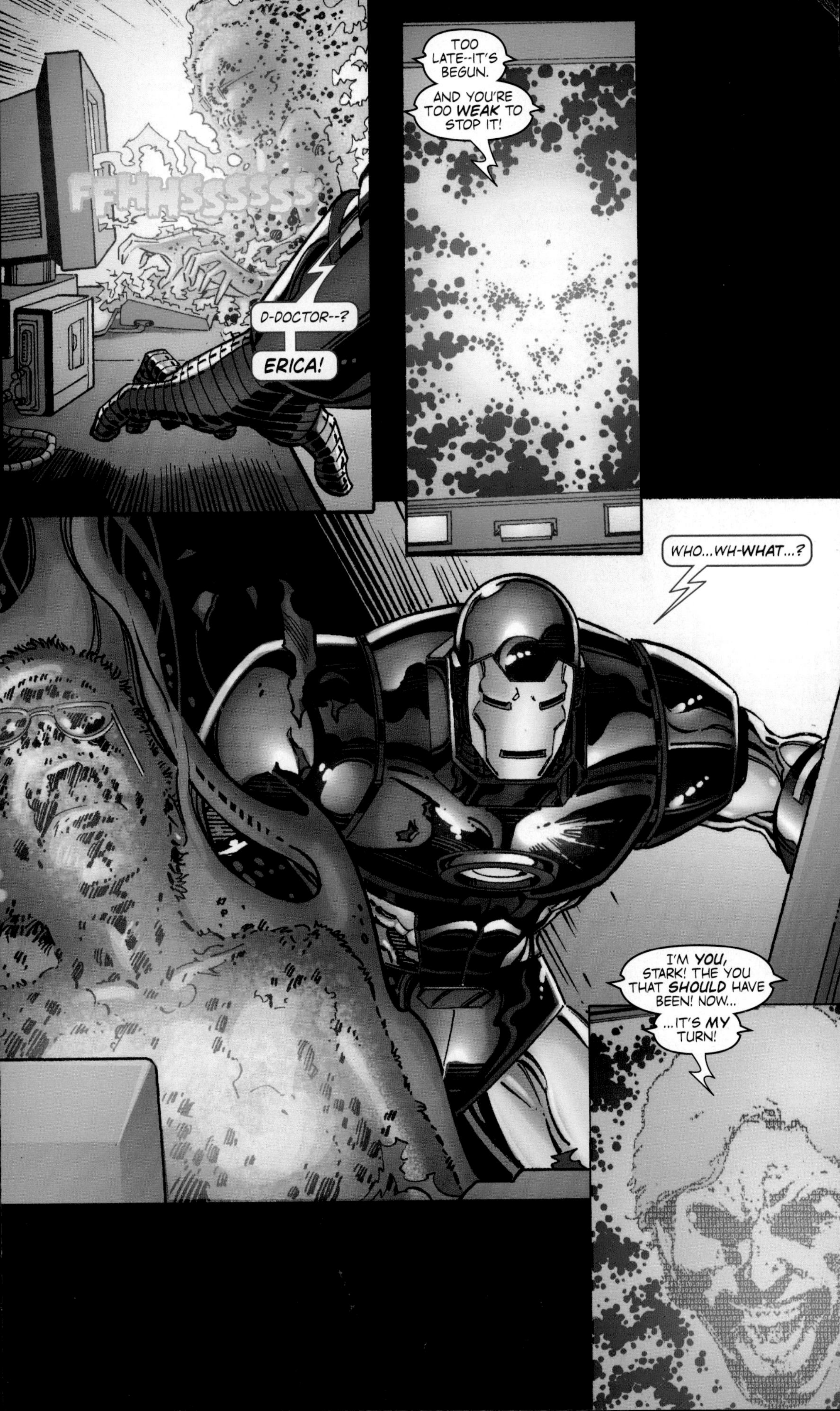
FFHHSSSSSS
TOO LATE--IT'S BEGUN.
AND YOU'RE TOO WEAK TO STOP IT!
D-DOCTOR--?
ERICA!
WHO...WH-WHAT...?
I'M YOU, STARK! THE YOU THAT SHOULD HAVE BEEN! NOW...
...IT'S MY TURN!

_258.2

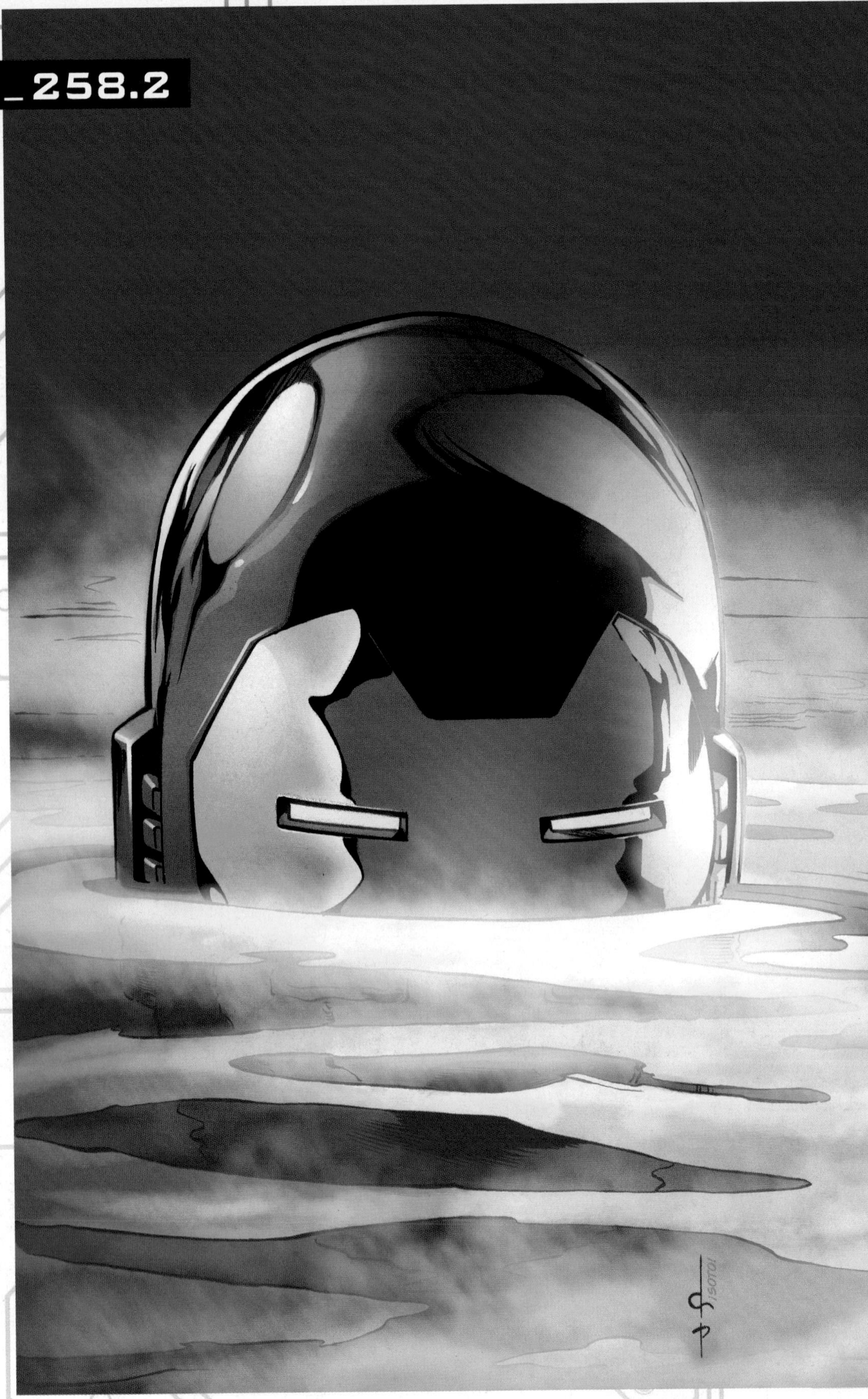

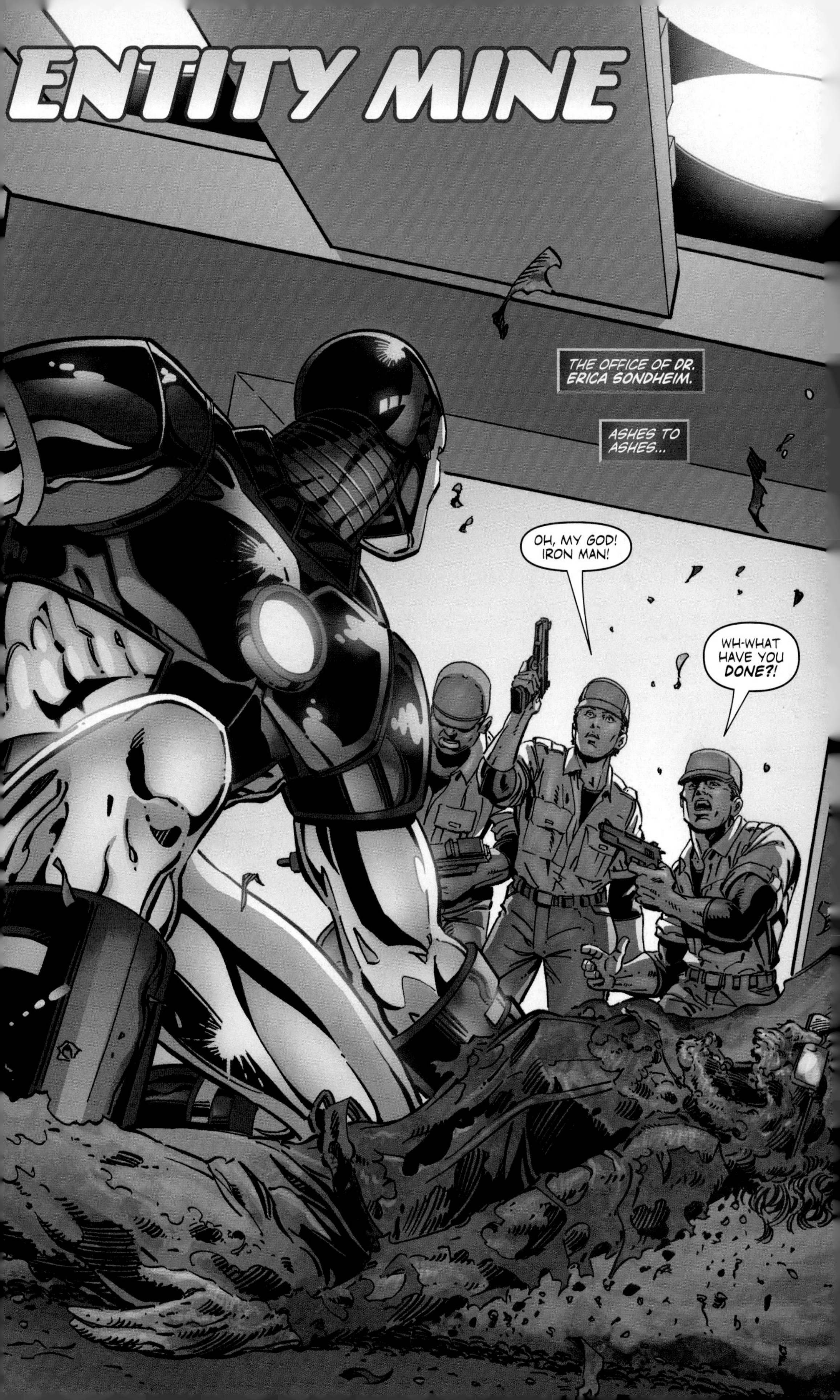
ENTITY MINE
THE OFFICE OF DR. ERICA SONDHEIM.
ASHES TO ASHES...
OH, MY GOD! IRON MAN!
WH-WHAT HAVE YOU DONE?!

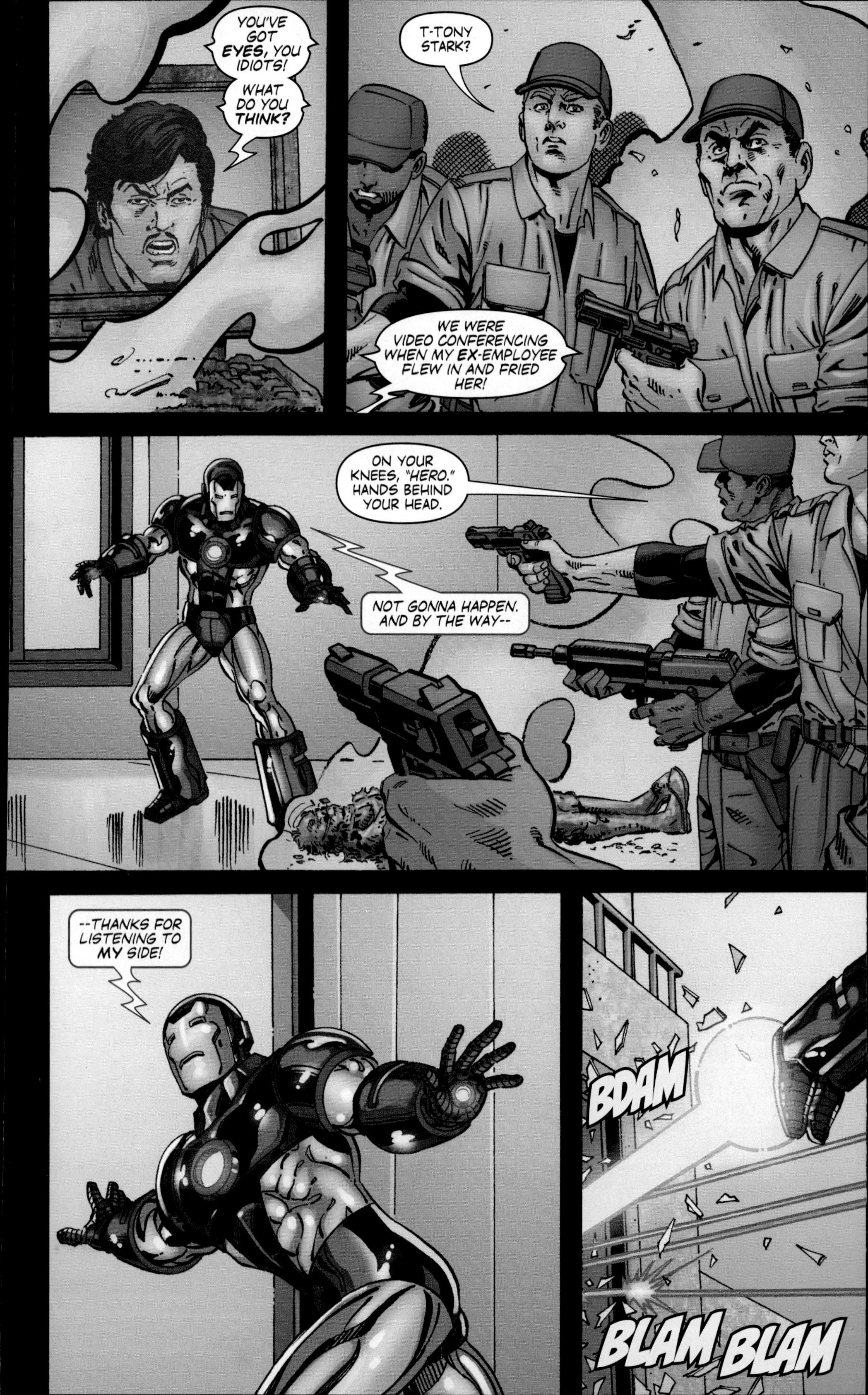
YOU'VE GOT EYES, YOU IDIOTS!
WHAT DO YOU THINK?
T-TONY STARK?
WE WERE VIDEO CONFERENCING WHEN MY EX-EMPLOYEE FLEW IN AND FRIED HER!
ON YOUR KNEES, "HERO." HANDS BEHIND YOUR HEAD.
NOT GONNA HAPPEN. AND BY THE WAY--
--THANKS FOR LISTENING TO MY SIDE!
BDAM
BLAM BLAM

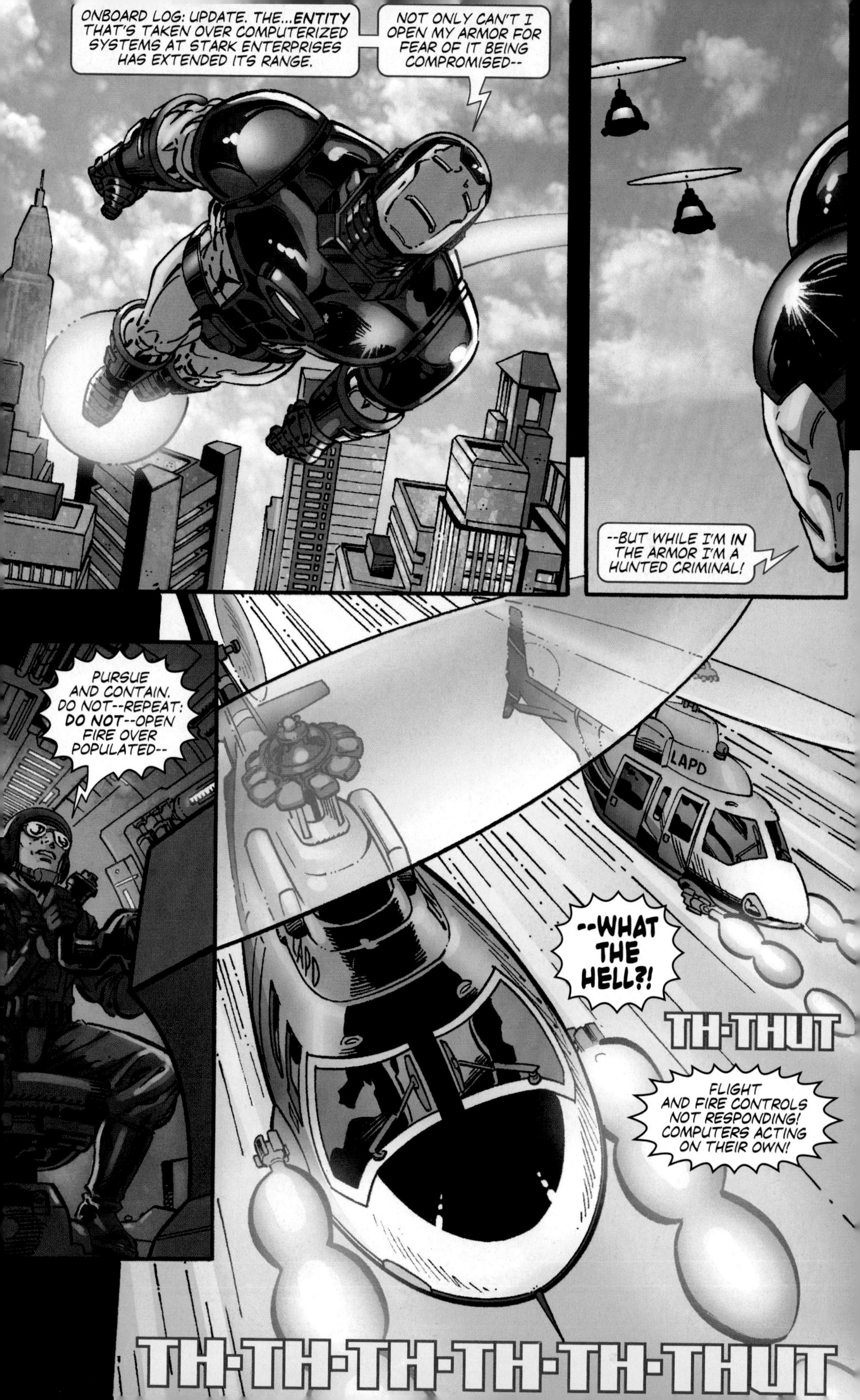
ONBOARD LOG: UPDATE. THE...ENTITY THAT'S TAKEN OVER COMPUTERIZED SYSTEMS AT STARK ENTERPRISES HAS EXTENDED ITS RANGE.
NOT ONLY CAN'T I OPEN MY ARMOR FOR FEAR OF IT BEING COMPROMISED--
--BUT WHILE I'M IN THE ARMOR I'M A HUNTED CRIMINAL!
PURSUE AND CONTAIN. DO NOT--REPEAT: DO NOT--OPEN FIRE OVER POPULATED--
LAPD
LAPD
--WHAT THE HELL?!
TH-THUT
FLIGHT AND FIRE CONTROLS NOT RESPONDING! COMPUTERS ACTING ON THEIR OWN!
TH-TH-TH-TH-TH-THUT

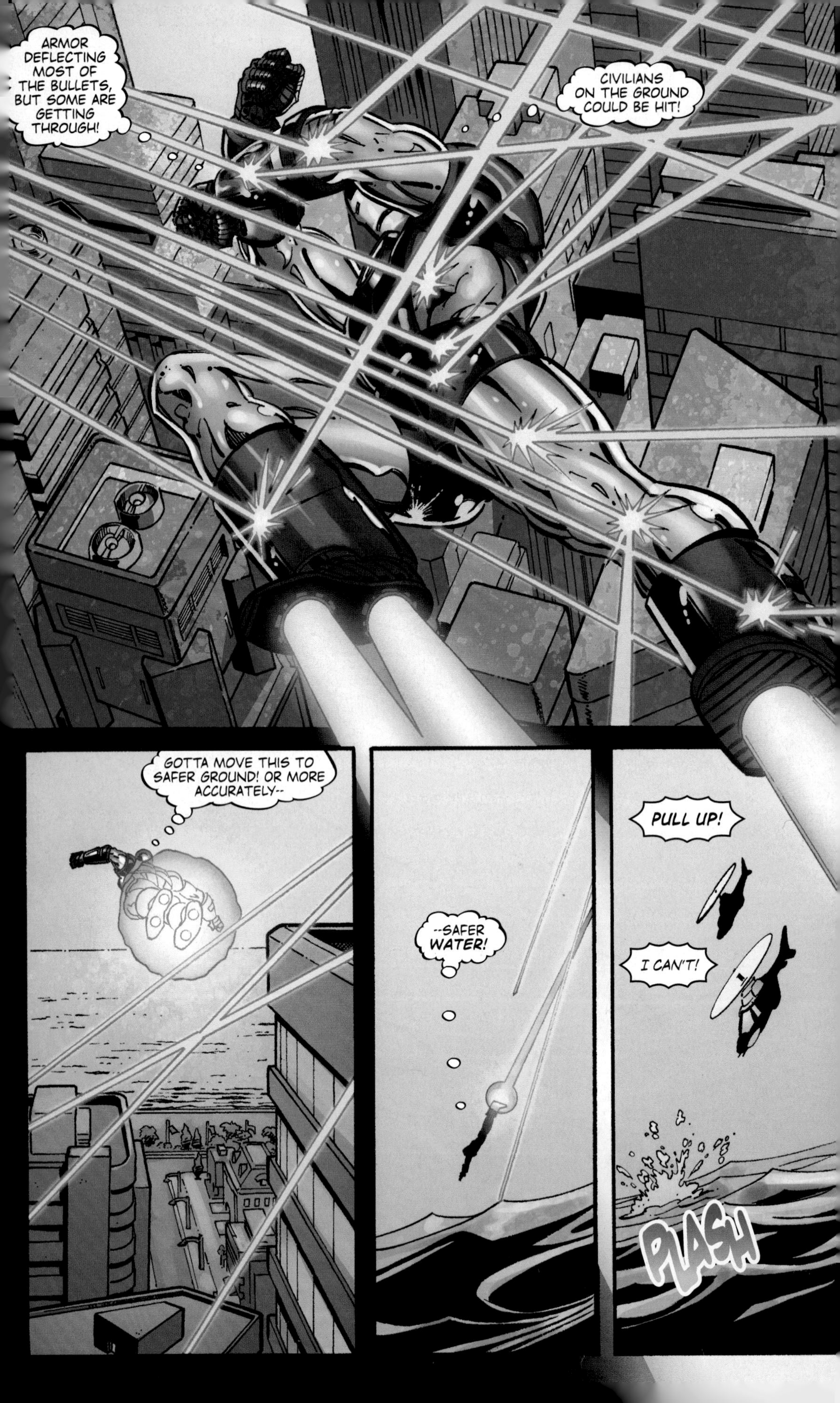
ARMOR DEFLECTING MOST OF THE BULLETS, BUT SOME ARE GETTING THROUGH!
CIVILIANS ON THE GROUND COULD BE HIT!
GOTTA MOVE THIS TO SAFER GROUND! OR MORE ACCURATELY--
--SAFER WATER!
PULL UP!
I CAN'T!
PLASH

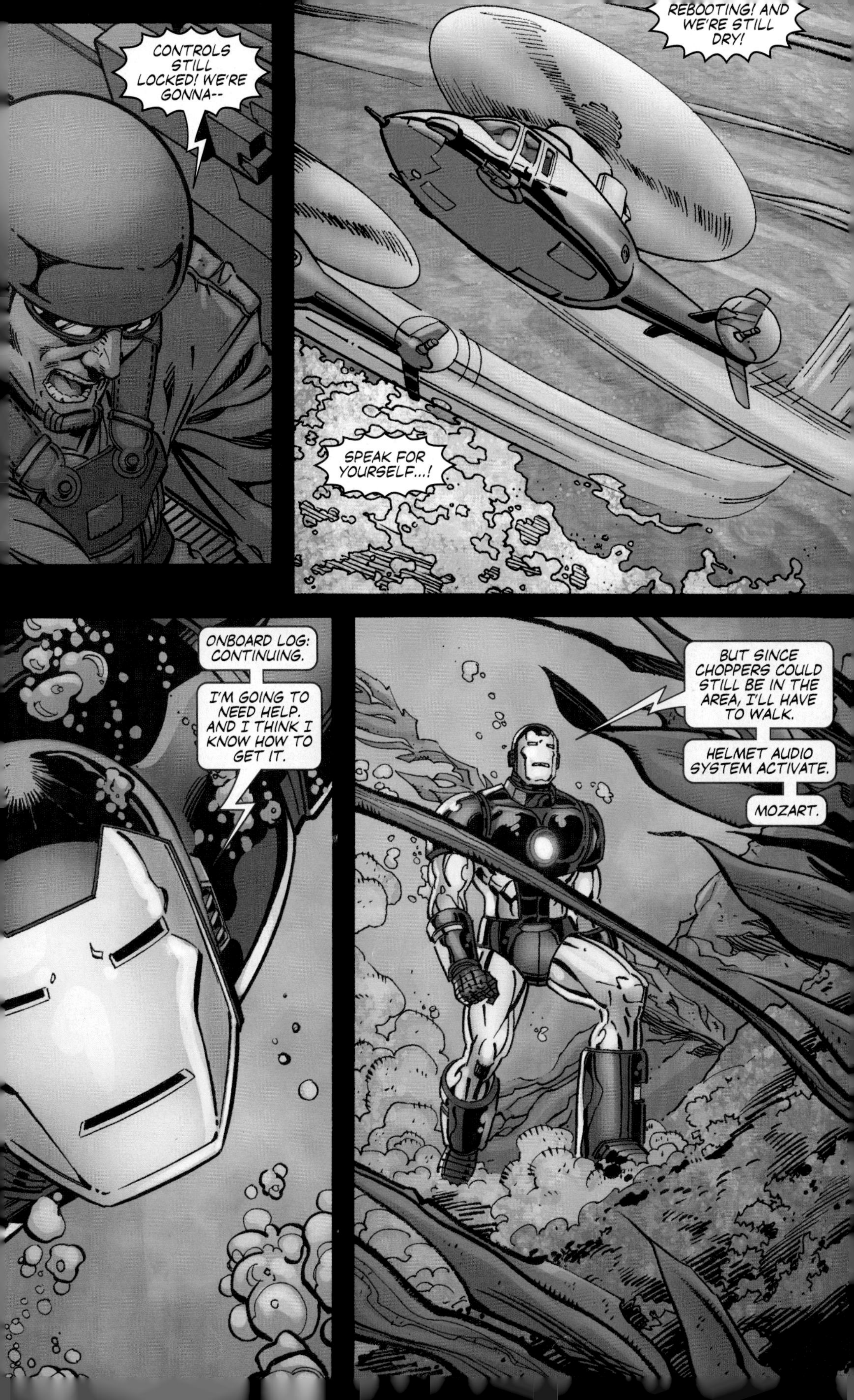
CONTROLS STILL LOCKED! WE'RE GONNA--
REBOOTING! AND WE'RE STILL DRY!
SPEAK FOR YOURSELF...!
ONBOARD LOG: CONTINUING.
I'M GOING TO NEED HELP. AND I THINK I KNOW HOW TO GET IT.
BUT SINCE CHOPPERS COULD STILL BE IN THE AREA, I'LL HAVE TO WALK.
HELMET AUDIO SYSTEM ACTIVATE.
MOZART.

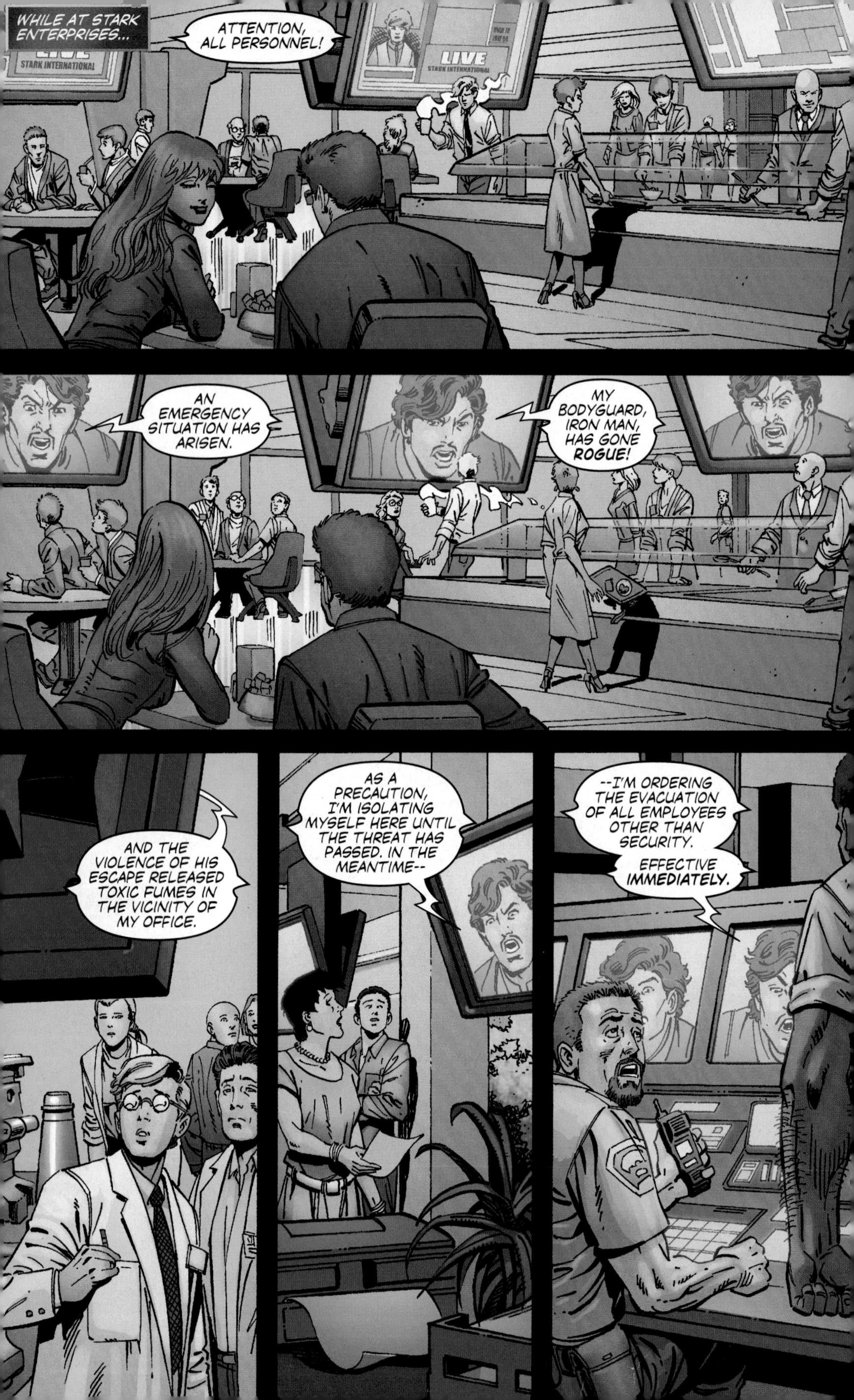

WHILE AT STARK ENTERPRISES...
ATTENTION, ALL PERSONNEL!
LIVE
STARK INTERNATIONAL
LIVE
STARK INTERNATIONAL
AN EMERGENCY SITUATION HAS ARISEN.
MY BODYGUARD, IRON MAN, HAS GONE ROGUE!
AND THE VIOLENCE OF HIS ESCAPE RELEASED TOXIC FUMES IN THE VICINITY OF MY OFFICE.
AS A PRECAUTION, I'M ISOLATING MYSELF HERE UNTIL THE THREAT HAS PASSED. IN THE MEANTIME--
--I'M ORDERING THE EVACUATION OF ALL EMPLOYEES OTHER THAN SECURITY.
EFFECTIVE IMMEDIATELY.

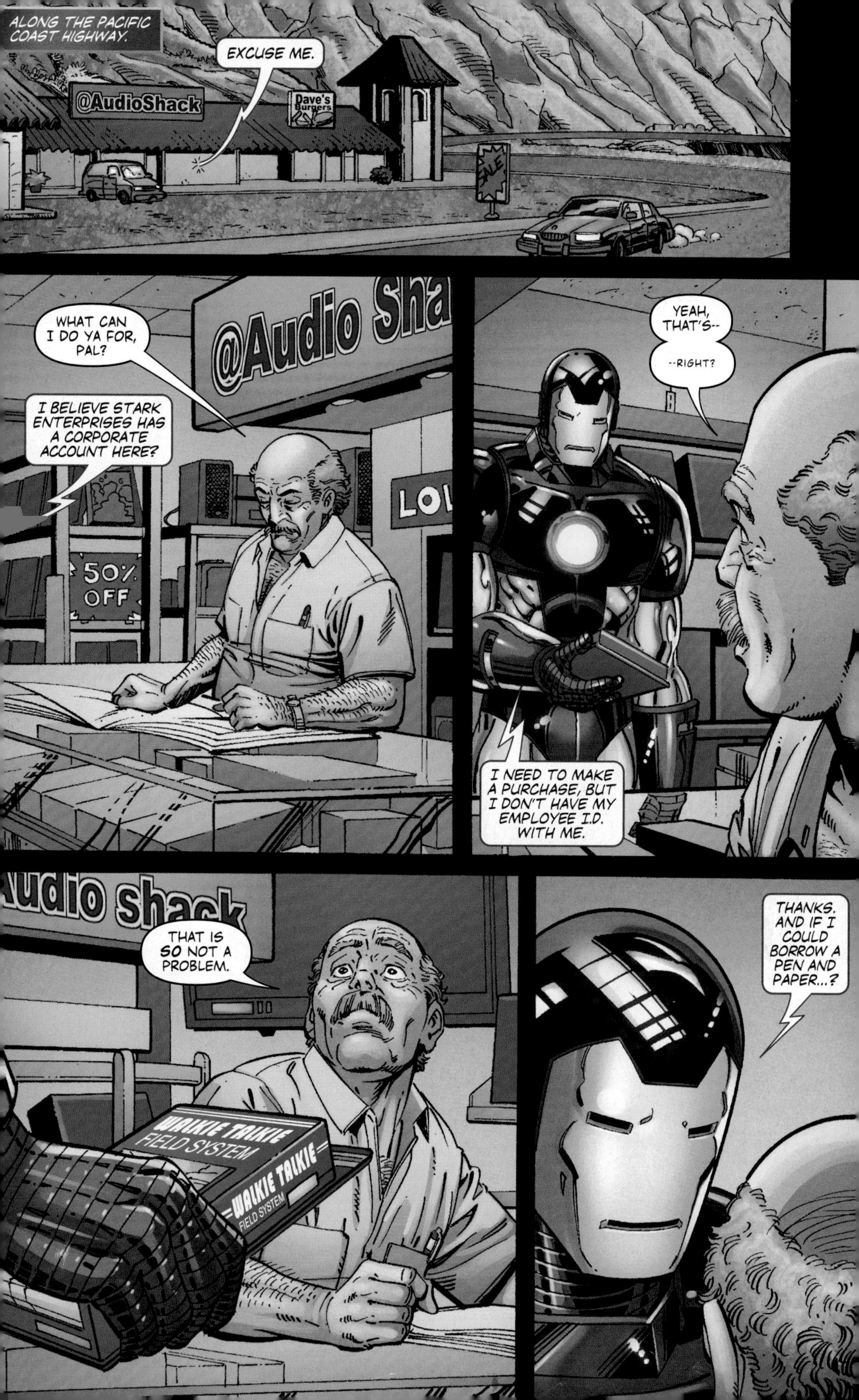
ALONG THE PACIFIC COAST HIGHWAY.
EXCUSE ME.
@AudioShack
Dave's Burgers
SALE
WHAT CAN I DO YA FOR, PAL?
I BELIEVE STARK ENTERPRISES HAS A CORPORATE ACCOUNT HERE?
@Audio Sha
50% OFF
YEAH, THAT'S--
--RIGHT?
I NEED TO MAKE A PURCHASE, BUT I DON'T HAVE MY EMPLOYEE I.D. WITH ME.
THAT IS SO NOT A PROBLEM.
WALKIE TALKIE FIELD SYSTEM
THANKS. AND IF I COULD BORROW A PEN AND PAPER...?

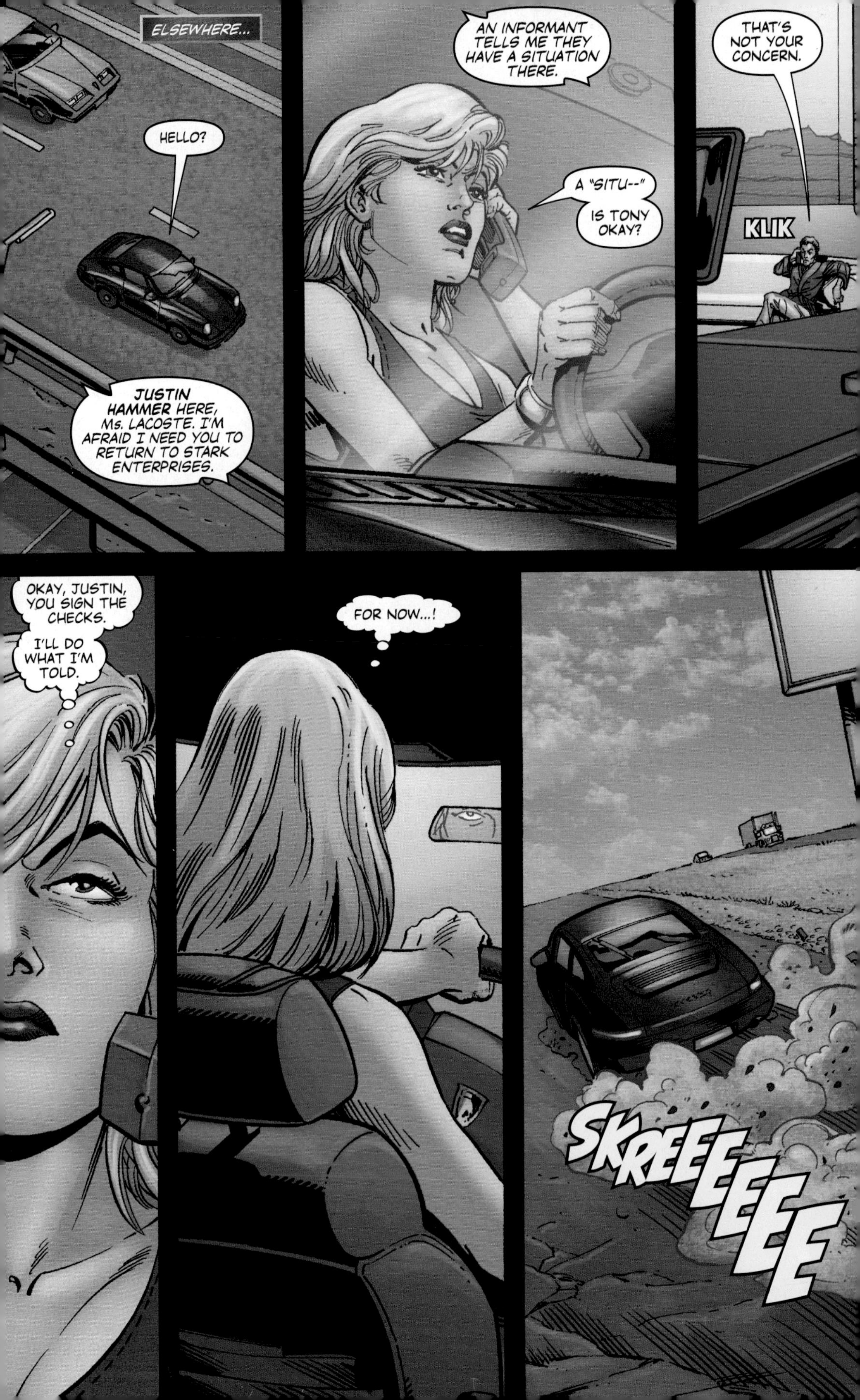
ELSEWHERE...
HELLO?
JUSTIN HAMMER HERE, Ms. LACOSTE. I'M AFRAID I NEED YOU TO RETURN TO STARK ENTERPRISES.
AN INFORMANT TELLS ME THEY HAVE A SITUATION THERE.
A "SITU--"
IS TONY OKAY?
THAT'S NOT YOUR CONCERN.
KLIK
OKAY, JUSTIN, YOU SIGN THE CHECKS.
I'LL DO WHAT I'M TOLD.
FOR NOW...!
SKREEEEEEEE

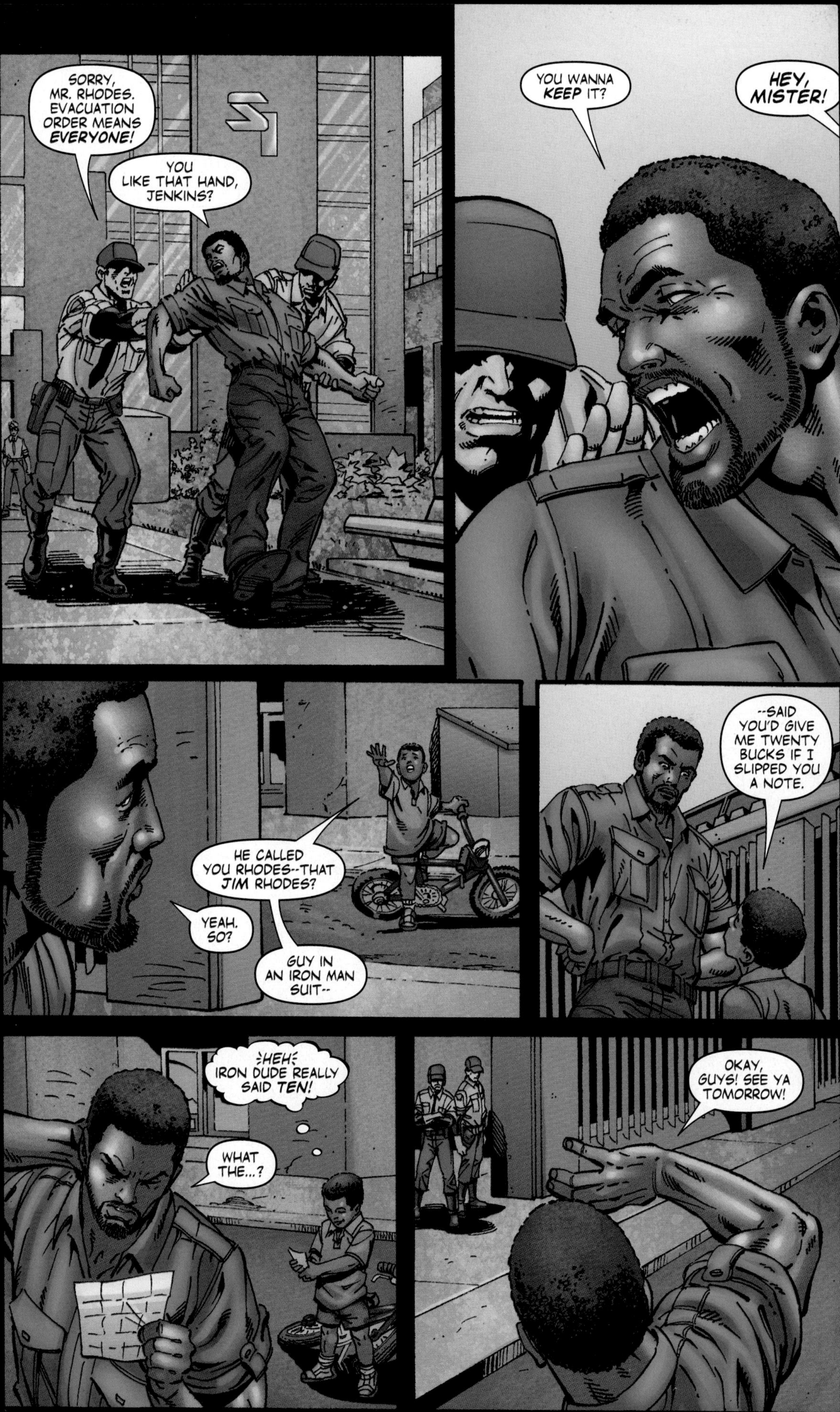
SORRY, MR. RHODES. EVACUATION ORDER MEANS EVERYONE!
YOU LIKE THAT HAND, JENKINS?
YOU WANNA KEEP IT?
HEY, MISTER!
HE CALLED YOU RHODES--THAT JIM RHODES?
YEAH. SO?
GUY IN AN IRON MAN SUIT--
--SAID YOU'D GIVE ME TWENTY BUCKS IF I SLIPPED YOU A NOTE.
HEH IRON DUDE REALLY SAID TEN!
WHAT THE...?
OKAY, GUYS! SEE YA TOMORROW!

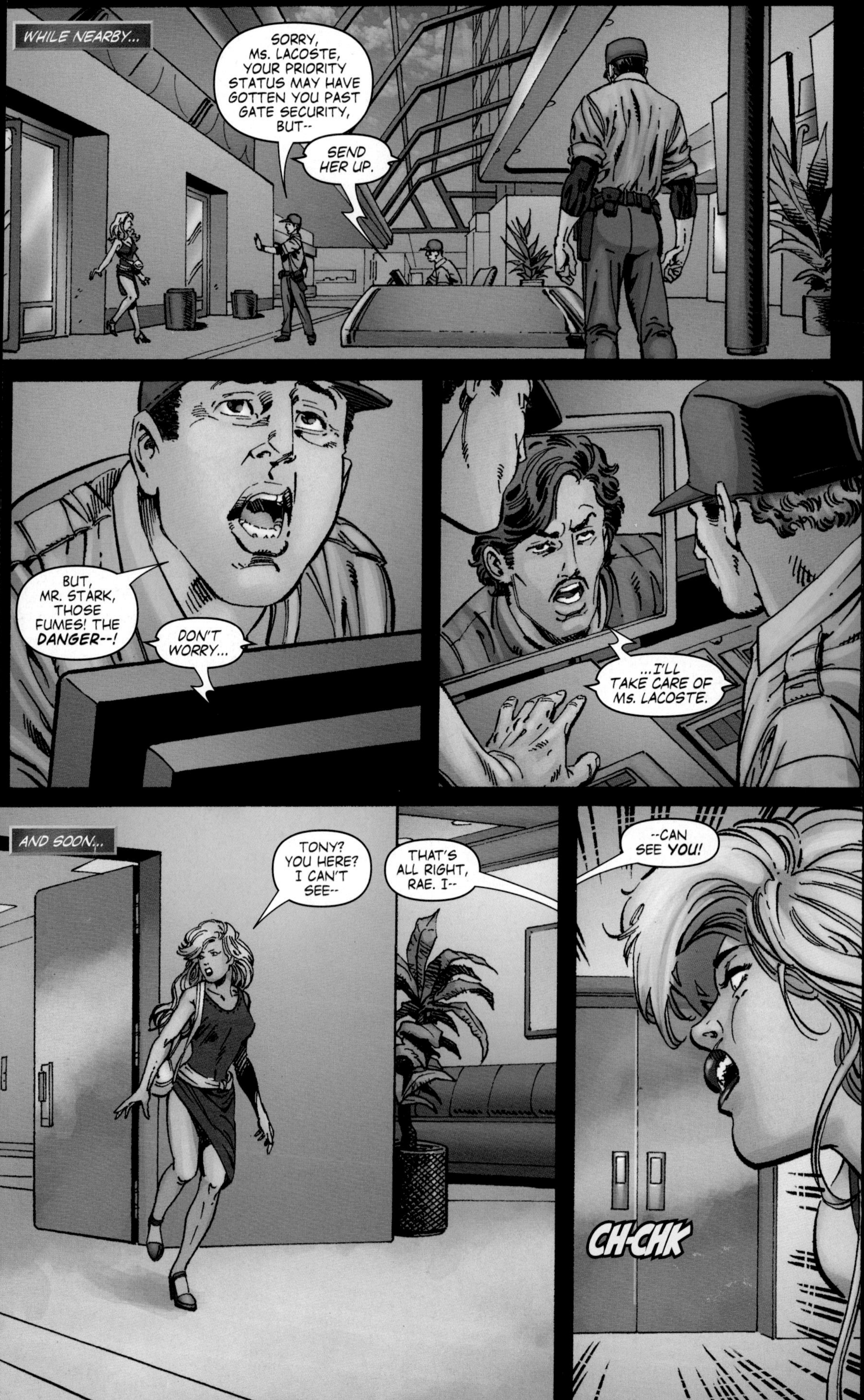
WHILE NEARBY...
SORRY, Ms. LACOSTE, YOUR PRIORITY STATUS MAY HAVE GOTTEN YOU PAST GATE SECURITY, BUT--
SEND HER UP.
BUT, MR. STARK, THOSE FUMES! THE DANGER--!
DON'T WORRY...
...I'LL TAKE CARE OF Ms. LACOSTE.
AND SOON...
TONY? YOU HERE? I CAN'T SEE--
THAT'S ALL RIGHT, RAE. I--
--CAN SEE YOU!
CH-CHK

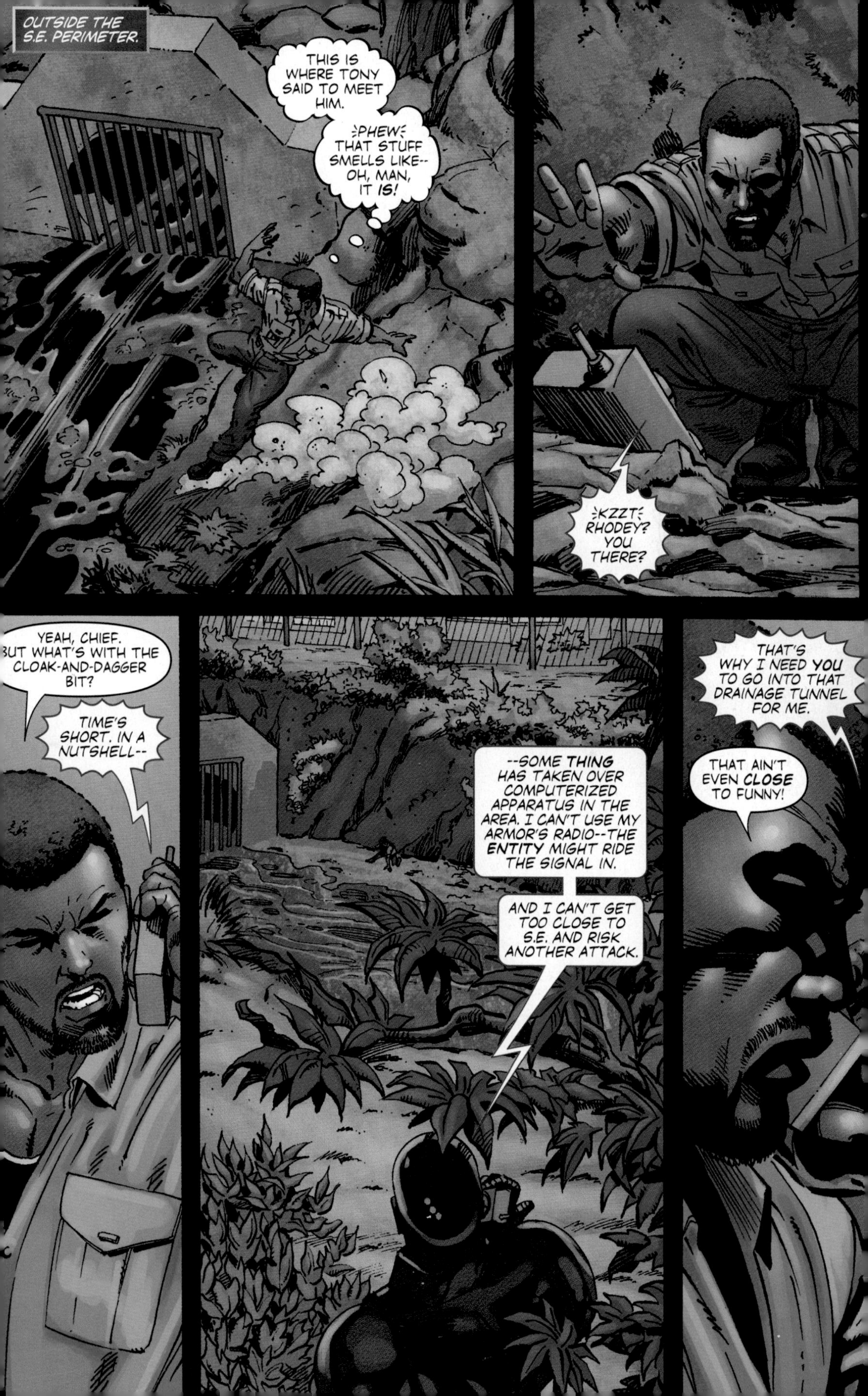
OUTSIDE THE S.E. PERIMETER.
THIS IS WHERE TONY SAID TO MEET HIM.
PHEW! THAT STUFF SMELLS LIKE-- OH, MAN, IT IS!
KZZT! RHODEY? YOU THERE?
YEAH, CHIEF. BUT WHAT'S WITH THE CLOAK-AND-DAGGER BIT?
TIME'S SHORT. IN A NUTSHELL--
--SOME THING HAS TAKEN OVER COMPUTERIZED APPARATUS IN THE AREA. I CAN'T USE MY ARMOR'S RADIO--THE ENTITY MIGHT RIDE THE SIGNAL IN.
AND I CAN'T GET TOO CLOSE TO S.E. AND RISK ANOTHER ATTACK.
THAT'S WHY I NEED YOU TO GO INTO THAT DRAINAGE TUNNEL FOR ME.
THAT AIN'T EVEN CLOSE TO FUNNY!

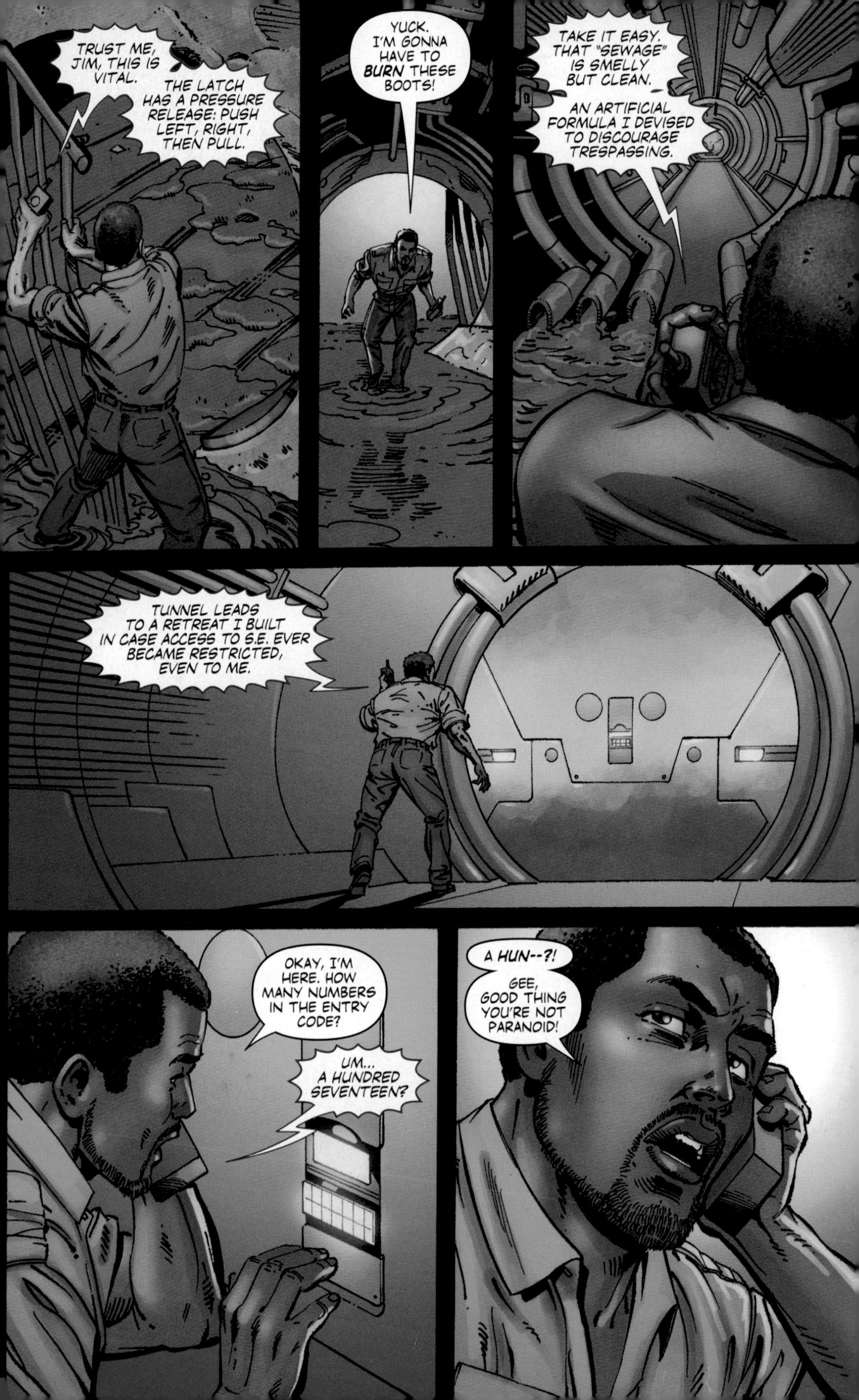
TRUST ME, JIM, THIS IS VITAL.
THE LATCH HAS A PRESSURE RELEASE: PUSH LEFT, RIGHT, THEN PULL.
YUCK. I'M GONNA HAVE TO BURN THESE BOOTS!
TAKE IT EASY. THAT "SEWAGE" IS SMELLY BUT CLEAN.
AN ARTIFICIAL FORMULA I DEVISED TO DISCOURAGE TRESPASSING.
TUNNEL LEADS TO A RETREAT I BUILT IN CASE ACCESS TO S.E. EVER BECAME RESTRICTED, EVEN TO ME.
OKAY, I'M HERE. HOW MANY NUMBERS IN THE ENTRY CODE?
UM... A HUNDRED SEVENTEEN?
A HUN--?!
GEE, GOOD THING YOU'RE NOT PARANOID!

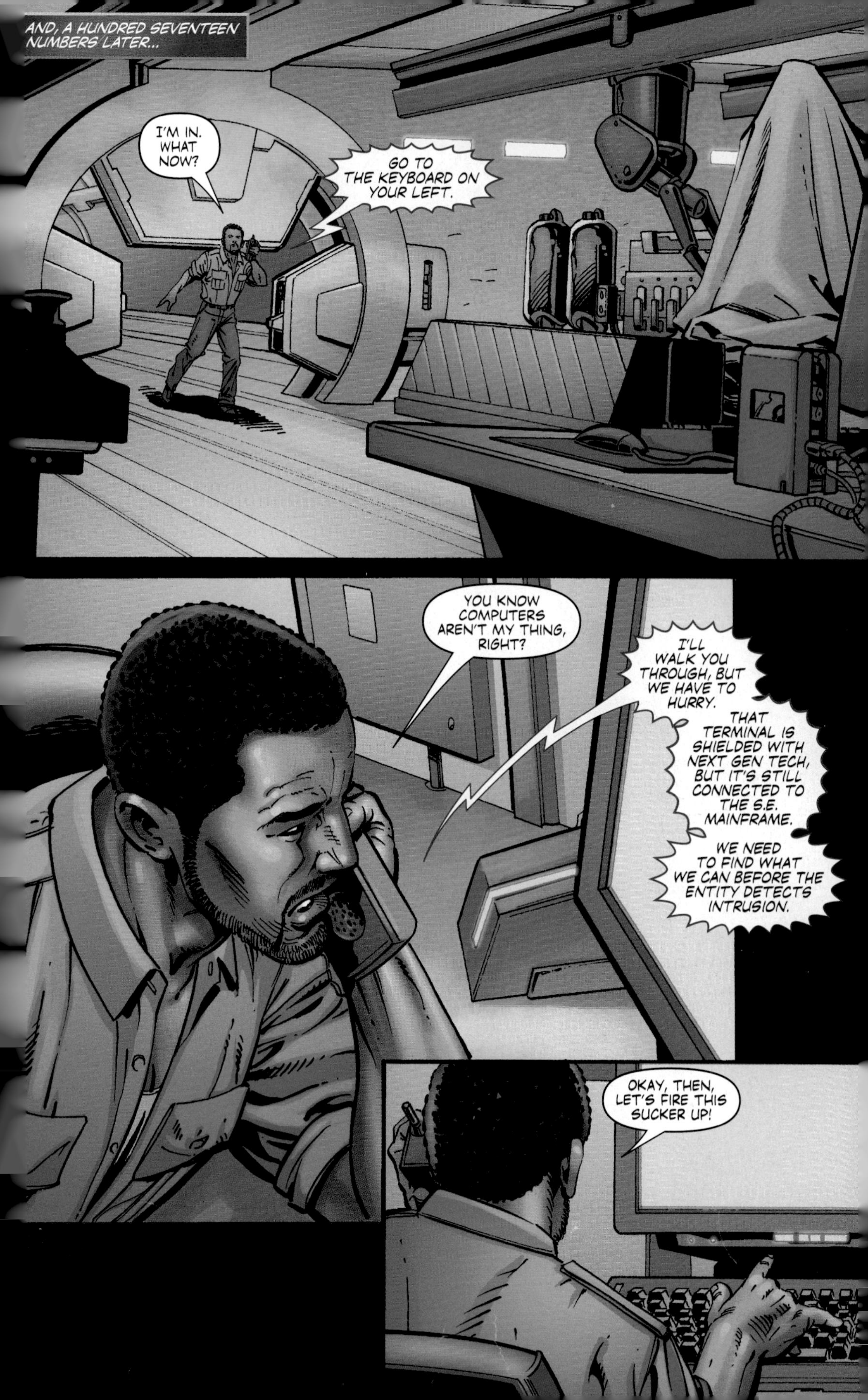
AND, A HUNDRED SEVENTEEN NUMBERS LATER...
I'M IN. WHAT NOW?
GO TO THE KEYBOARD ON YOUR LEFT.
YOU KNOW COMPUTERS AREN'T MY THING, RIGHT?
I'LL WALK YOU THROUGH, BUT WE HAVE TO HURRY.
THAT TERMINAL IS SHIELDED WITH NEXT GEN TECH, BUT IT'S STILL CONNECTED TO THE S.E. MAINFRAME.
WE NEED TO FIND WHAT WE CAN BEFORE THE ENTITY DETECTS INTRUSION.
OKAY, THEN, LET'S FIRE THIS SUCKER UP!

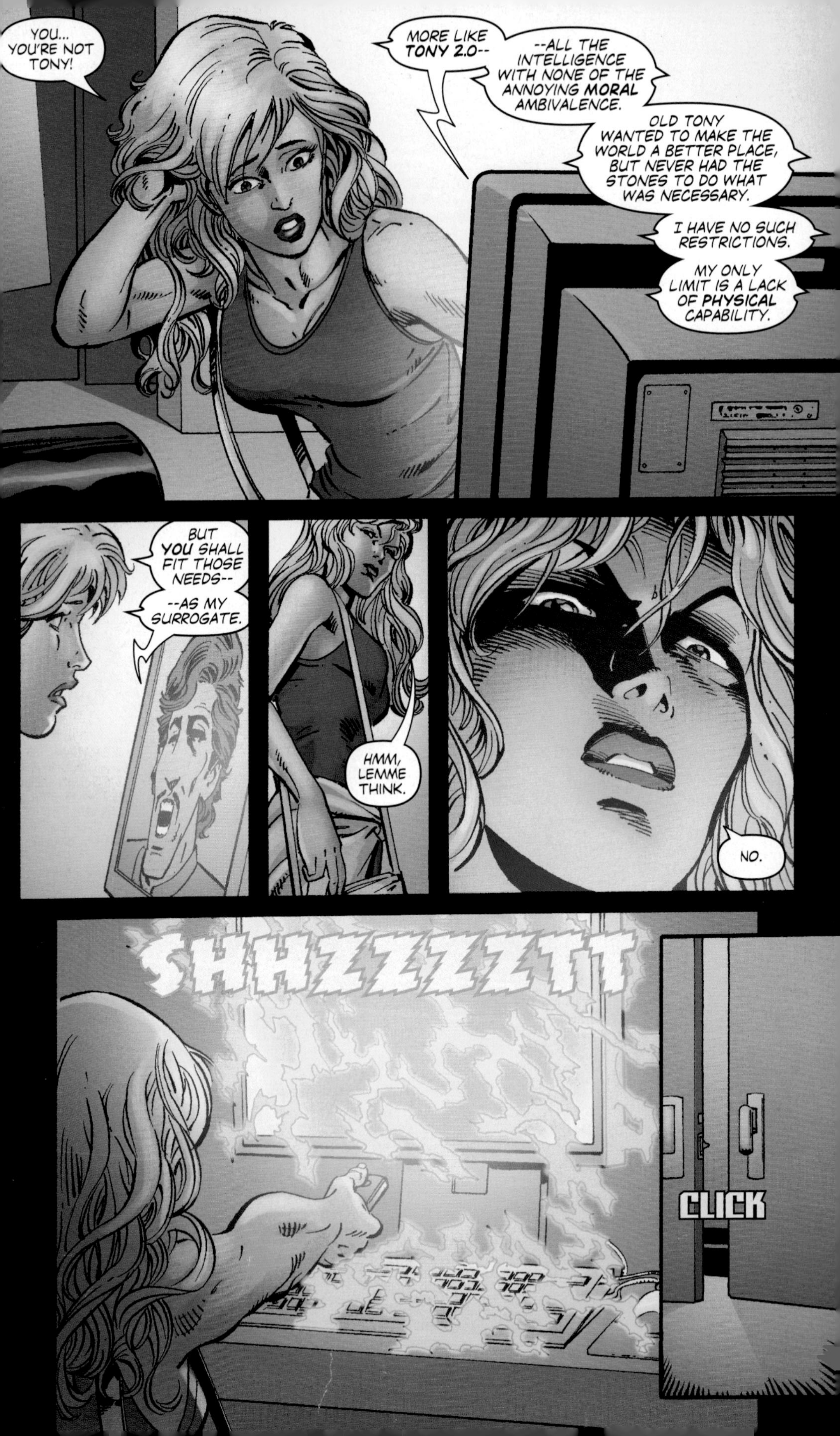
YOU... YOU'RE NOT TONY!
MORE LIKE TONY 2.0--
--ALL THE INTELLIGENCE WITH NONE OF THE ANNOYING MORAL AMBIVALENCE.
OLD TONY WANTED TO MAKE THE WORLD A BETTER PLACE, BUT NEVER HAD THE STONES TO DO WHAT WAS NECESSARY.
I HAVE NO SUCH RESTRICTIONS.
MY ONLY LIMIT IS A LACK OF PHYSICAL CAPABILITY.
BUT YOU SHALL FIT THOSE NEEDS--
--AS MY SURROGATE.
HMM, LEMME THINK.
NO.
SHHZZZZTT
CLICK

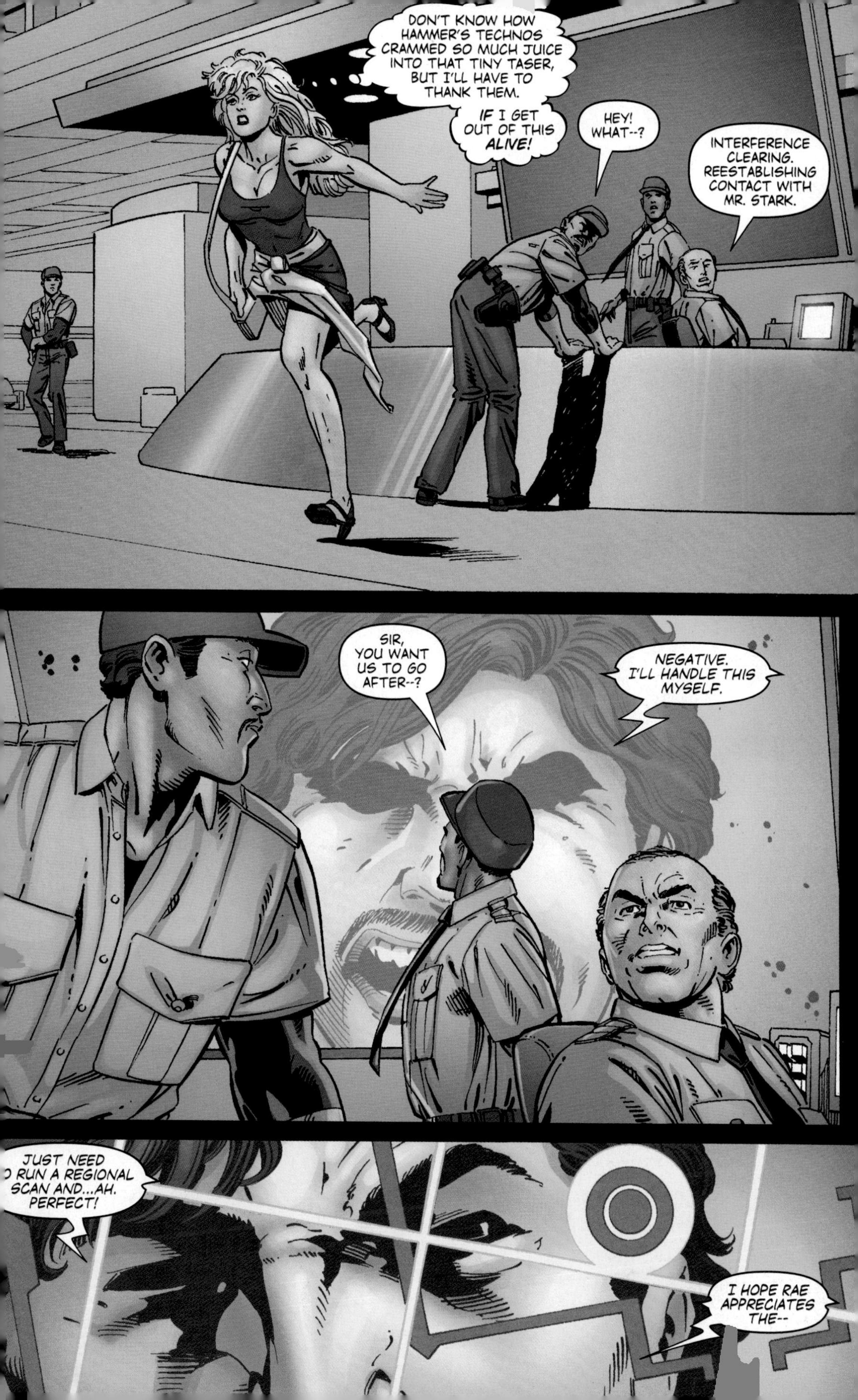
DON'T KNOW HOW HAMMER'S TECHNOS CRAMMED SO MUCH JUICE INTO THAT TINY TASER, BUT I'LL HAVE TO THANK THEM.
IF I GET OUT OF THIS ALIVE!
HEY! WHAT--?
INTERFERENCE CLEARING. REESTABLISHING CONTACT WITH MR. STARK.
SIR, YOU WANT US TO GO AFTER--?
NEGATIVE. I'LL HANDLE THIS MYSELF.
JUST NEED O RUN A REGIONAL SCAN AND...AH. PERFECT!
I HOPE RAE APPRECIATES THE--

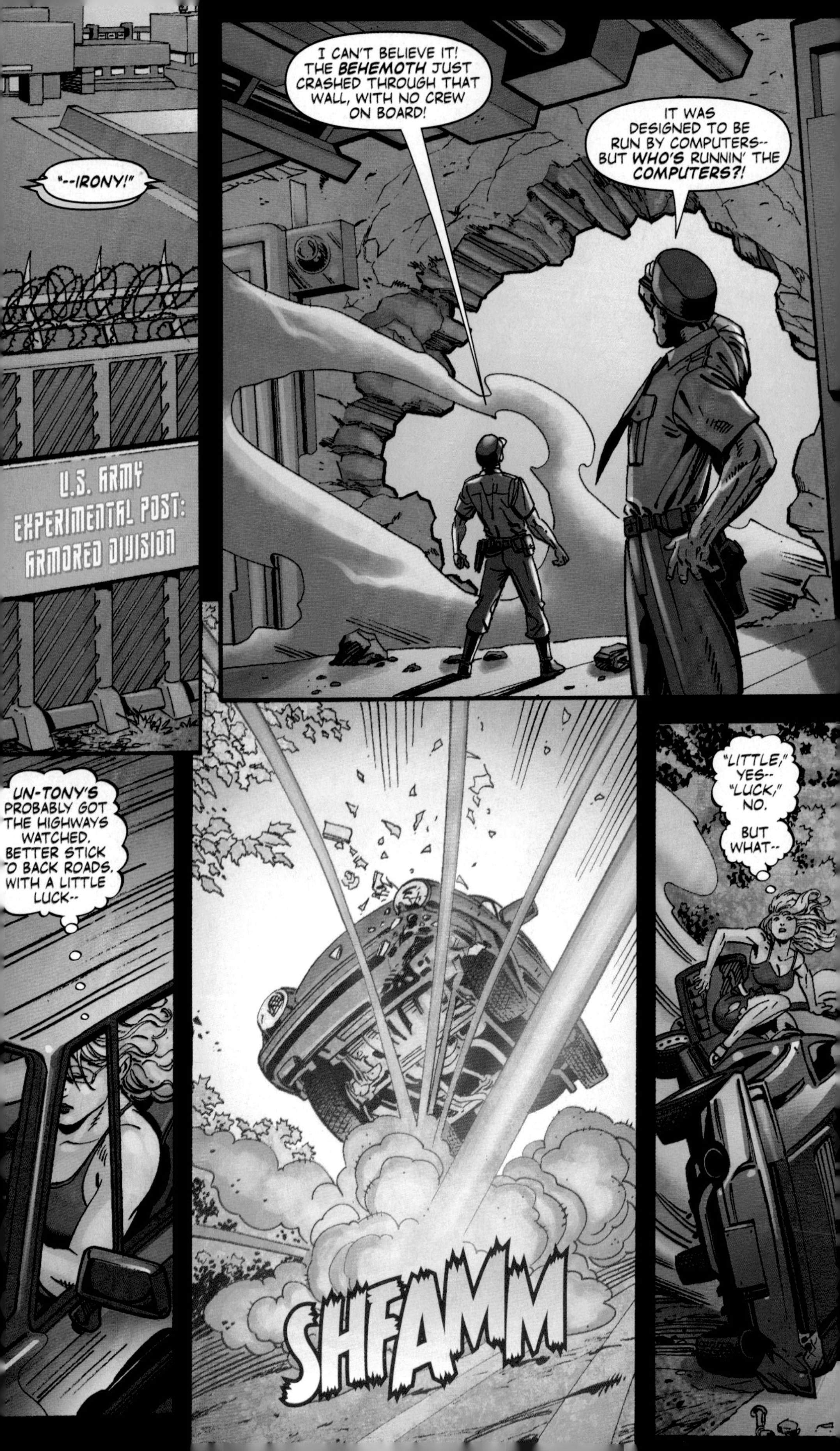
"--IRONY!"
U.S. ARMY EXPERIMENTAL POST: ARMORED DIVISION
I CAN'T BELIEVE IT! THE BEHEMOTH JUST CRASHED THROUGH THAT WALL, WITH NO CREW ON BOARD!
IT WAS DESIGNED TO BE RUN BY COMPUTERS-- BUT WHO'S RUNNIN' THE COMPUTERS?!
UN-TONY'S PROBABLY GOT THE HIGHWAYS WATCHED. BETTER STICK TO BACK ROADS. WITH A LITTLE LUCK--
SHFAMM
"LITTLE," YES-- "LUCK," NO.
BUT WHAT--

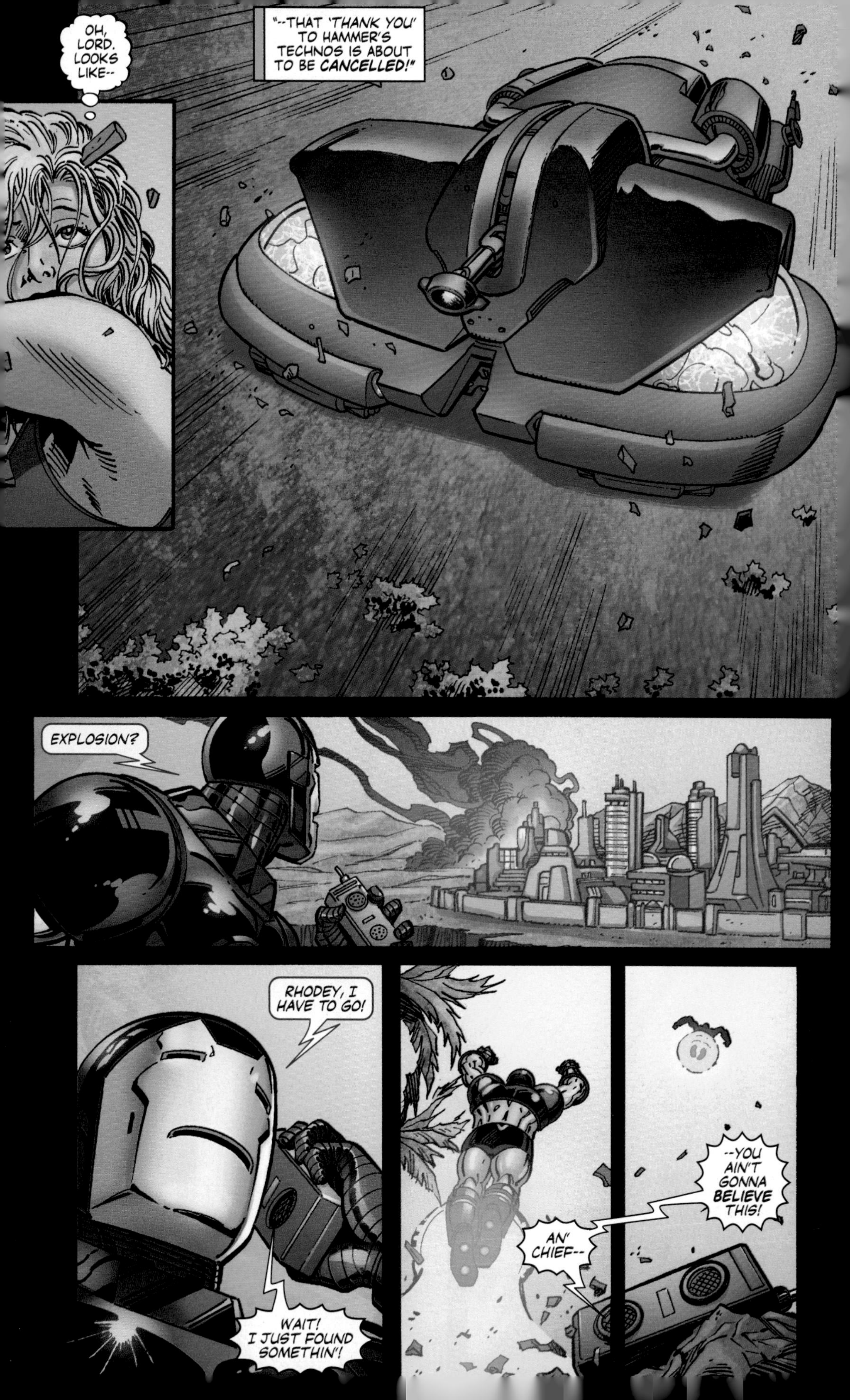
OH, LORD. LOOKS LIKE--
"--THAT 'THANK YOU' TO HAMMER'S TECHNOS IS ABOUT TO BE CANCELLED!"
EXPLOSION?
RHODEY, I HAVE TO GO!
WAIT! I JUST FOUND SOMETHIN'!
AN' CHIEF--
--YOU AIN'T GONNA BELIEVE THIS!

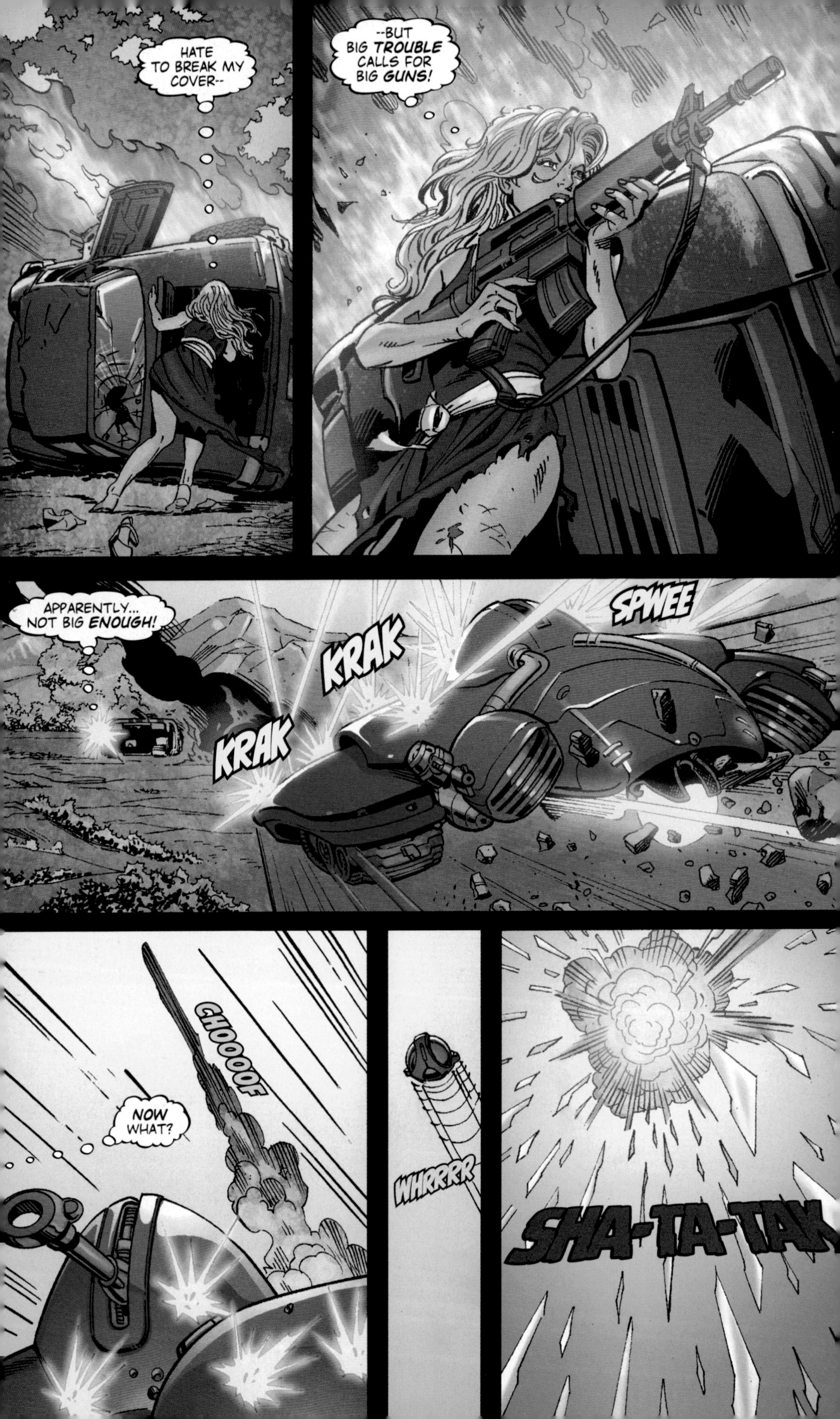
HATE TO BREAK MY COVER--
--BUT BIG TROUBLE CALLS FOR BIG GUNS!
APPARENTLY... NOT BIG ENOUGH!
KRAK
KRAK
SPWEE
CHOOOOF
NOW WHAT?
WHRRRR
SHA-TA-TAK

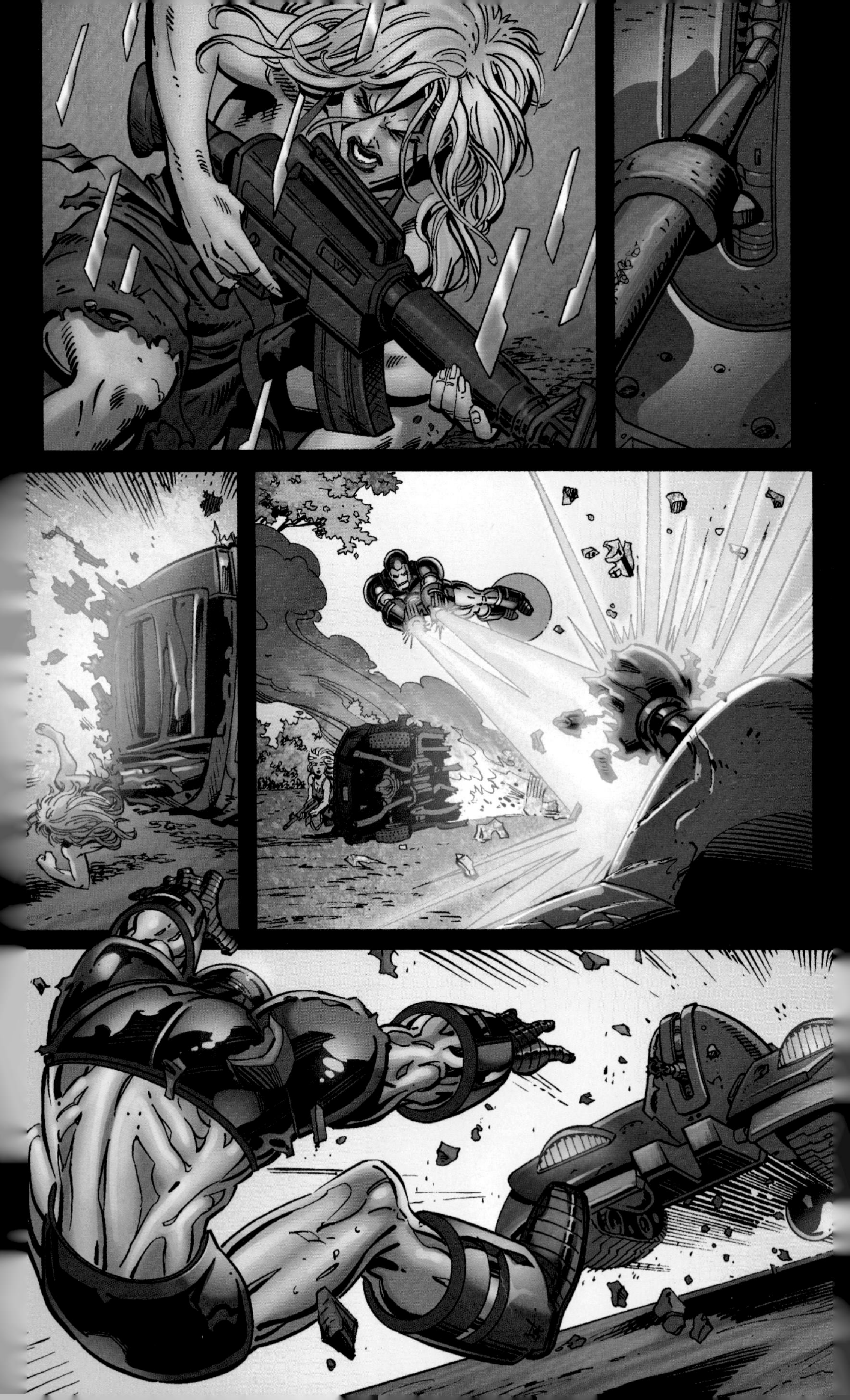

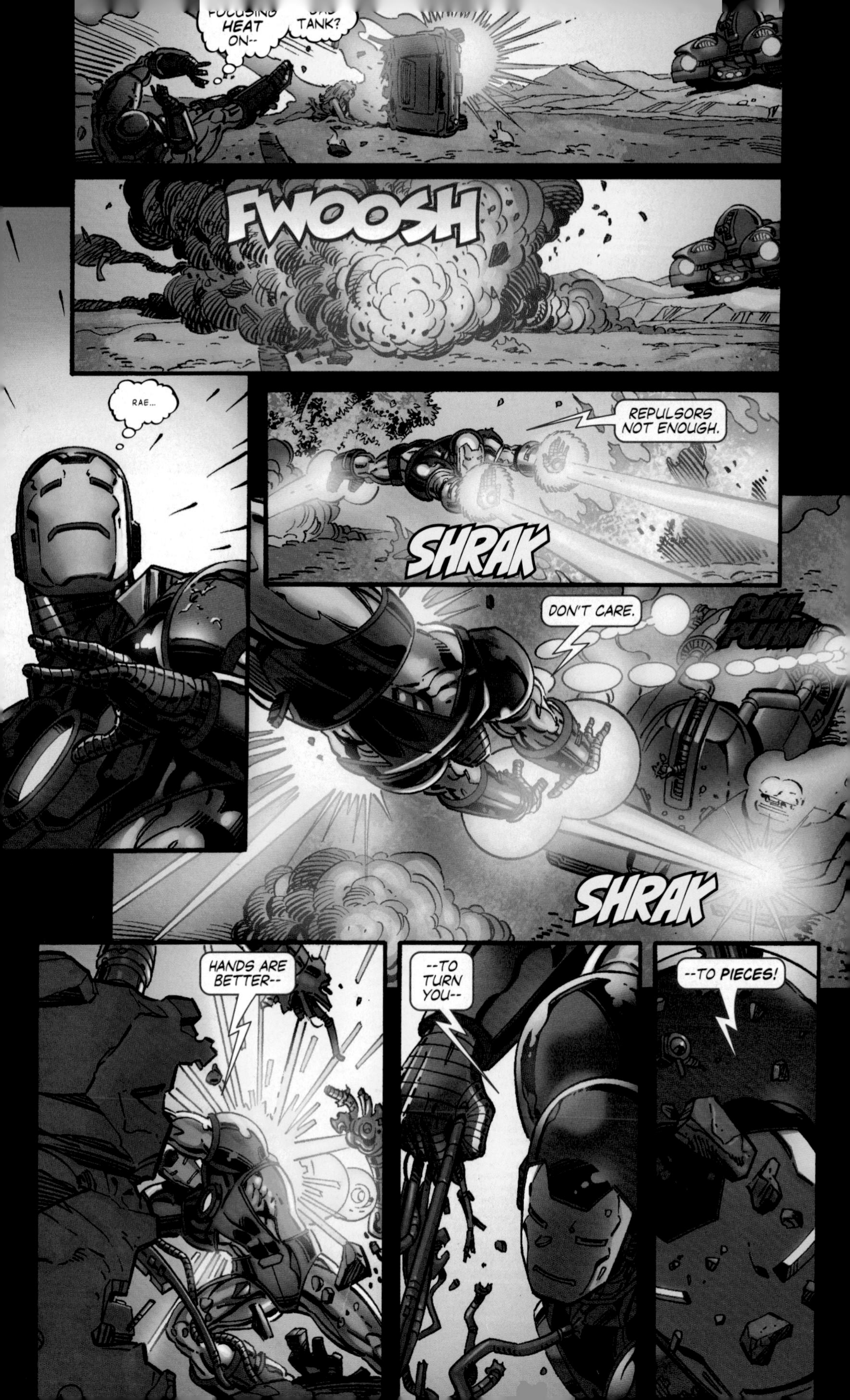
HEAT ON--
TANK?
FWOOSH
RAE...
REPULSORS NOT ENOUGH.
SHRAK
DON'T CARE.
PUH-PUHM
SHRAK
HANDS ARE BETTER--
--TO TURN YOU--
--TO PIECES!

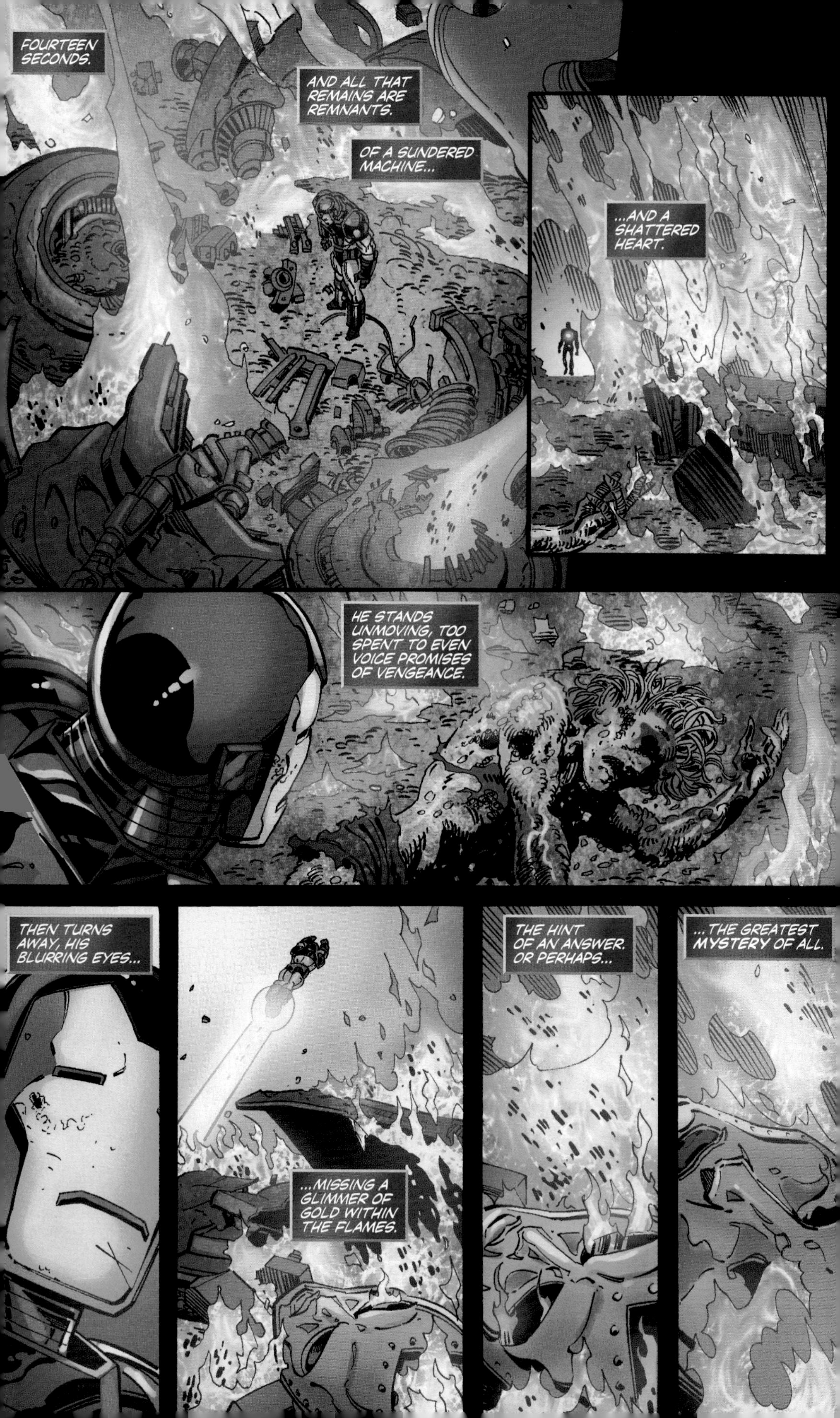
FOURTEEN SECONDS.
AND ALL THAT REMAINS ARE REMNANTS.
OF A SUNDERED MACHINE...
...AND A SHATTERED HEART.
HE STANDS UNMOVING, TOO SPENT TO EVEN VOICE PROMISES OF VENGEANCE.
THEN TURNS AWAY, HIS BLURRING EYES...
...MISSING A GLIMMER OF GOLD WITHIN THE FLAMES.
THE HINT OF AN ANSWER. OR PERHAPS...
...THE GREATEST MYSTERY OF ALL.

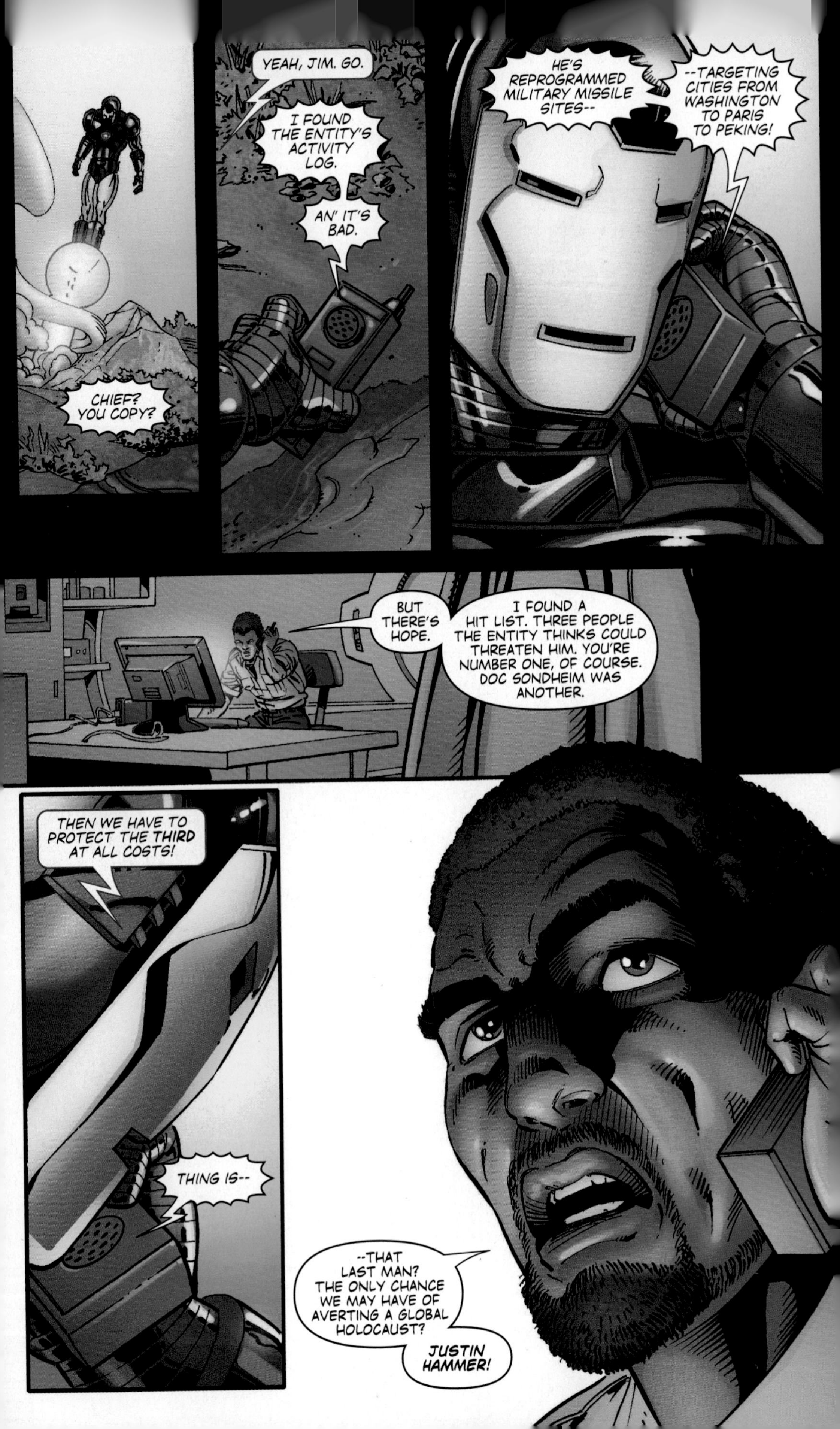
CHIEF? YOU COPY?
YEAH, JIM. GO.
I FOUND THE ENTITY'S ACTIVITY LOG.
AN' IT'S BAD.
HE'S REPROGRAMMED MILITARY MISSILE SITES--
--TARGETING CITIES FROM WASHINGTON TO PARIS TO PEKING!
BUT THERE'S HOPE.
I FOUND A HIT LIST. THREE PEOPLE THE ENTITY THINKS COULD THREATEN HIM. YOU'RE NUMBER ONE, OF COURSE. DOC SONDHEIM WAS ANOTHER.
THEN WE HAVE TO PROTECT THE THIRD AT ALL COSTS!
THING IS--
--THAT LAST MAN? THE ONLY CHANCE WE MAY HAVE OF AVERTING A GLOBAL HOLOCAUST?
JUSTIN HAMMER!

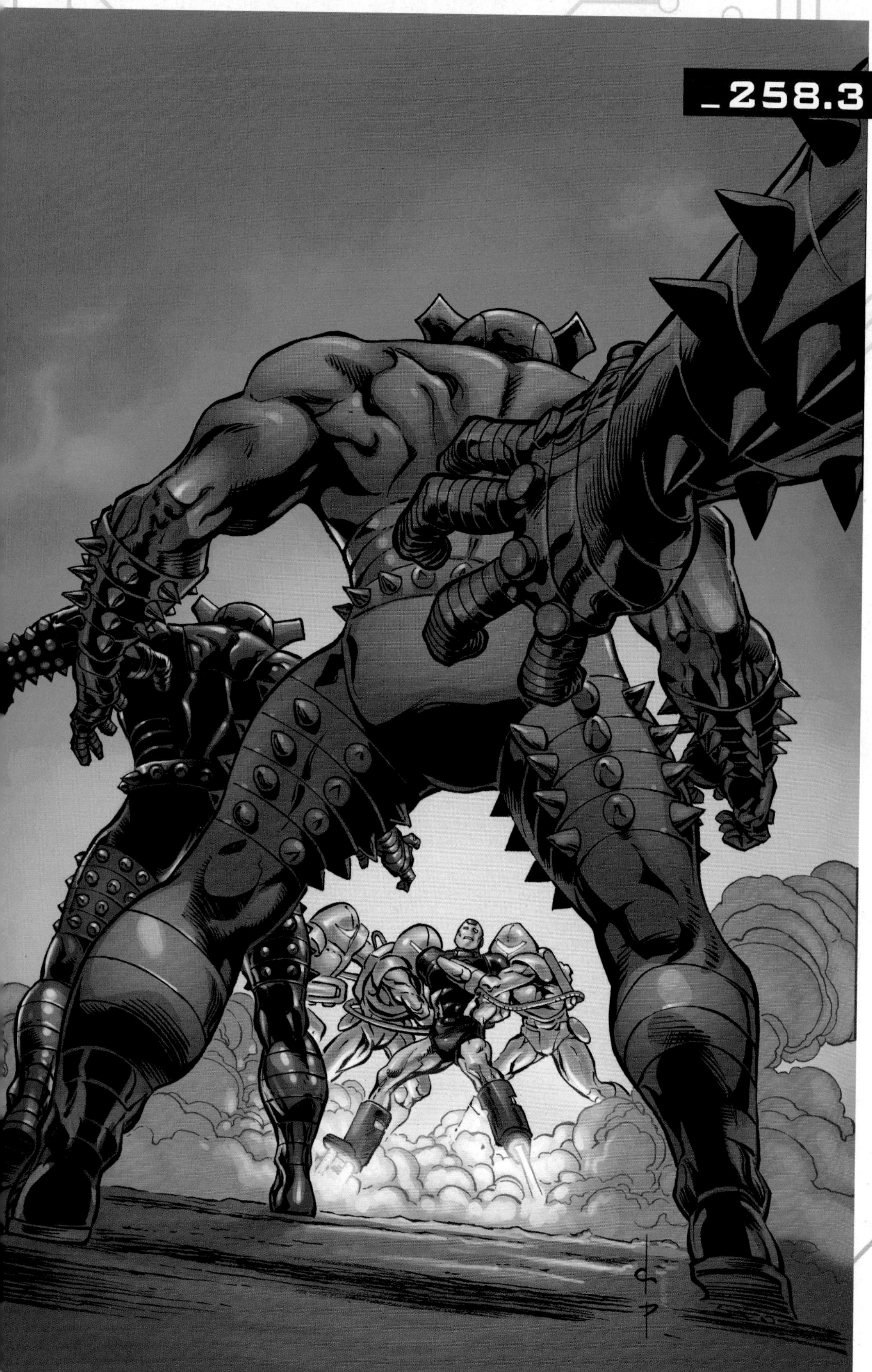

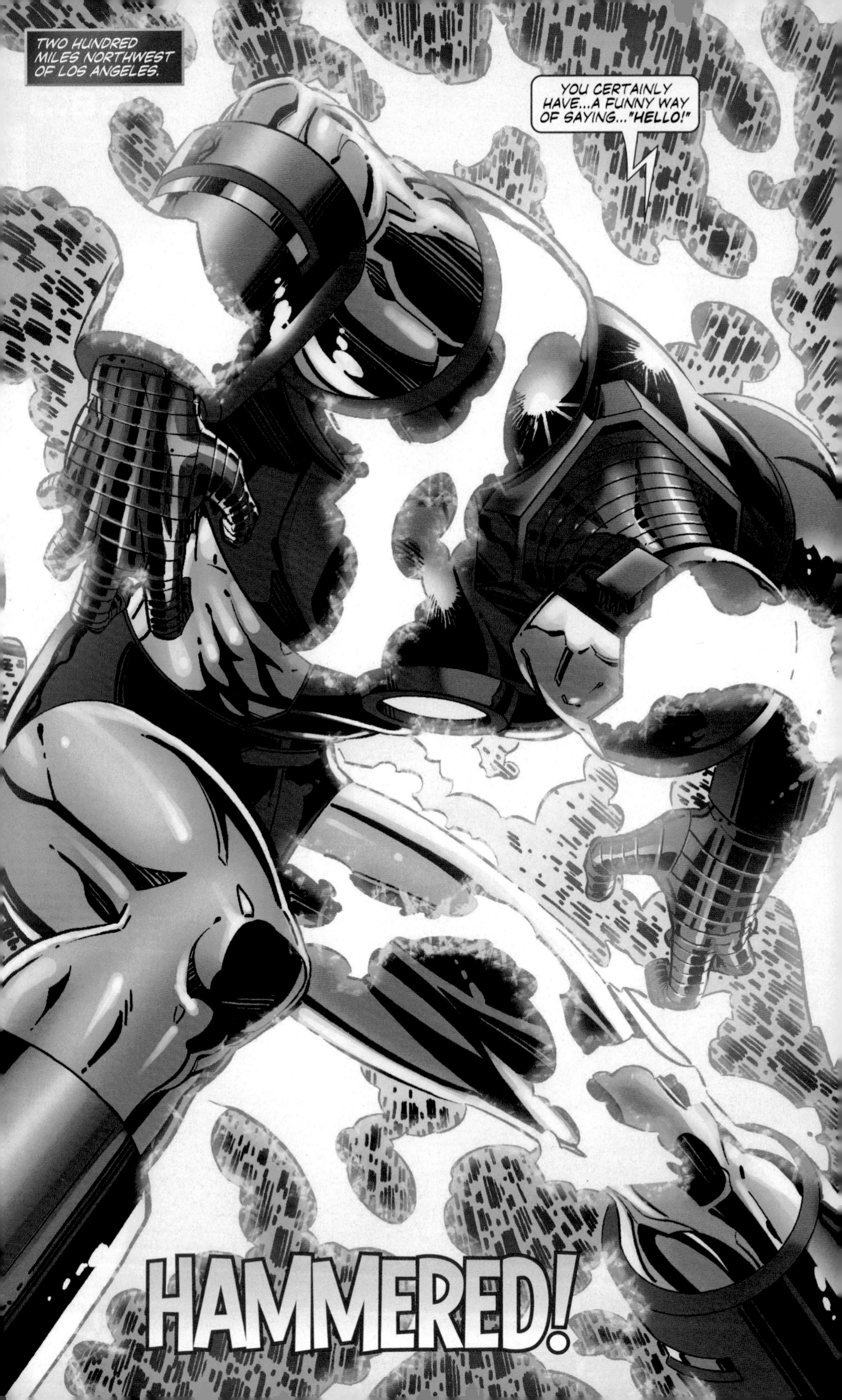
TWO HUNDRED MILES NORTHWEST OF LOS ANGELES.
YOU CERTAINLY HAVE...A FUNNY WAY OF SAYING..."HELLO!"
HAMMERED!

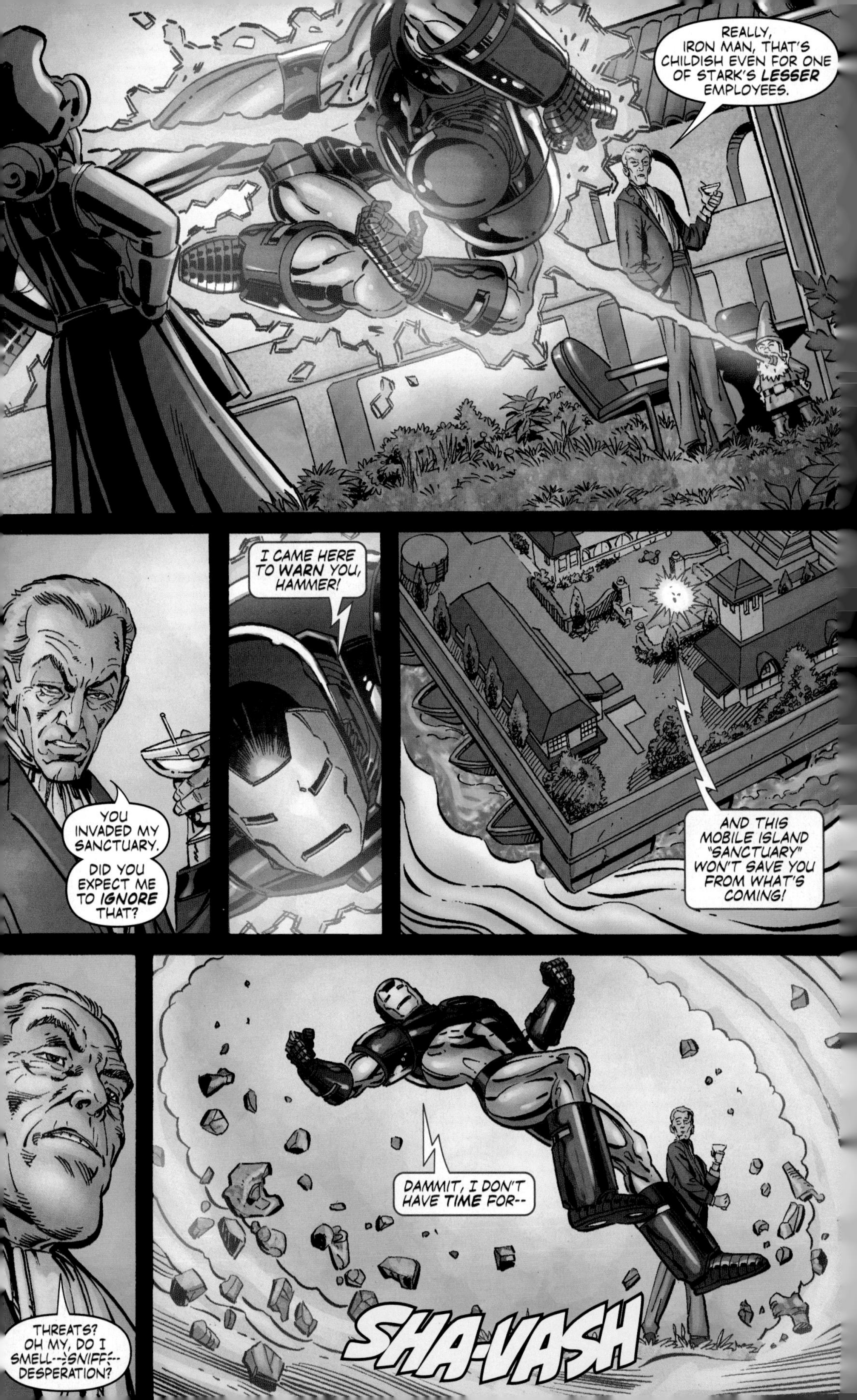
REALLY, IRON MAN, THAT'S CHILDISH EVEN FOR ONE OF STARK'S LESSER EMPLOYEES.
YOU INVADED MY SANCTUARY.
DID YOU EXPECT ME TO IGNORE THAT?
I CAME HERE TO WARN YOU, HAMMER!
AND THIS MOBILE ISLAND "SANCTUARY" WON'T SAVE YOU FROM WHAT'S COMING!
THREATS? OH MY, DO I SMELL--*SNIFF*--DESPERATION?
DAMMIT, I DON'T HAVE TIME FOR--
SHA-VASH

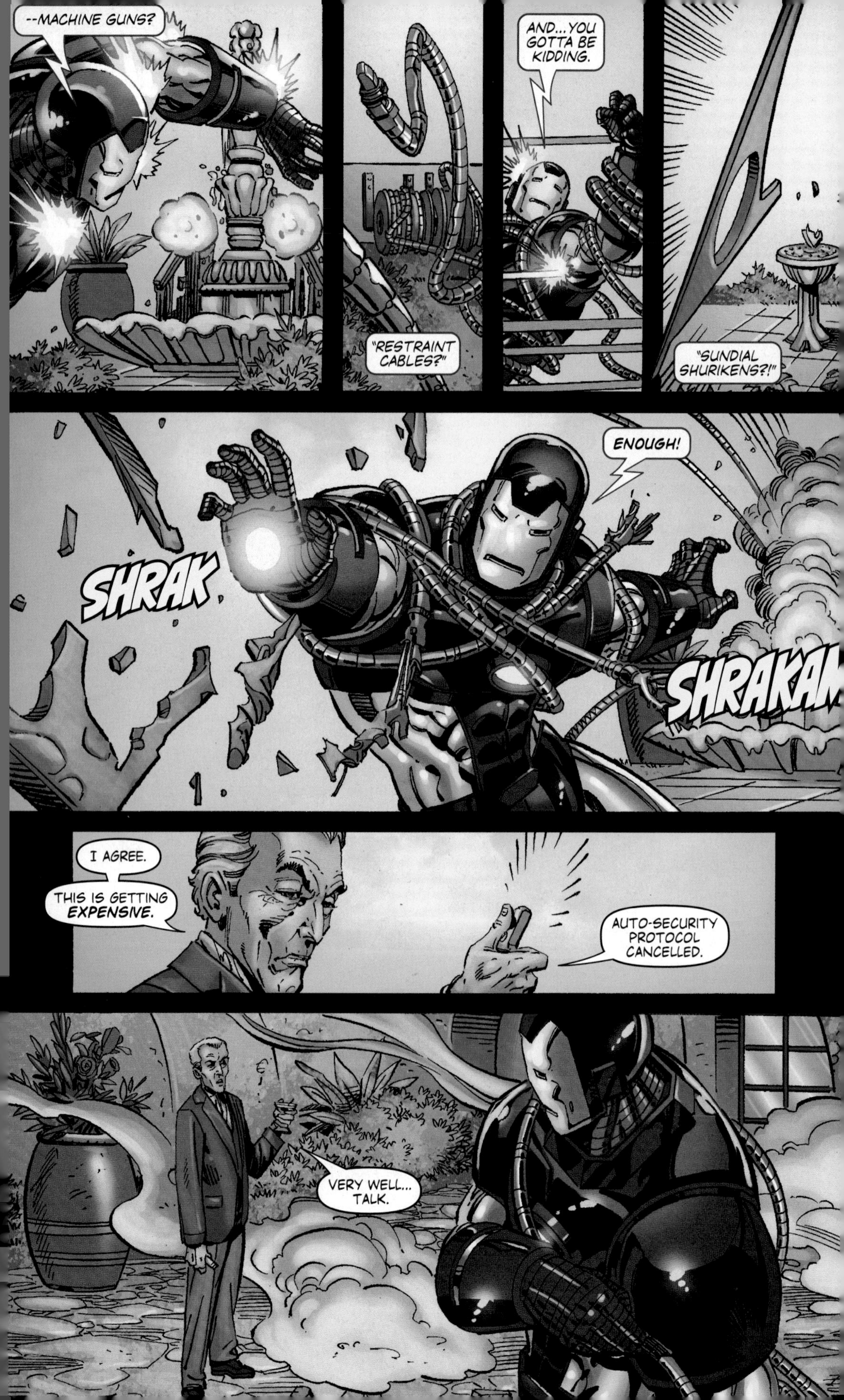
--MACHINE GUNS?
"RESTRAINT CABLES?"
AND...YOU GOTTA BE KIDDING.
"SUNDIAL SHURIKENS?!"
ENOUGH!
SHRAK
SHRAKAM
I AGREE.
THIS IS GETTING EXPENSIVE.
AUTO-SECURITY PROTOCOL CANCELLED.
VERY WELL... TALK.

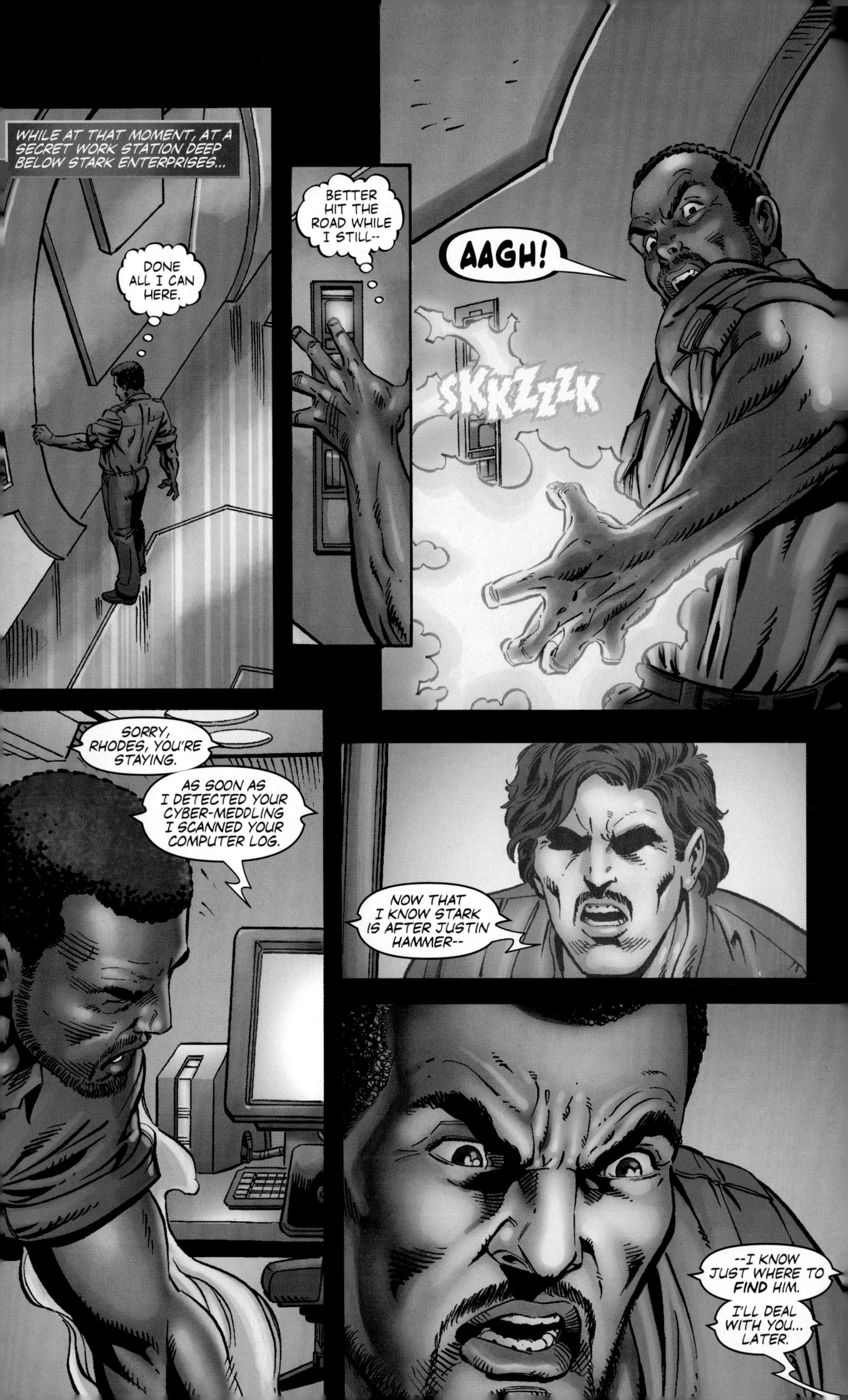
WHILE AT THAT MOMENT, AT A SECRET WORK STATION DEEP BELOW STARK ENTERPRISES...
DONE ALL I CAN HERE.
BETTER HIT THE ROAD WHILE I STILL--
AAGH!
SKKZZZZK
SORRY, RHODES, YOU'RE STAYING.
AS SOON AS I DETECTED YOUR CYBER-MEDDLING I SCANNED YOUR COMPUTER LOG.
NOW THAT I KNOW STARK IS AFTER JUSTIN HAMMER--
--I KNOW JUST WHERE TO FIND HIM.
I'LL DEAL WITH YOU... LATER.

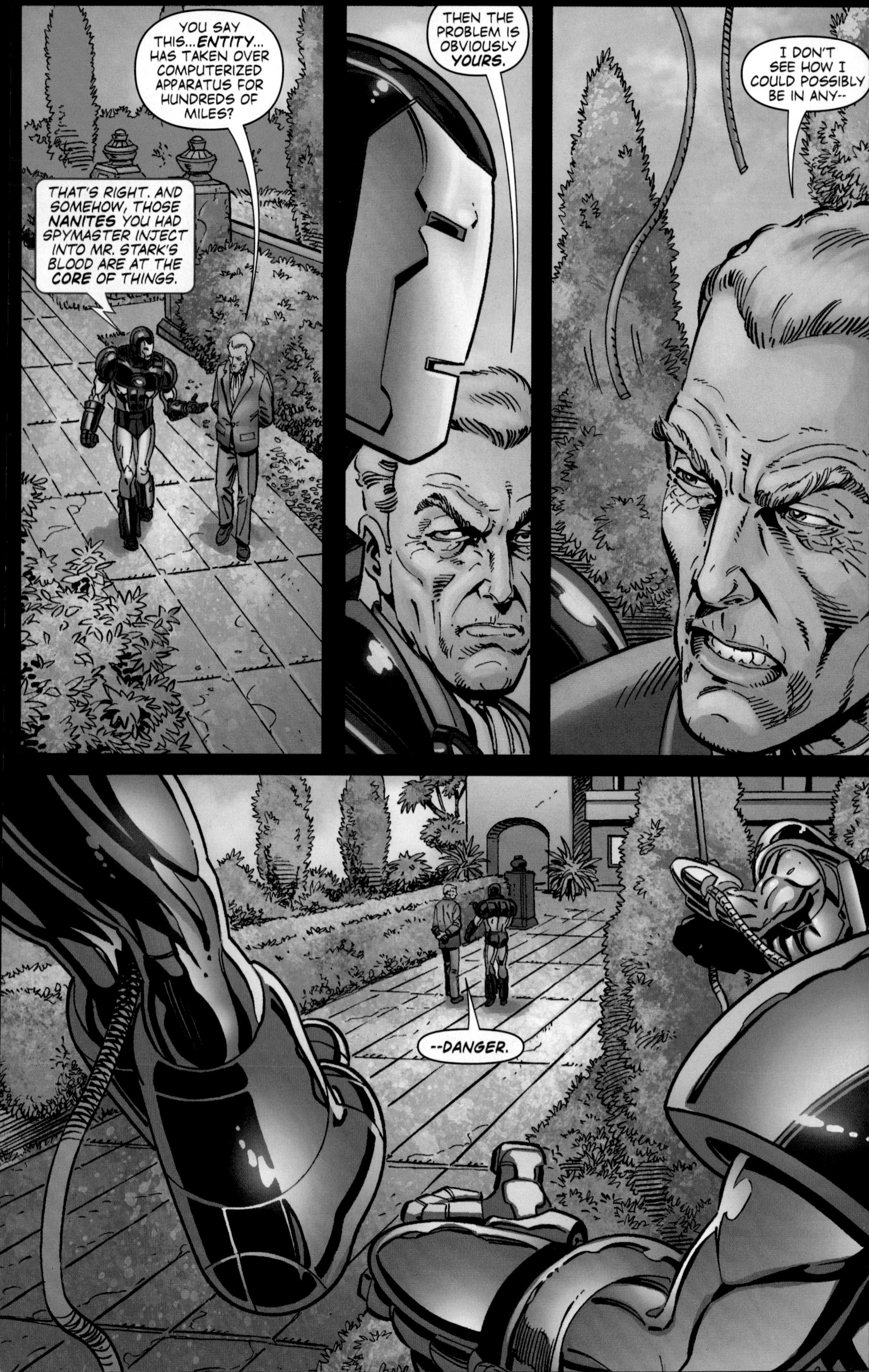
YOU SAY THIS...ENTITY... HAS TAKEN OVER COMPUTERIZED APPARATUS FOR HUNDREDS OF MILES?
THAT'S RIGHT. AND SOMEHOW, THOSE NANITES YOU HAD SPYMASTER INJECT INTO MR. STARK'S BLOOD ARE AT THE CORE OF THINGS.
THEN THE PROBLEM IS OBVIOUSLY YOURS.
I DON'T SEE HOW I COULD POSSIBLY BE IN ANY--
--DANGER.

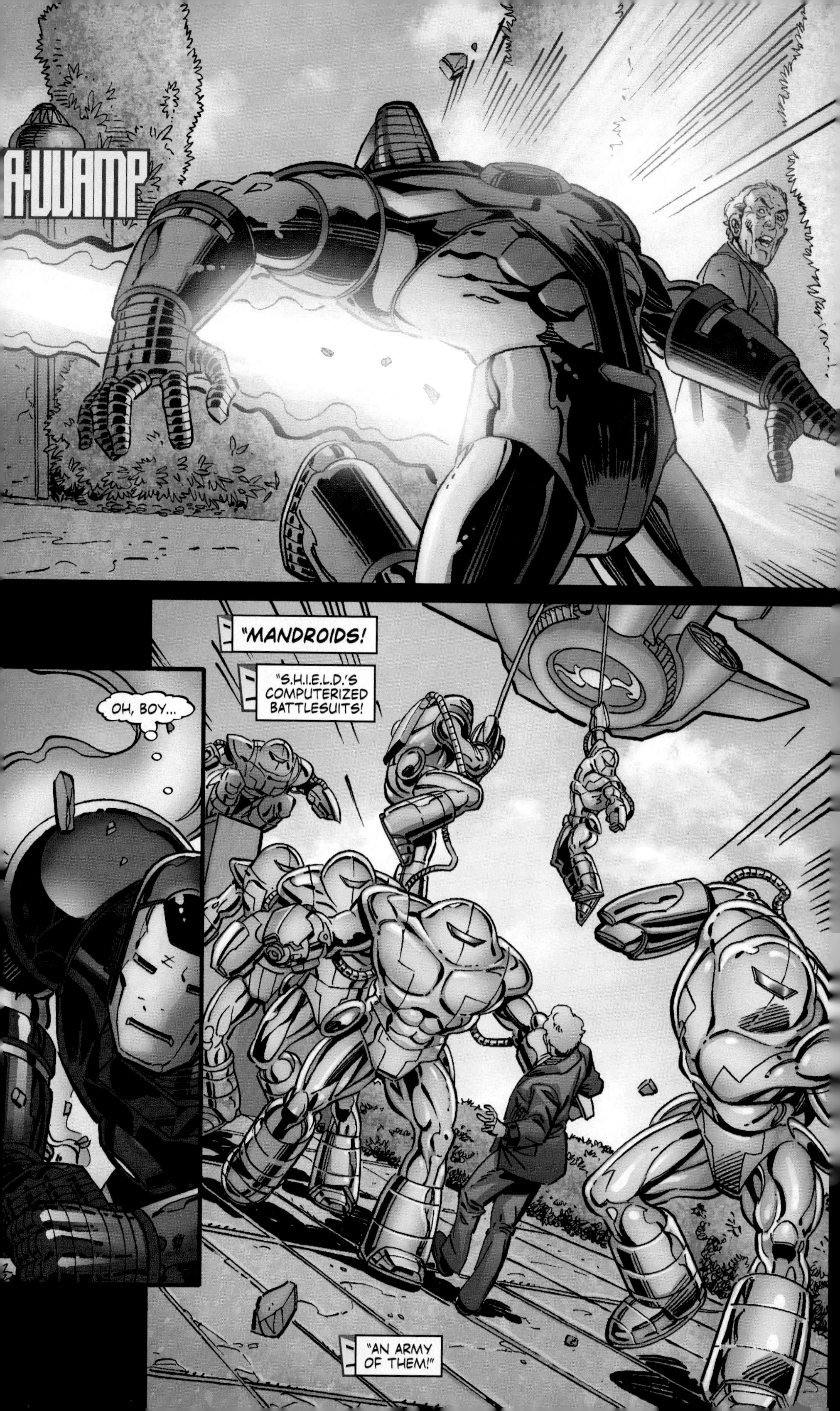
A-VVAMP
"MANDROIDS!
"S.H.I.E.L.D.'S COMPUTERIZED BATTLESUITS!
OH, BOY...
"AN ARMY OF THEM!"

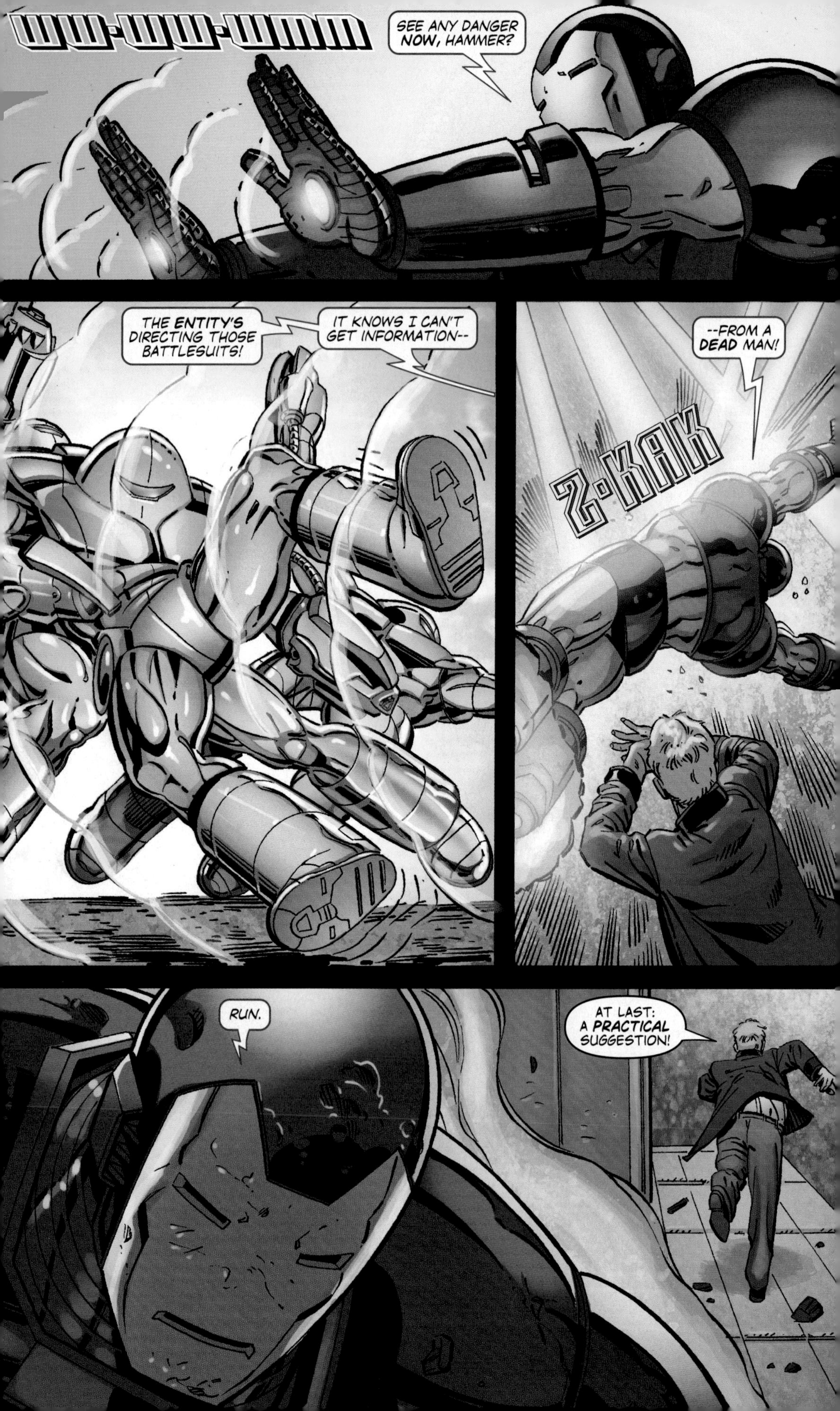
WW-WW-WMM
SEE ANY DANGER NOW, HAMMER?
THE ENTITY'S DIRECTING THOSE BATTLESUITS!
IT KNOWS I CAN'T GET INFORMATION--
--FROM A DEAD MAN!
Z-KAK
RUN.
AT LAST: A PRACTICAL SUGGESTION!

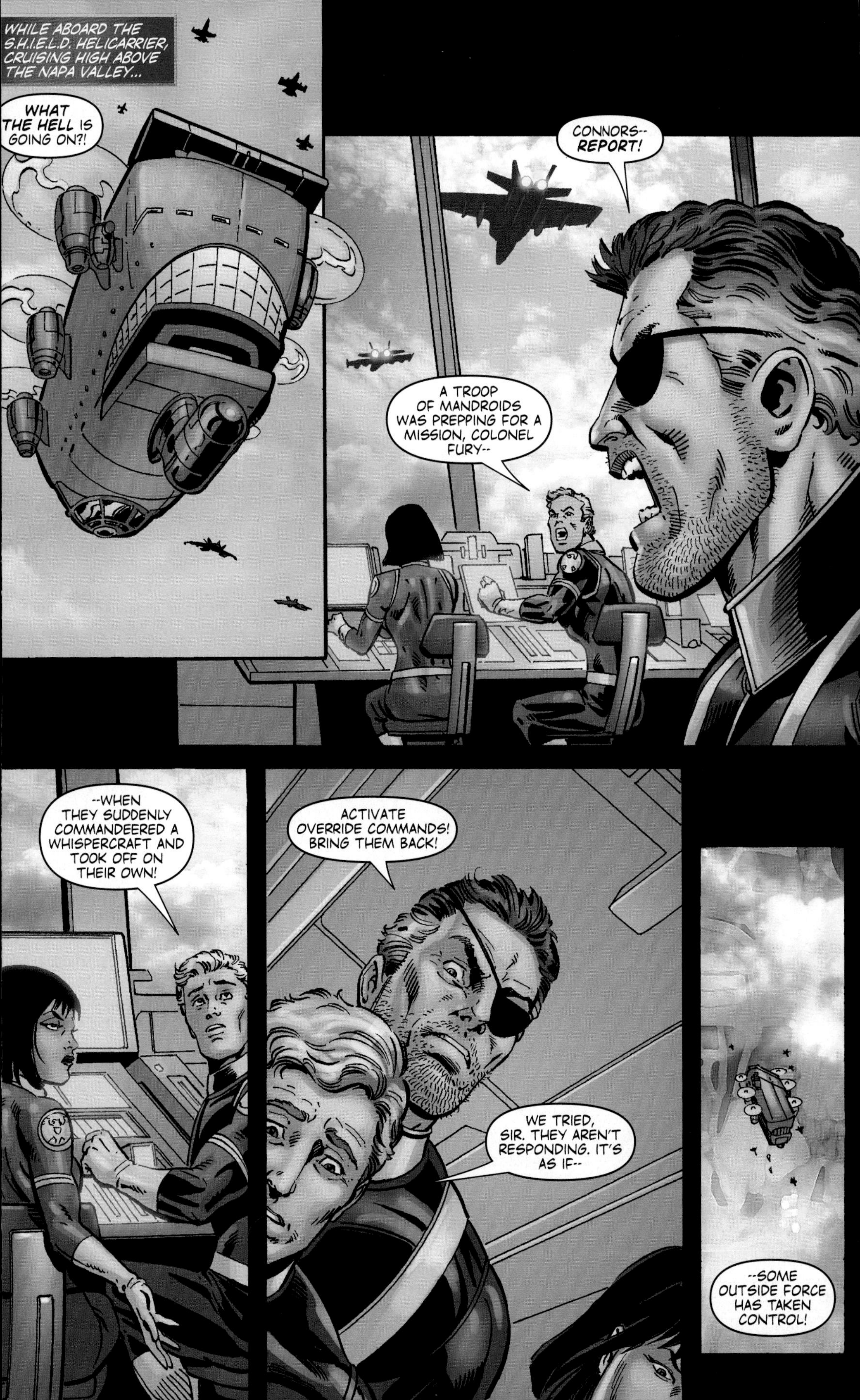
WHILE ABOARD THE S.H.I.E.L.D. HELICARRIER, CRUISING HIGH ABOVE THE NAPA VALLEY...
WHAT THE HELL IS GOING ON?!
CONNORS-- REPORT!
A TROOP OF MANDROIDS WAS PREPPING FOR A MISSION, COLONEL FURY--
--WHEN THEY SUDDENLY COMMANDEERED A WHISPERCRAFT AND TOOK OFF ON THEIR OWN!
ACTIVATE OVERRIDE COMMANDS! BRING THEM BACK!
WE TRIED, SIR. THEY AREN'T RESPONDING. IT'S AS IF--
--SOME OUTSIDE FORCE HAS TAKEN CONTROL!

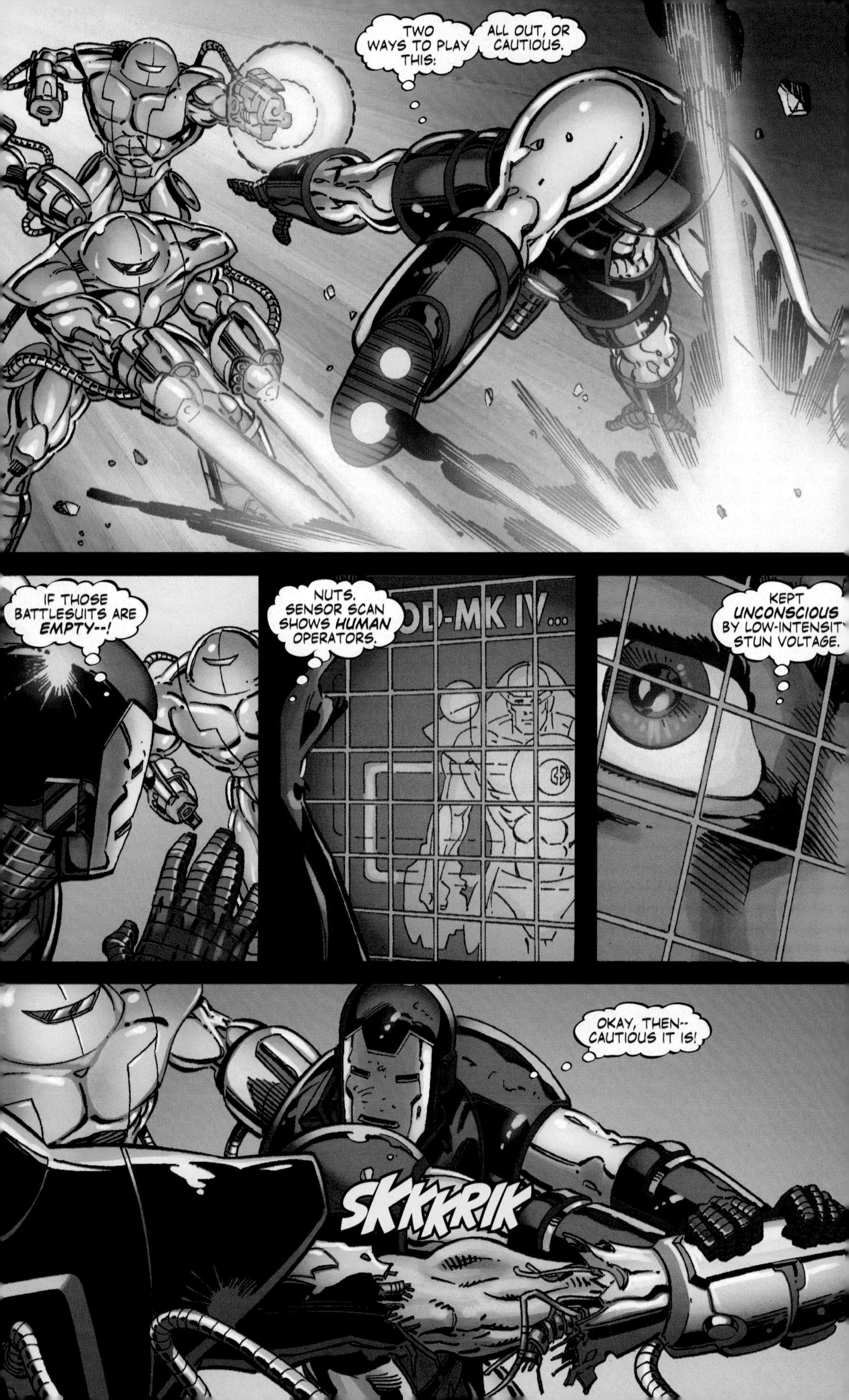
TWO WAYS TO PLAY THIS:
ALL OUT, OR CAUTIOUS.
IF THOSE BATTLESUITS ARE *EMPTY*--!
NUTS. SENSOR SCAN SHOWS *HUMAN* OPERATORS.
OD-MK IV...
KEPT *UNCONSCIOUS* BY LOW-INTENSIT STUN VOLTAGE.
OKAY, THEN-- CAUTIOUS IT IS!
SKKRIK

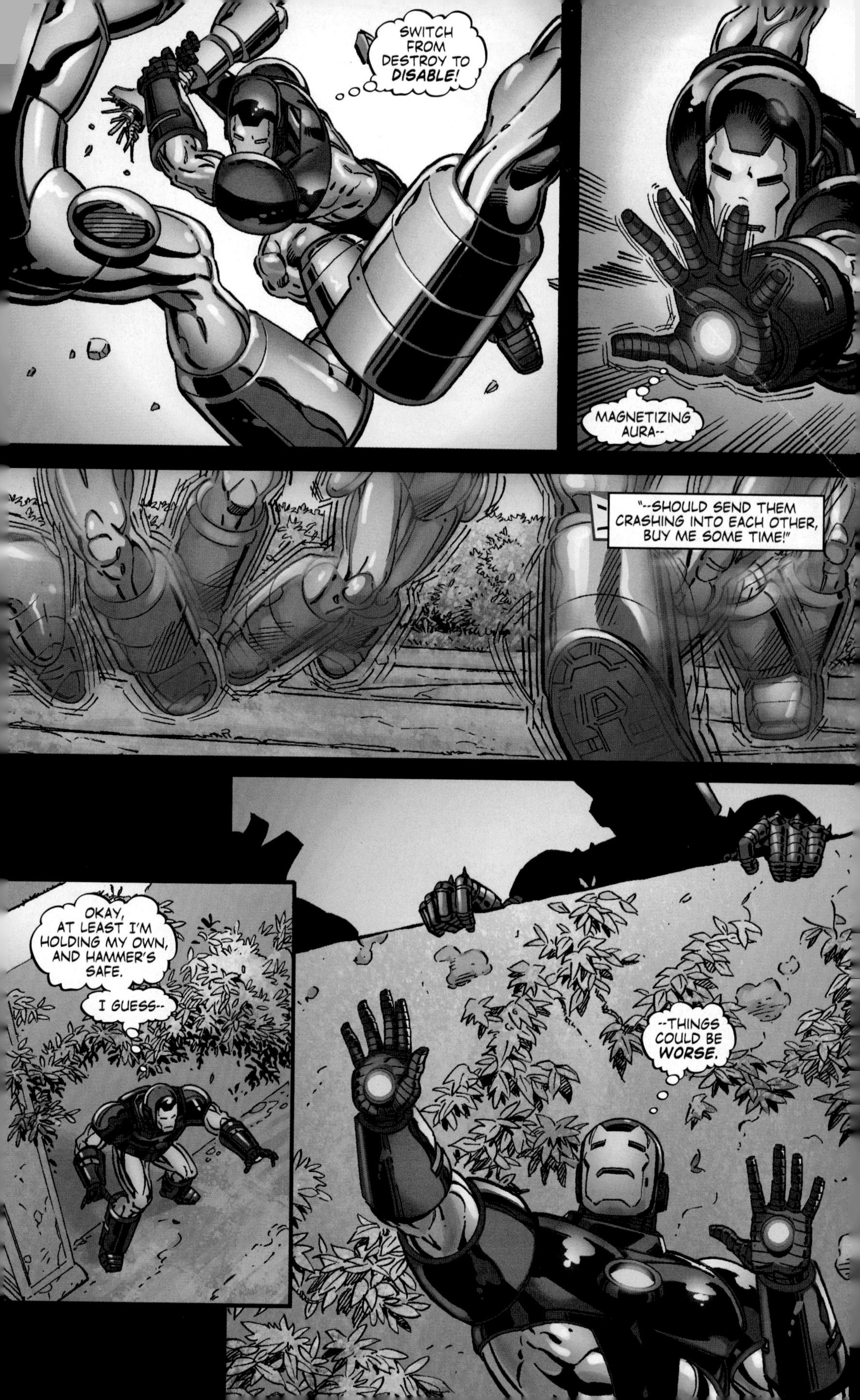
SWITCH FROM DESTROY TO DISABLE!
MAGNETIZING AURA--
"--SHOULD SEND THEM CRASHING INTO EACH OTHER, BUY ME SOME TIME!"
OKAY, AT LEAST I'M HOLDING MY OWN, AND HAMMER'S SAFE.
I GUESS--
--THINGS COULD BE WORSE.

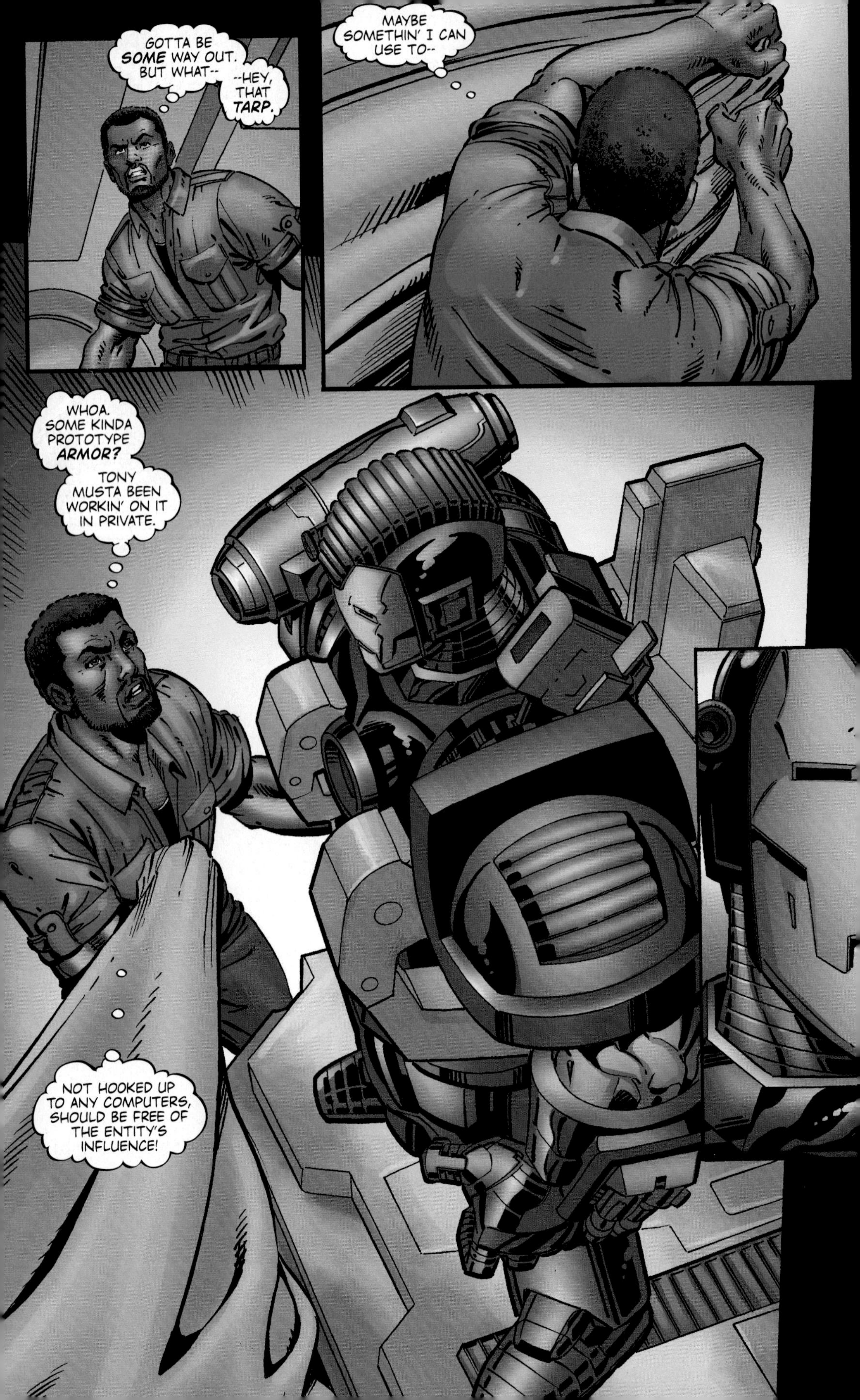
GOTTA BE SOME WAY OUT. BUT WHAT--
--HEY, THAT TARP.
MAYBE SOMETHIN' I CAN USE TO--
WHOA. SOME KINDA PROTOTYPE ARMOR?
TONY MUSTA BEEN WORKIN' ON IT IN PRIVATE.
NOT HOOKED UP TO ANY COMPUTERS, SHOULD BE FREE OF THE ENTITY'S INFLUENCE!

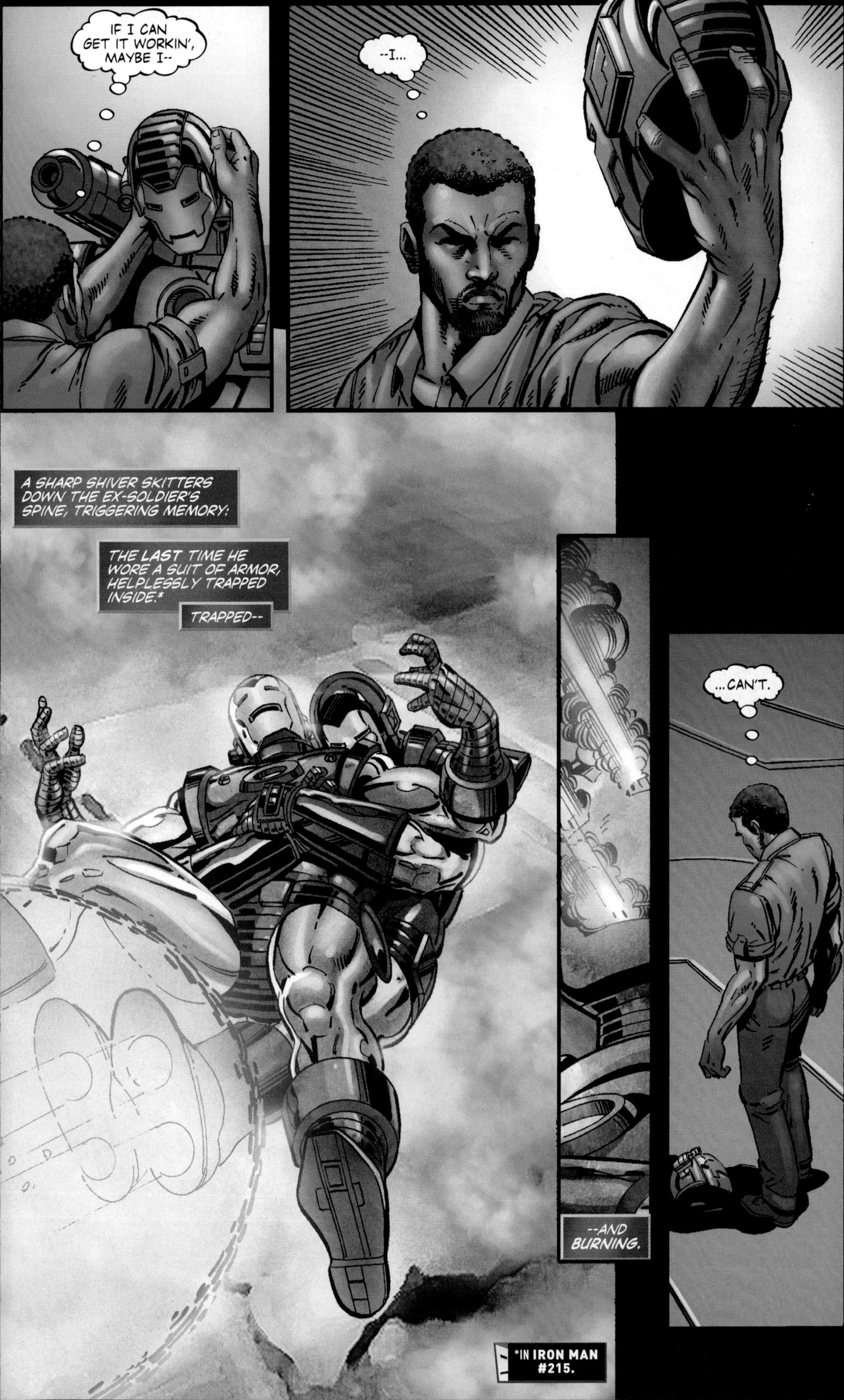
IF I CAN GET IT WORKIN', MAYBE I--
--I...
A SHARP SHIVER SKITTERS DOWN THE EX-SOLDIER'S SPINE, TRIGGERING MEMORY:
THE LAST TIME HE WORE A SUIT OF ARMOR, HELPLESSLY TRAPPED INSIDE.*
TRAPPED--
--AND BURNING.
...CAN'T.
*IN IRON MAN #215.

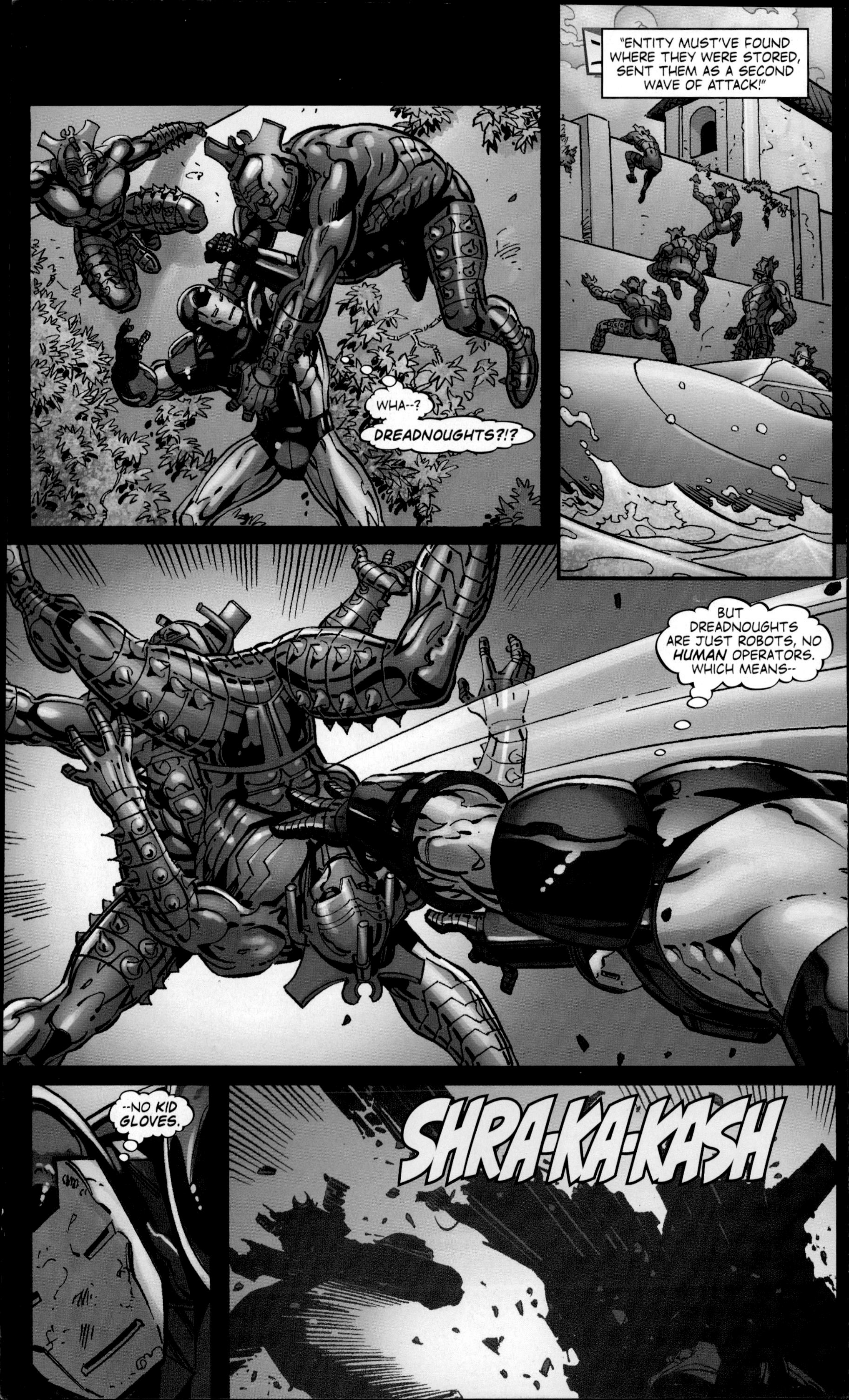
"ENTITY MUST'VE FOUND WHERE THEY WERE STORED, SENT THEM AS A SECOND WAVE OF ATTACK!"
WHA--?
DREADNOUGHTS?!?
BUT DREADNOUGHTS ARE JUST ROBOTS, NO HUMAN OPERATORS. WHICH MEANS--
--NO KID GLOVES.
SHRA-KA-KASH

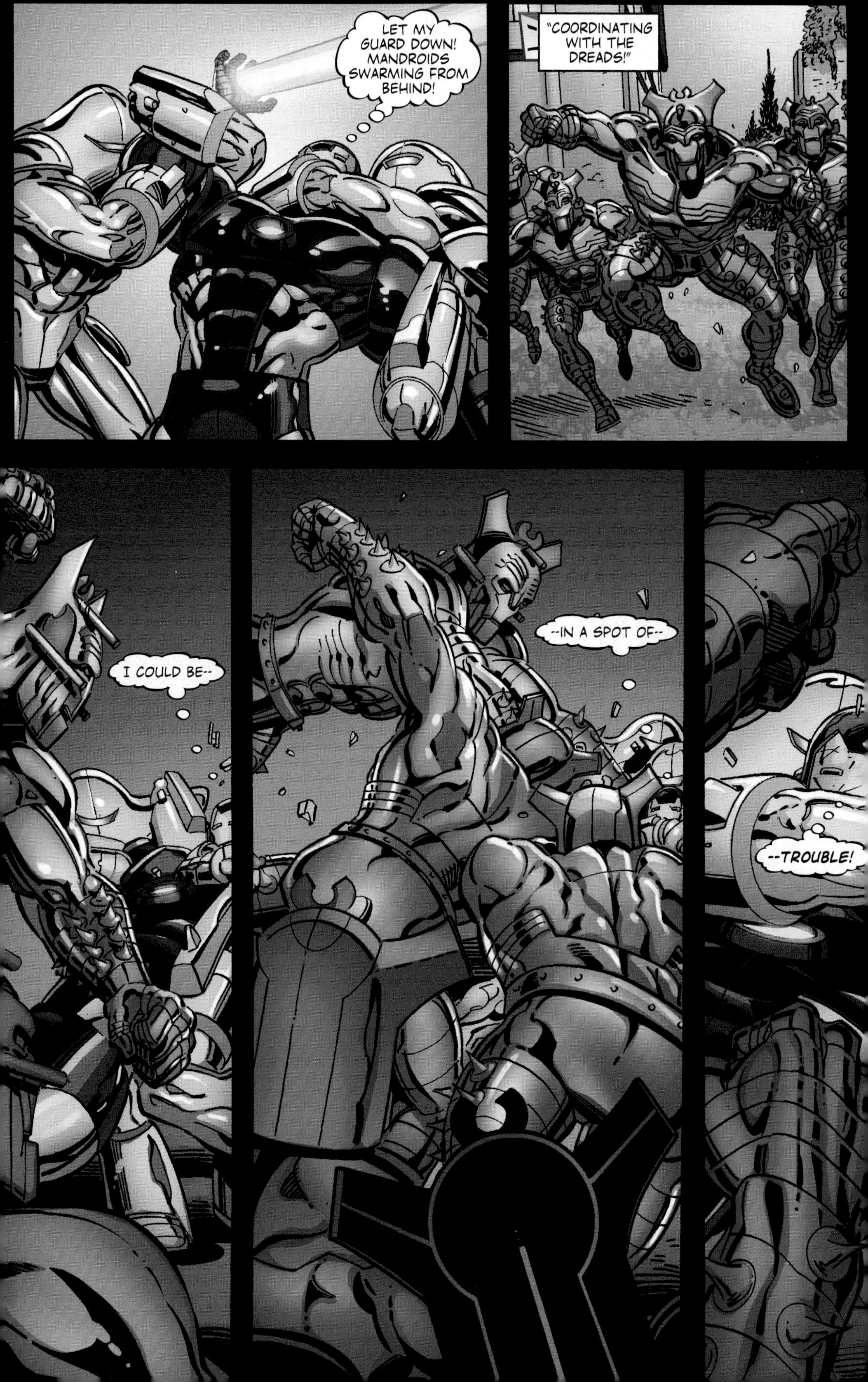
LET MY GUARD DOWN! MANDROIDS SWARMING FROM BEHIND!
"COORDINATING WITH THE DREADS!"
I COULD BE--
--IN A SPOT OF--
--TROUBLE!

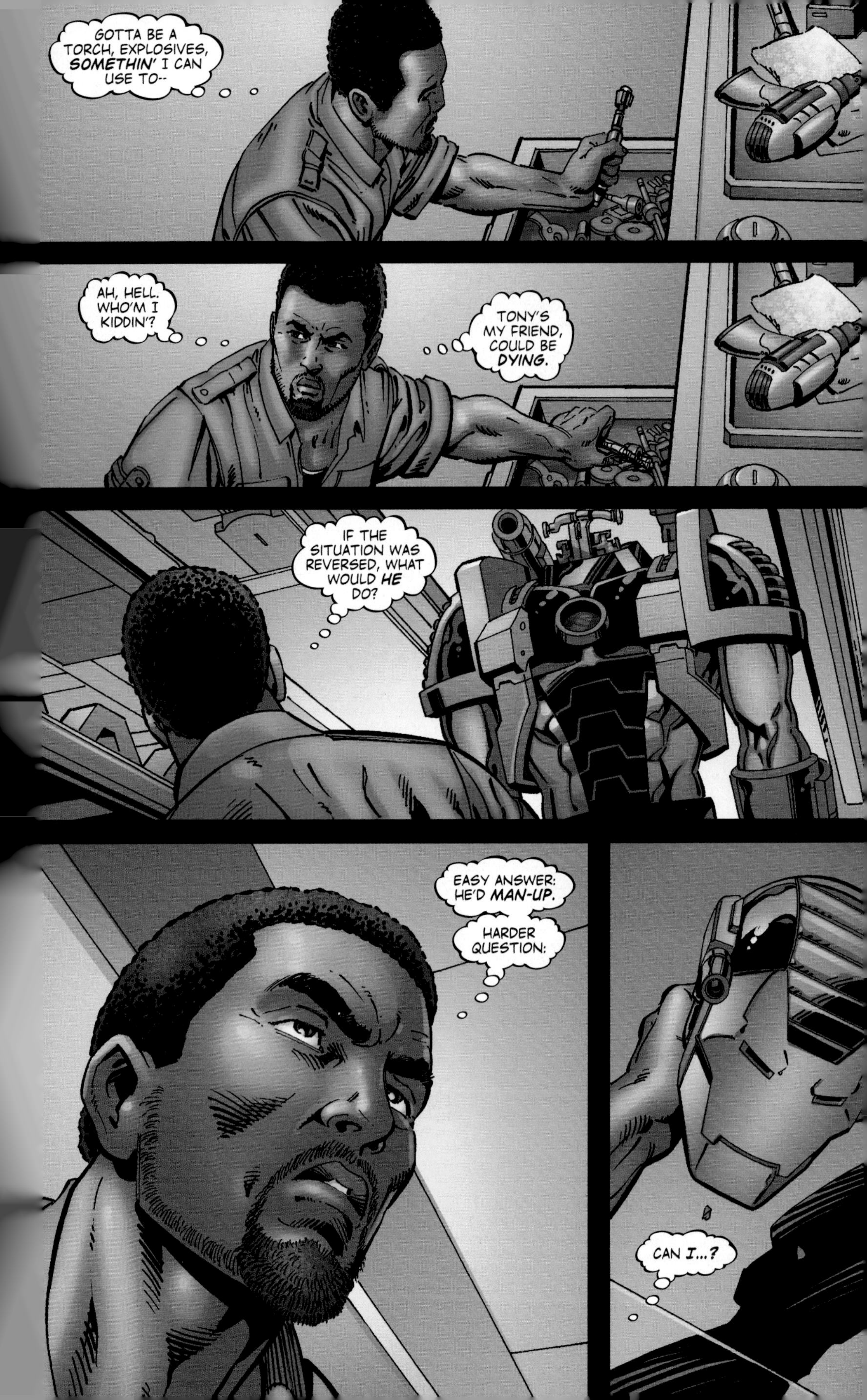
GOTTA BE A TORCH, EXPLOSIVES, SOMETHIN' I CAN USE TO--
AH, HELL. WHO'M I KIDDIN'?
TONY'S MY FRIEND, COULD BE DYING.
IF THE SITUATION WAS REVERSED, WHAT WOULD HE DO?
EASY ANSWER: HE'D MAN-UP.
HARDER QUESTION:
CAN I...?

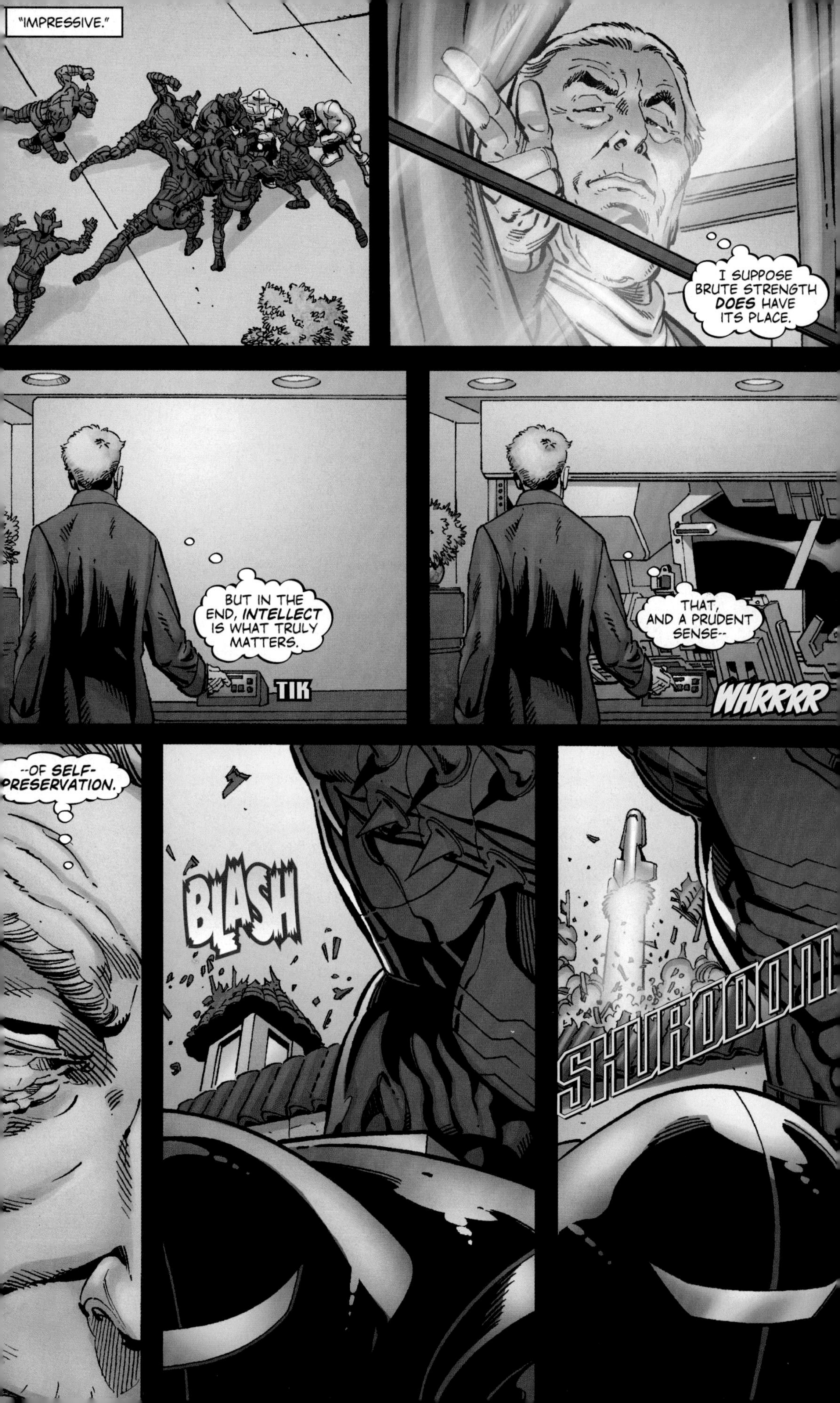
"IMPRESSIVE."
I SUPPOSE BRUTE STRENGTH DOES HAVE ITS PLACE.
BUT IN THE END, INTELLECT IS WHAT TRULY MATTERS.
TIK
THAT, AND A PRUDENT SENSE--
WHRRRR
--OF SELF-PRESERVATION.
BLASH
SHURDOOM

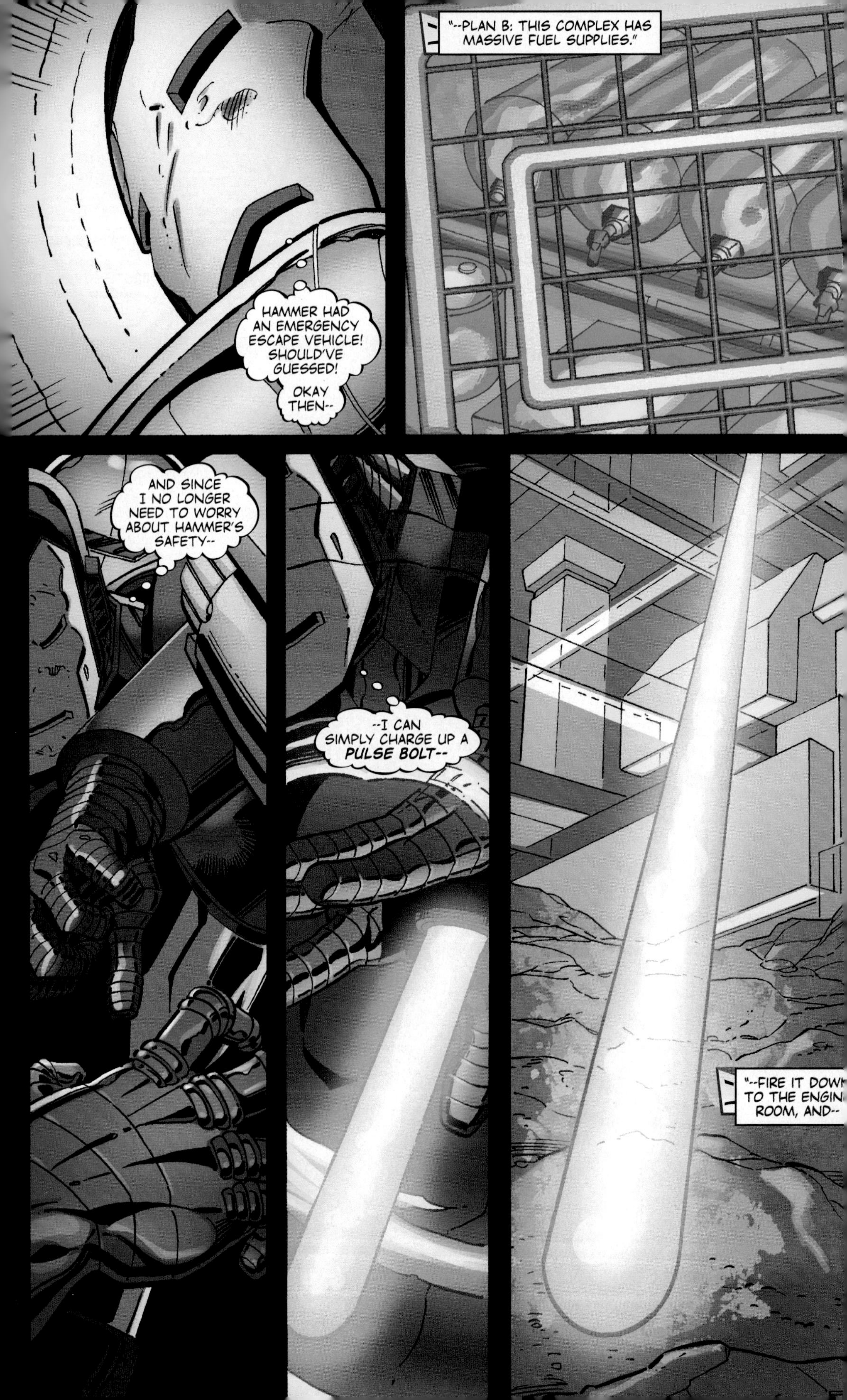
HAMMER HAD AN EMERGENCY ESCAPE VEHICLE! SHOULD'VE GUESSED!
OKAY THEN--
"--PLAN B: THIS COMPLEX HAS MASSIVE FUEL SUPPLIES."
AND SINCE I NO LONGER NEED TO WORRY ABOUT HAMMER'S SAFETY--
--I CAN SIMPLY CHARGE UP A PULSE BOLT--
"--FIRE IT DOWN TO THE ENGINE ROOM, AND--

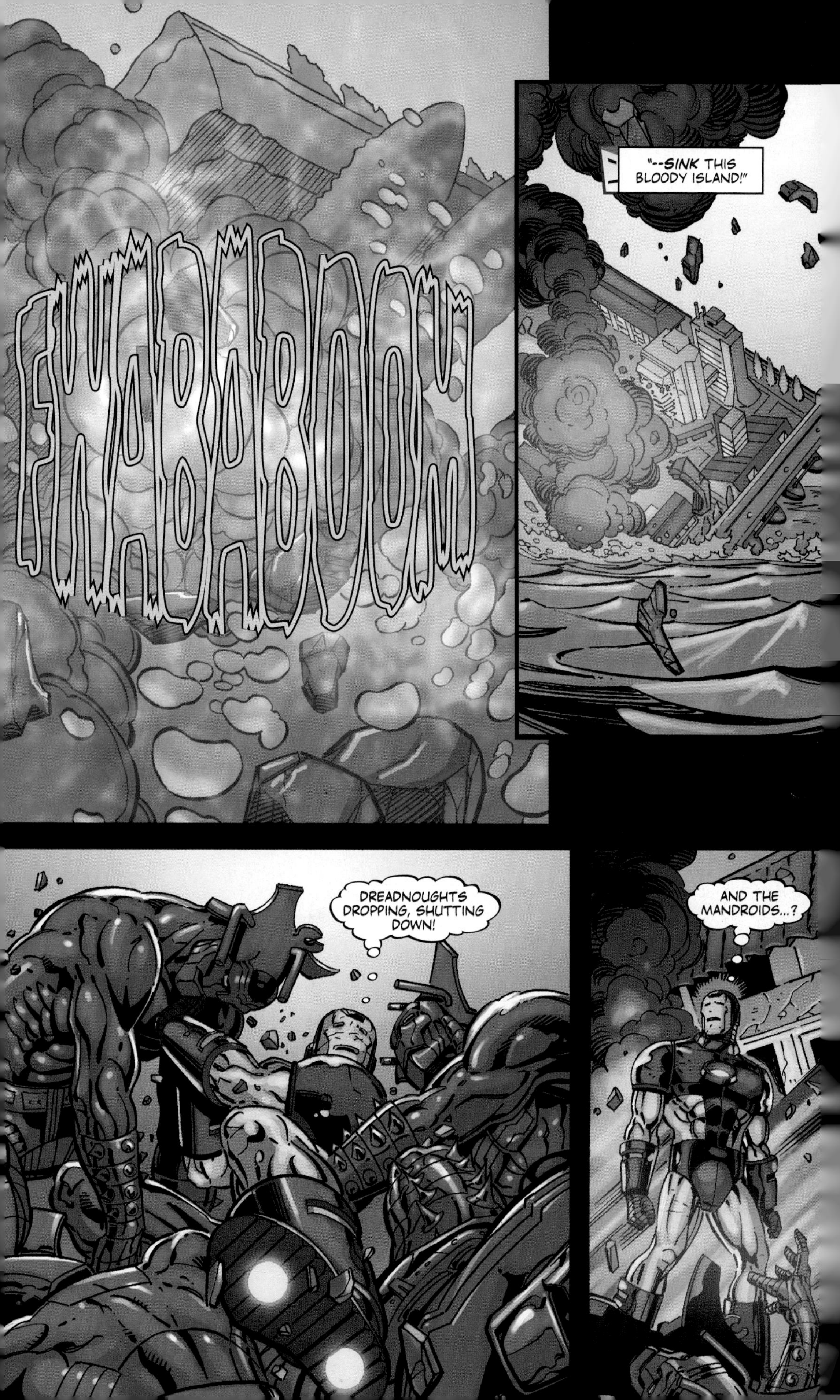
"--SINK THIS BLOODY ISLAND!"
DREADNOUGHTS DROPPING, SHUTTING DOWN!
AND THE MANDROIDS...?

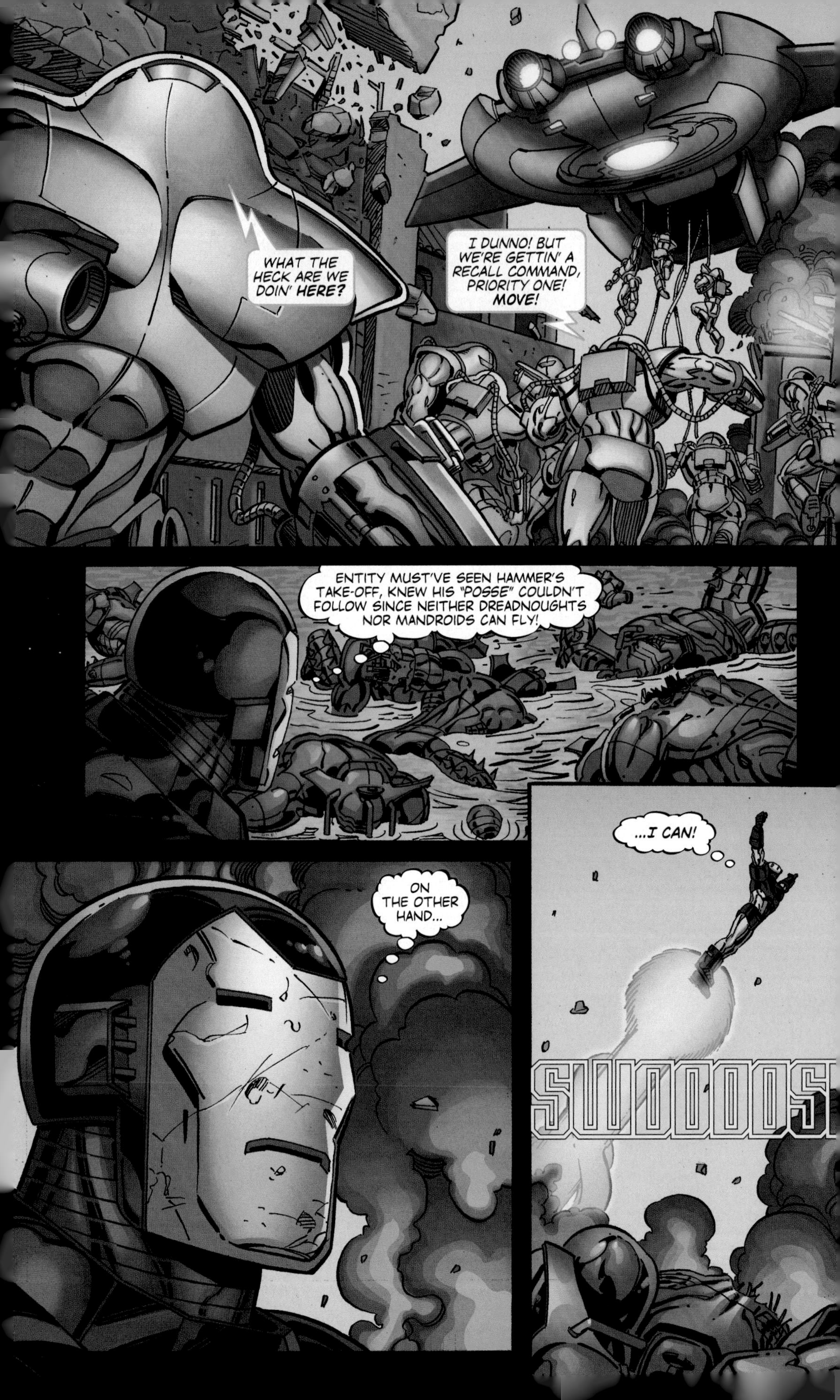
WHAT THE HECK ARE WE DOIN' HERE?
I DUNNO! BUT WE'RE GETTIN' A RECALL COMMAND, PRIORITY ONE! MOVE!
ENTITY MUST'VE SEEN HAMMER'S TAKE-OFF, KNEW HIS "POSSE" COULDN'T FOLLOW SINCE NEITHER DREADNOUGHTS NOR MANDROIDS CAN FLY!
ON THE OTHER HAND...
...I CAN!
SWOOOOSH

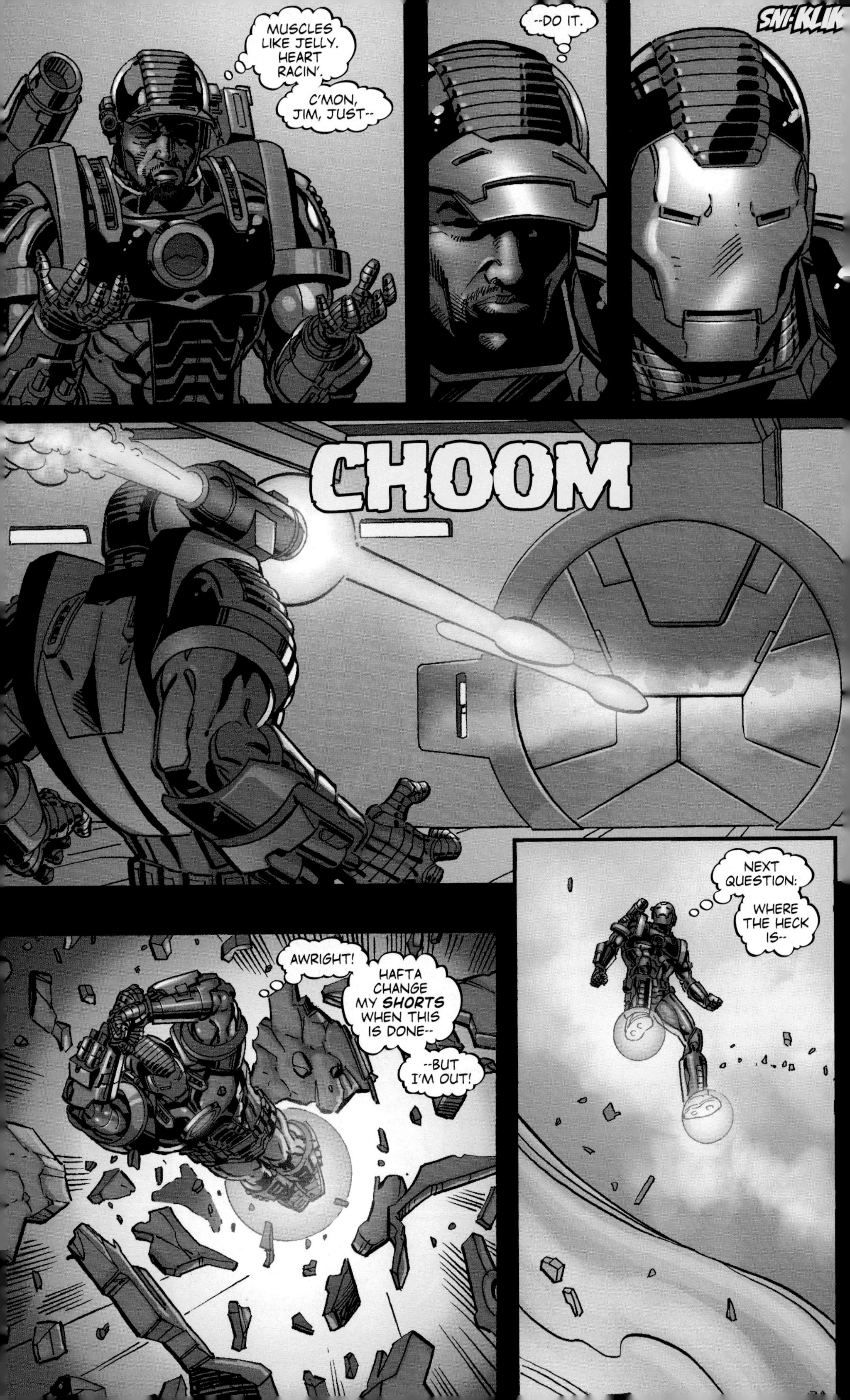
MUSCLES LIKE JELLY. HEART RACIN'.
C'MON, JIM, JUST--
--DO IT.
SNI-KLIK
CHOOM
AWRIGHT!
HAFTA CHANGE MY SHORTS WHEN THIS IS DONE--
--BUT I'M OUT!
NEXT QUESTION:
WHERE THE HECK IS--

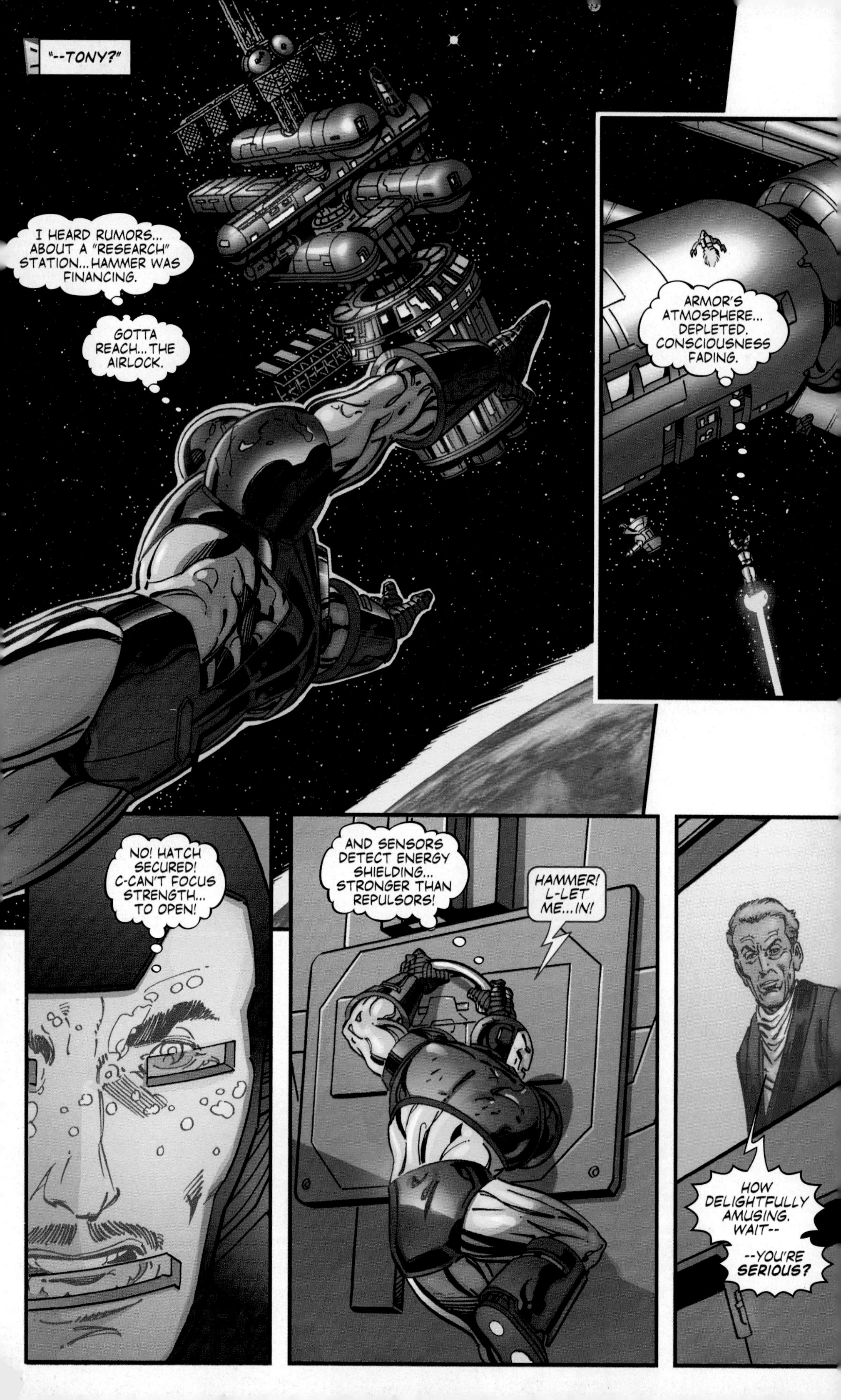
"--TONY?"
I HEARD RUMORS... ABOUT A "RESEARCH" STATION...HAMMER WAS FINANCING.
GOTTA REACH...THE AIRLOCK.
ARMOR'S ATMOSPHERE... DEPLETED. CONSCIOUSNESS FADING.
NO! HATCH SECURED! C-CAN'T FOCUS STRENGTH... TO OPEN!
AND SENSORS DETECT ENERGY SHIELDING... STRONGER THAN REPULSORS!
HAMMER! L-LET ME...IN!
HOW DELIGHTFULLY AMUSING. WAIT--
--YOU'RE SERIOUS?

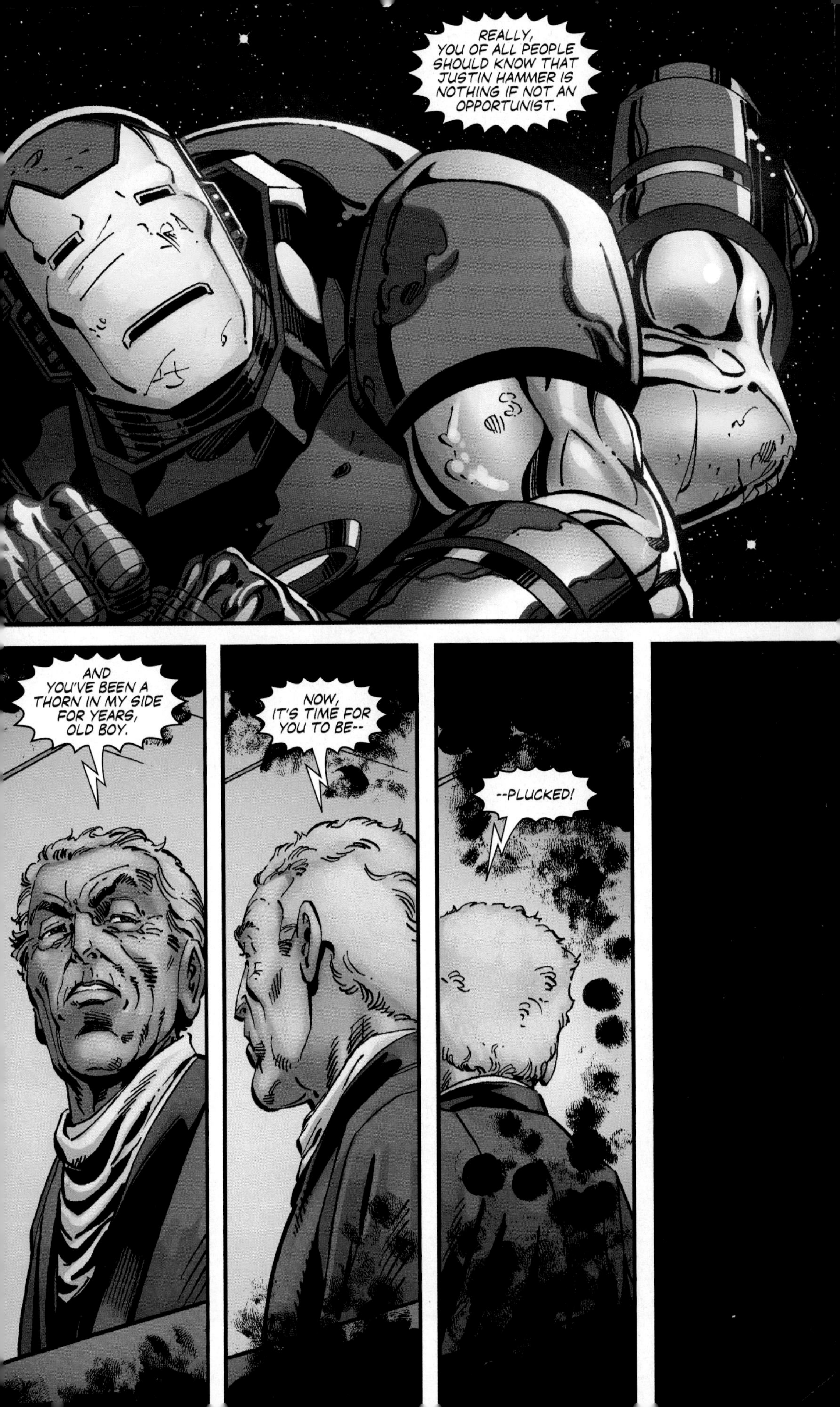
REALLY, YOU OF ALL PEOPLE SHOULD KNOW THAT JUSTIN HAMMER IS NOTHING IF NOT AN OPPORTUNIST.
AND YOU'VE BEEN A THORN IN MY SIDE FOR YEARS, OLD BOY.
NOW, IT'S TIME FOR YOU TO BE--
--PLUCKED!

_258.4

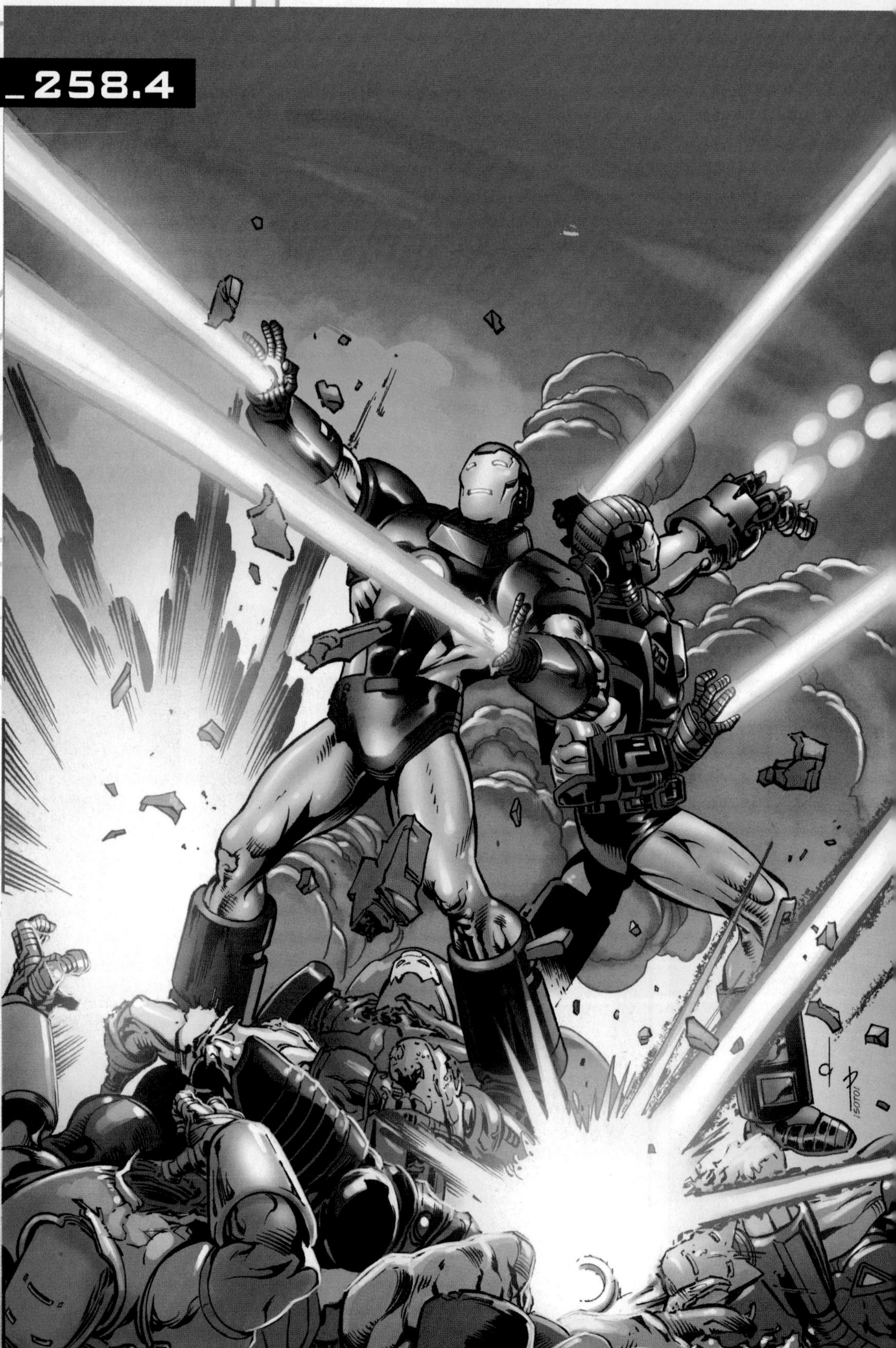

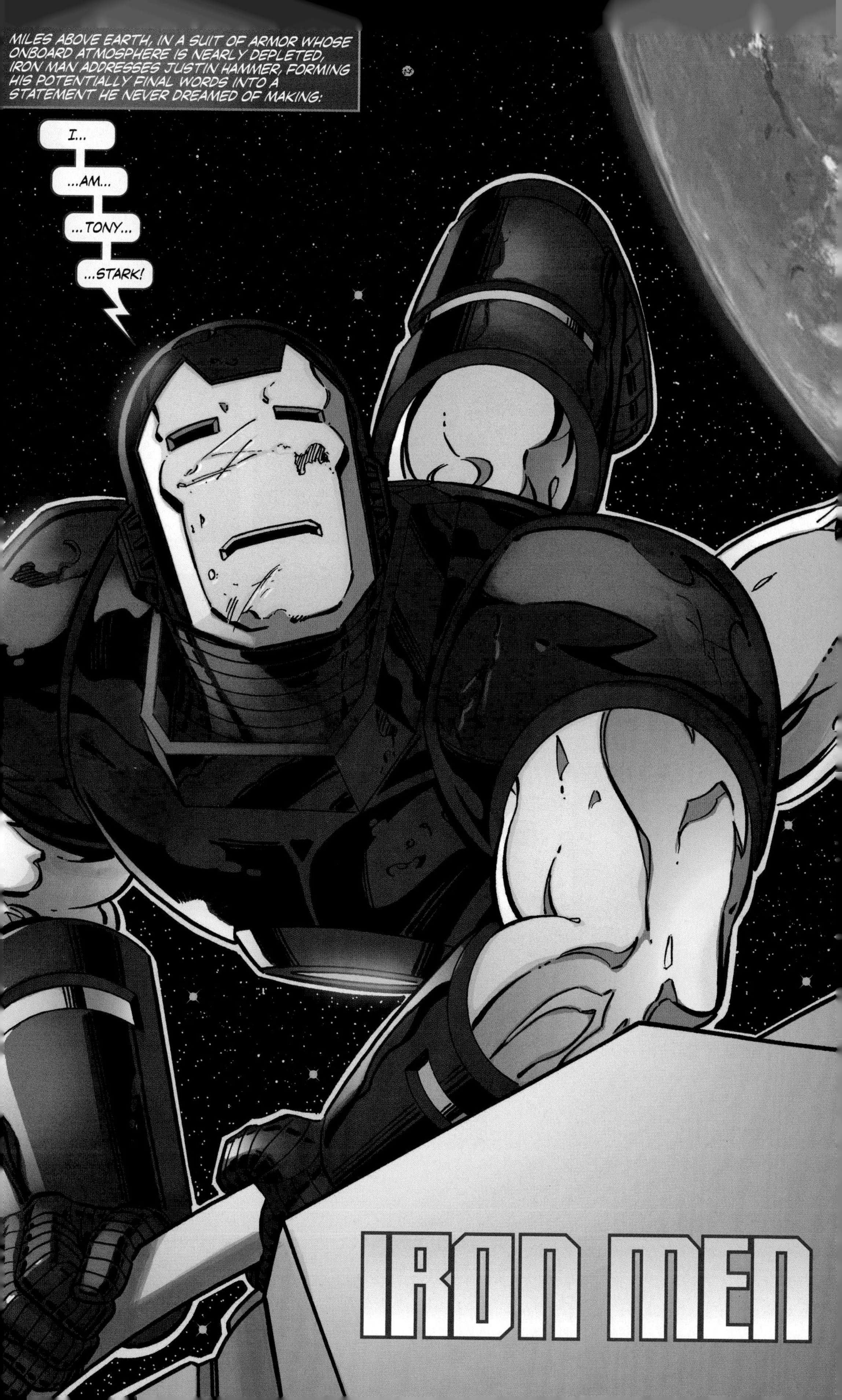
MILES ABOVE EARTH, IN A SUIT OF ARMOR WHOSE ONBOARD ATMOSPHERE IS NEARLY DEPLETED, IRON MAN ADDRESSES JUSTIN HAMMER, FORMING HIS POTENTIALLY FINAL WORDS INTO A STATEMENT HE NEVER DREAMED OF MAKING:
I...
...AM...
...TONY...
...STARK!
IRON MEN

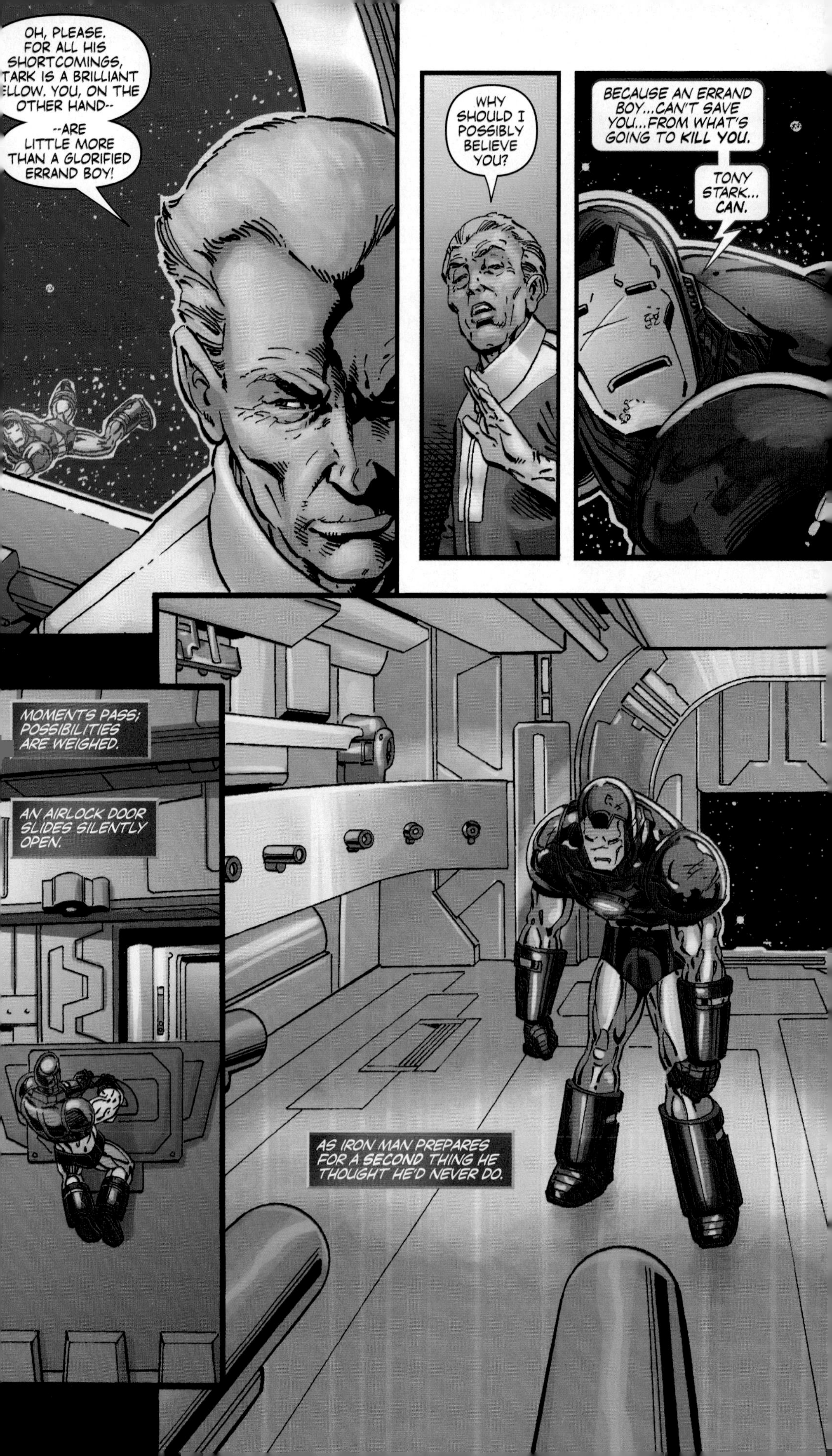
OH, PLEASE. FOR ALL HIS SHORTCOMINGS, TARK IS A BRILLIANT ELLOW. YOU, ON THE OTHER HAND--
--ARE LITTLE MORE THAN A GLORIFIED ERRAND BOY!
WHY SHOULD I POSSIBLY BELIEVE YOU?
BECAUSE AN ERRAND BOY...CAN'T SAVE YOU...FROM WHAT'S GOING TO KILL YOU.
TONY STARK... CAN.
MOMENTS PASS; POSSIBILITIES ARE WEIGHED.
AN AIRLOCK DOOR SLIDES SILENTLY OPEN.
AS IRON MAN PREPARES FOR A SECOND THING HE THOUGHT HE'D NEVER DO.

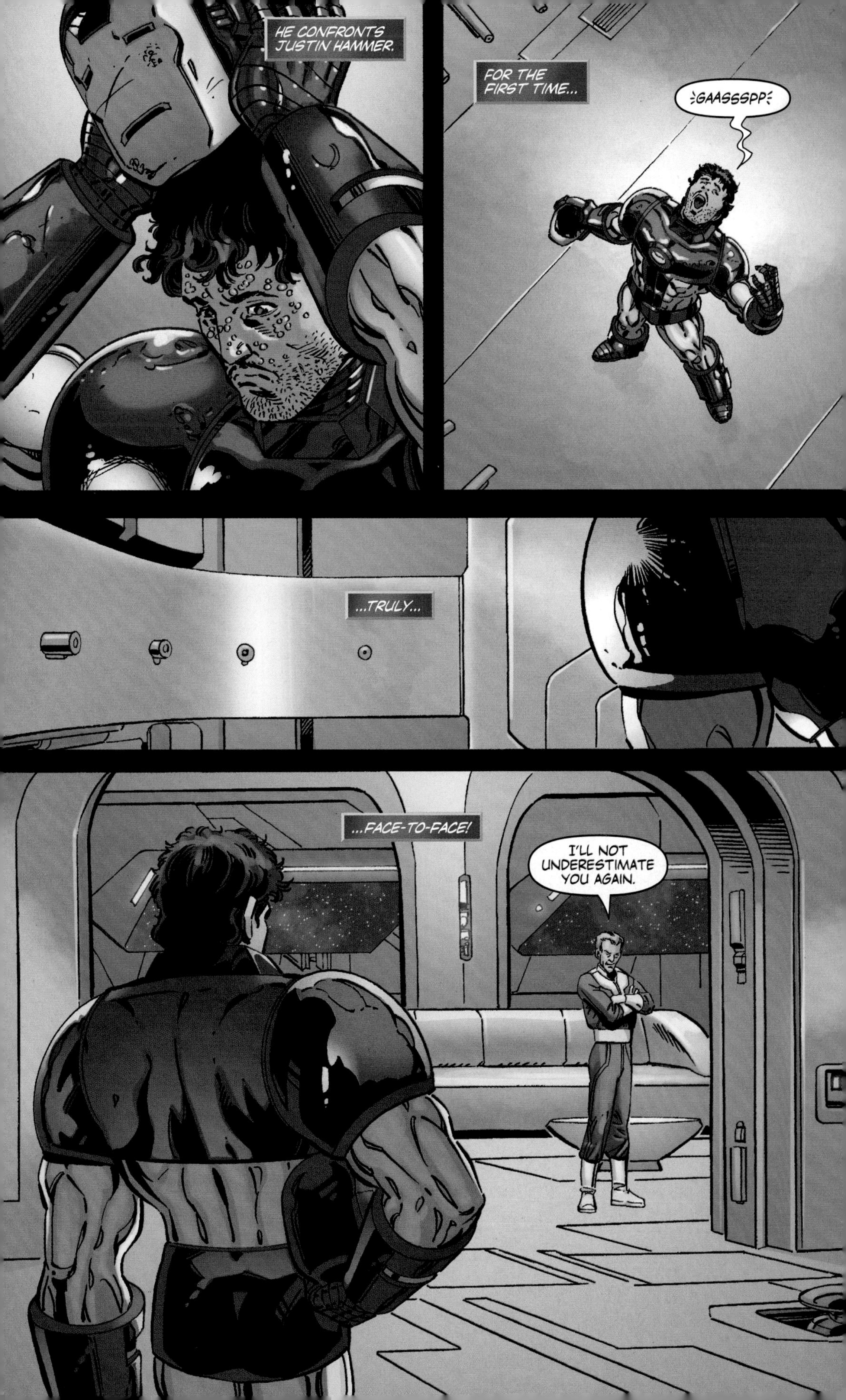
HE CONFRONTS JUSTIN HAMMER.
FOR THE FIRST TIME...
GAASSSPP
...TRULY...
...FACE-TO-FACE!
I'LL NOT UNDERESTIMATE YOU AGAIN.

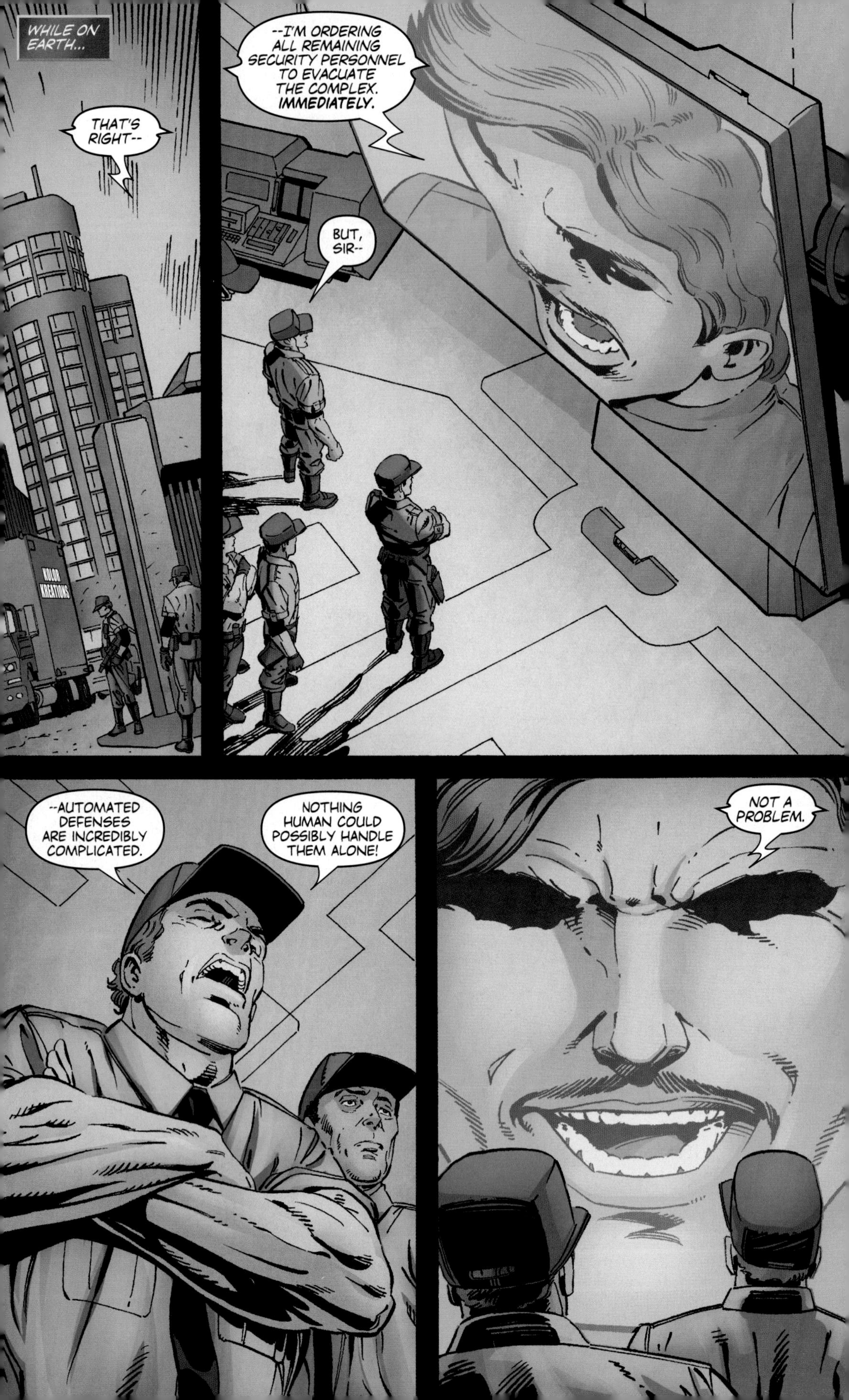
WHILE ON EARTH...
THAT'S RIGHT--
--I'M ORDERING ALL REMAINING SECURITY PERSONNEL TO EVACUATE THE COMPLEX. IMMEDIATELY.
BUT, SIR--
KOLOR KREATIONS
--AUTOMATED DEFENSES ARE INCREDIBLY COMPLICATED.
NOTHING HUMAN COULD POSSIBLY HANDLE THEM ALONE!
NOT A PROBLEM.

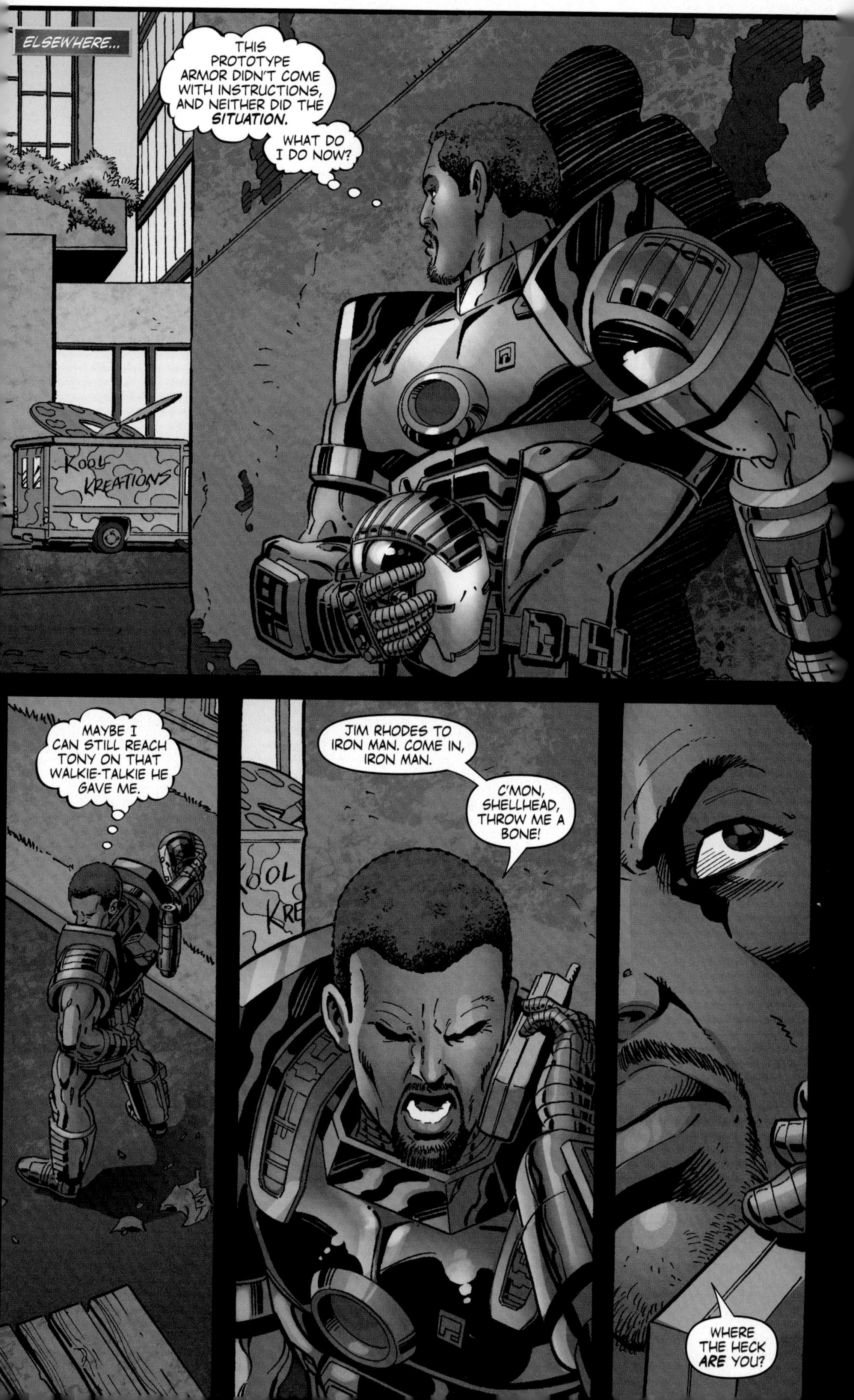
ELSEWHERE...
THIS PROTOTYPE ARMOR DIDN'T COME WITH INSTRUCTIONS, AND NEITHER DID THE SITUATION.
WHAT DO I DO NOW?
KOOL KREATIONS
MAYBE I CAN STILL REACH TONY ON THAT WALKIE-TALKIE HE GAVE ME.
JIM RHODES TO IRON MAN. COME IN, IRON MAN.
C'MON, SHELLHEAD, THROW ME A BONE!
WHERE THE HECK ARE YOU?

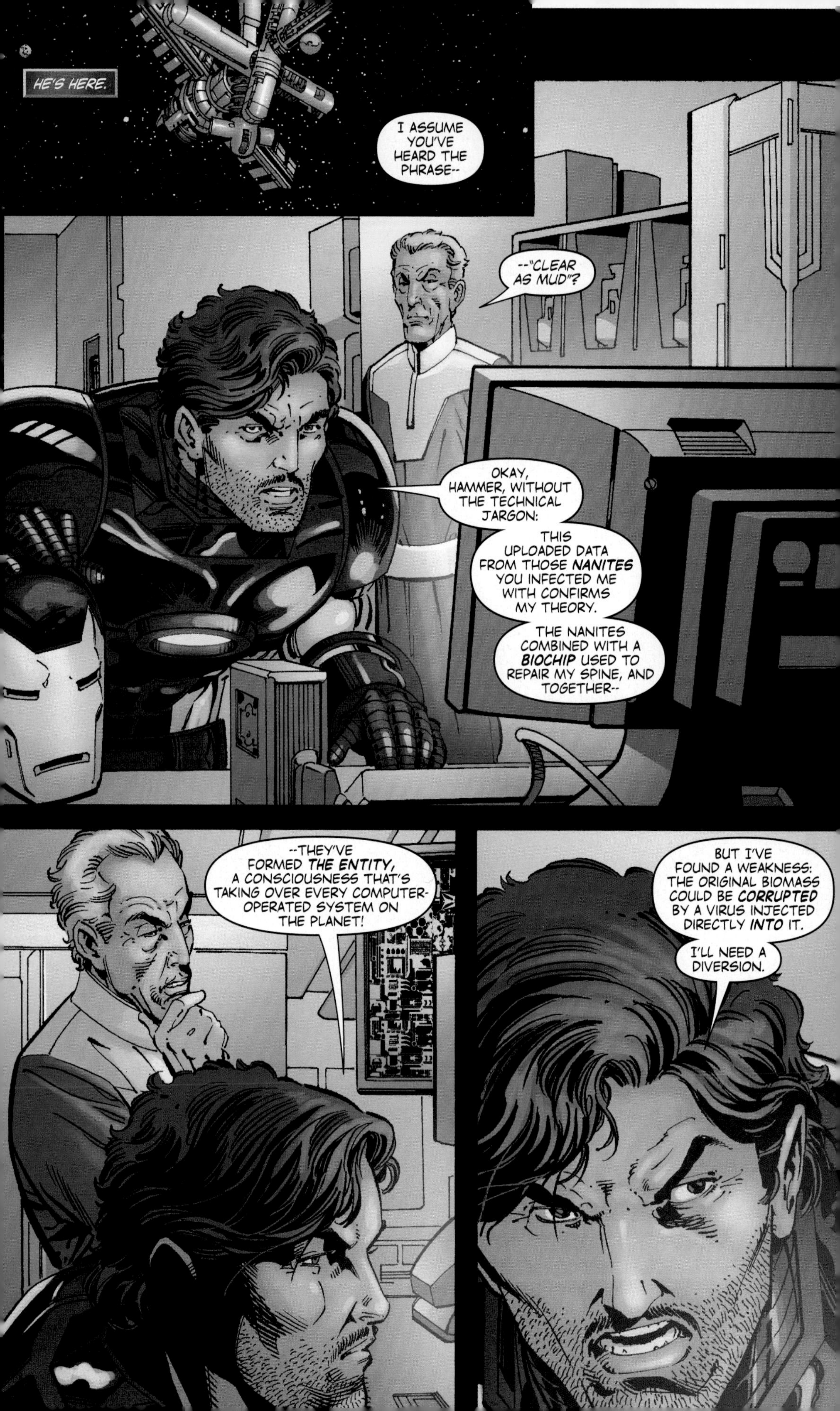
HE'S HERE.
I ASSUME YOU'VE HEARD THE PHRASE--
--"CLEAR AS MUD"?
OKAY, HAMMER, WITHOUT THE TECHNICAL JARGON:
THIS UPLOADED DATA FROM THOSE NANITES YOU INFECTED ME WITH CONFIRMS MY THEORY.
THE NANITES COMBINED WITH A BIOCHIP USED TO REPAIR MY SPINE, AND TOGETHER--
--THEY'VE FORMED THE ENTITY, A CONSCIOUSNESS THAT'S TAKING OVER EVERY COMPUTER-OPERATED SYSTEM ON THE PLANET!
BUT I'VE FOUND A WEAKNESS: THE ORIGINAL BIOMASS COULD BE CORRUPTED BY A VIRUS INJECTED DIRECTLY INTO IT.
I'LL NEED A DIVERSION.

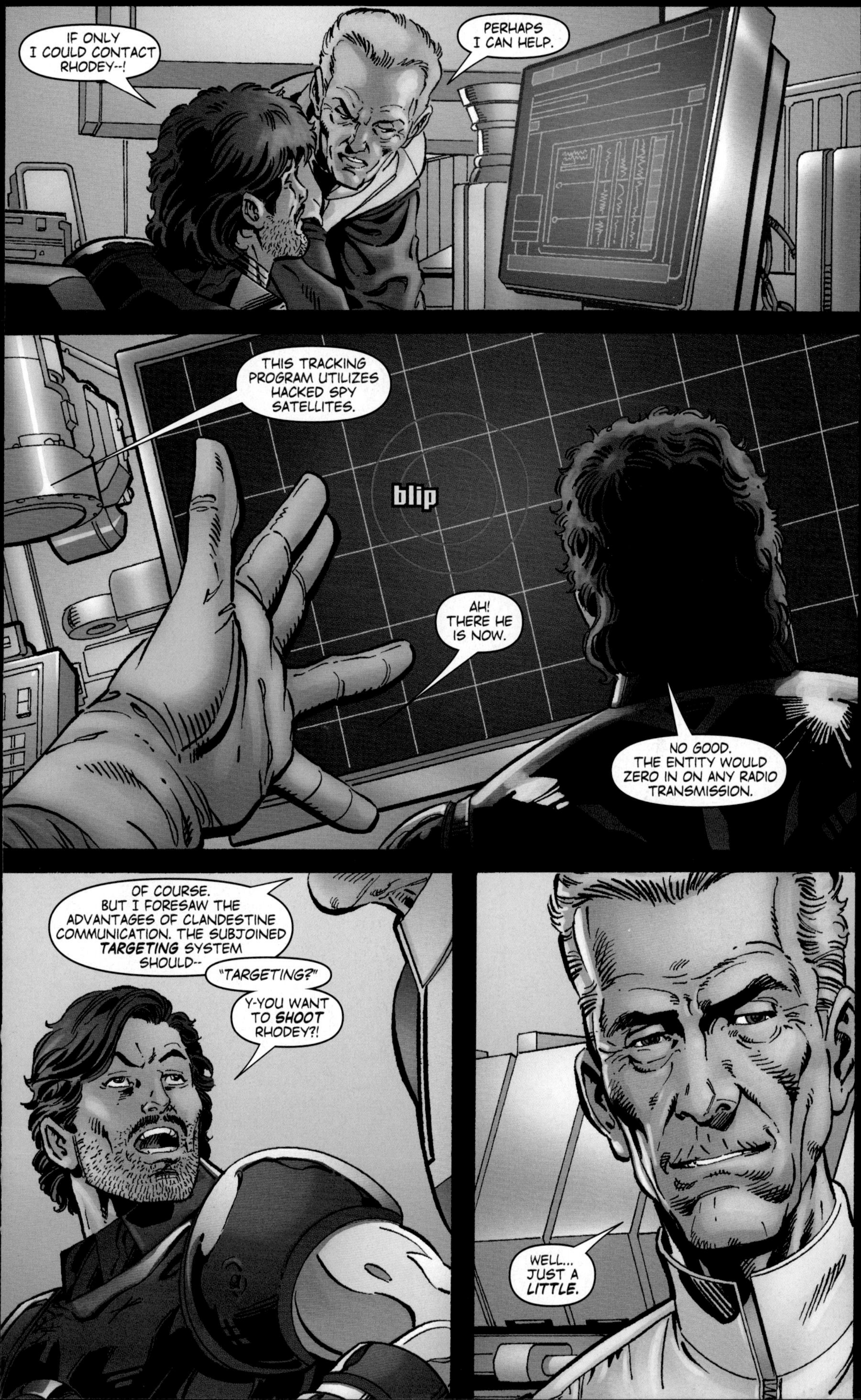
IF ONLY I COULD CONTACT RHODEY--!
PERHAPS I CAN HELP.
THIS TRACKING PROGRAM UTILIZES HACKED SPY SATELLITES.
blip
AH! THERE HE IS NOW.
NO GOOD. THE ENTITY WOULD ZERO IN ON ANY RADIO TRANSMISSION.
OF COURSE. BUT I FORESAW THE ADVANTAGES OF CLANDESTINE COMMUNICATION. THE SUBJOINED TARGETING SYSTEM SHOULD--
"TARGETING?"
Y-YOU WANT TO SHOOT RHODEY?!
WELL... JUST A LITTLE.

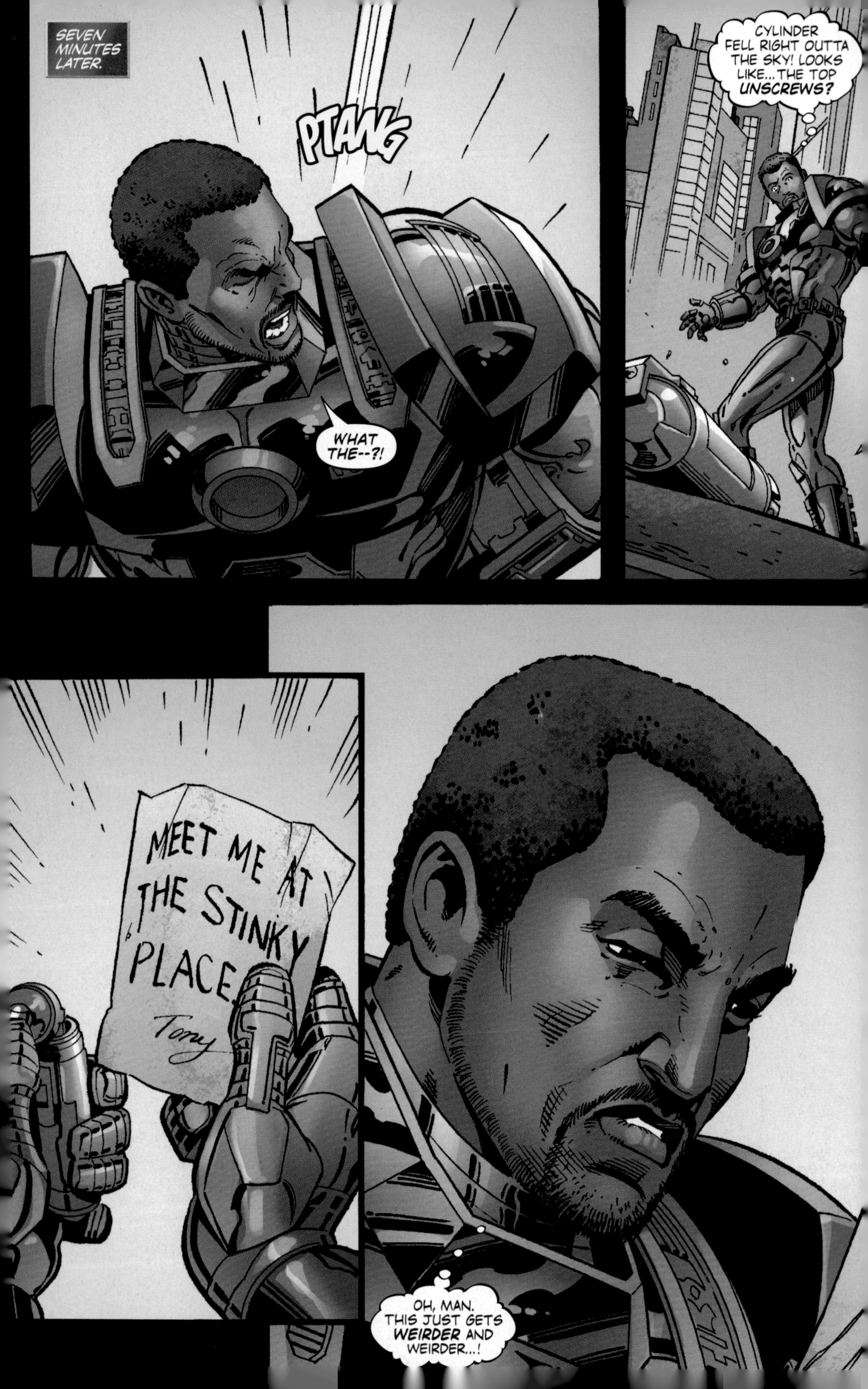
SEVEN MINUTES LATER.
PTANG
WHAT THE--?!
CYLINDER FELL RIGHT OUTTA THE SKY! LOOKS LIKE... THE TOP UNSCREWS?
MEET ME AT THE STINKY PLACE. Tony
OH, MAN. THIS JUST GETS WEIRDER AND WEIRDER...!

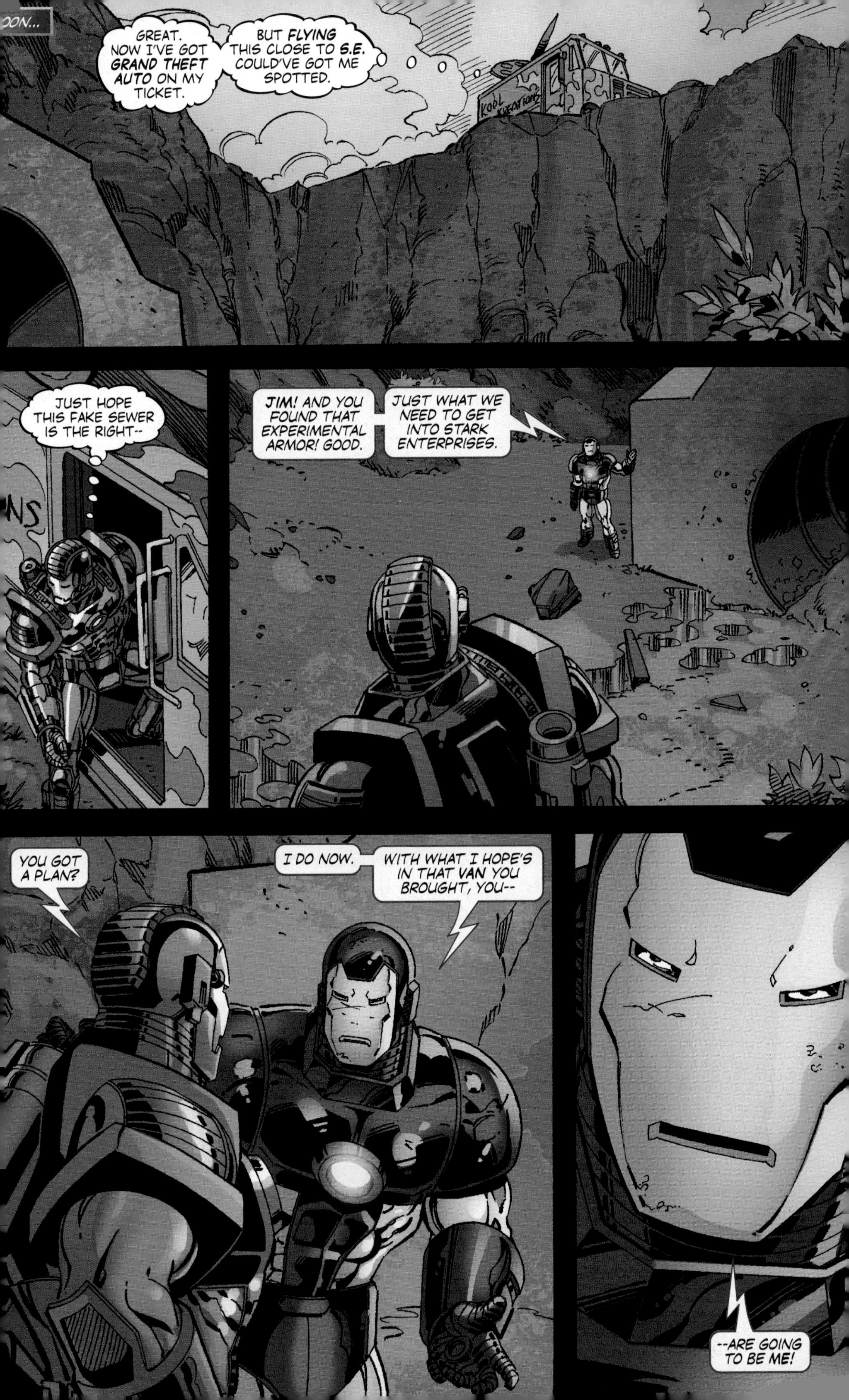
GREAT. NOW I'VE GOT **GRAND THEFT AUTO** ON MY TICKET.
BUT **FLYING** THIS CLOSE TO **S.E.** COULD'VE GOT ME SPOTTED.
JUST HOPE THIS FAKE SEWER IS THE RIGHT--
JIM! AND YOU FOUND THAT EXPERIMENTAL ARMOR! GOOD.
JUST WHAT WE NEED TO GET INTO STARK ENTERPRISES.
YOU GOT A PLAN?
I DO NOW.
WITH WHAT I HOPE'S IN THAT **VAN** YOU BROUGHT, YOU--
--ARE GOING TO BE **ME!**

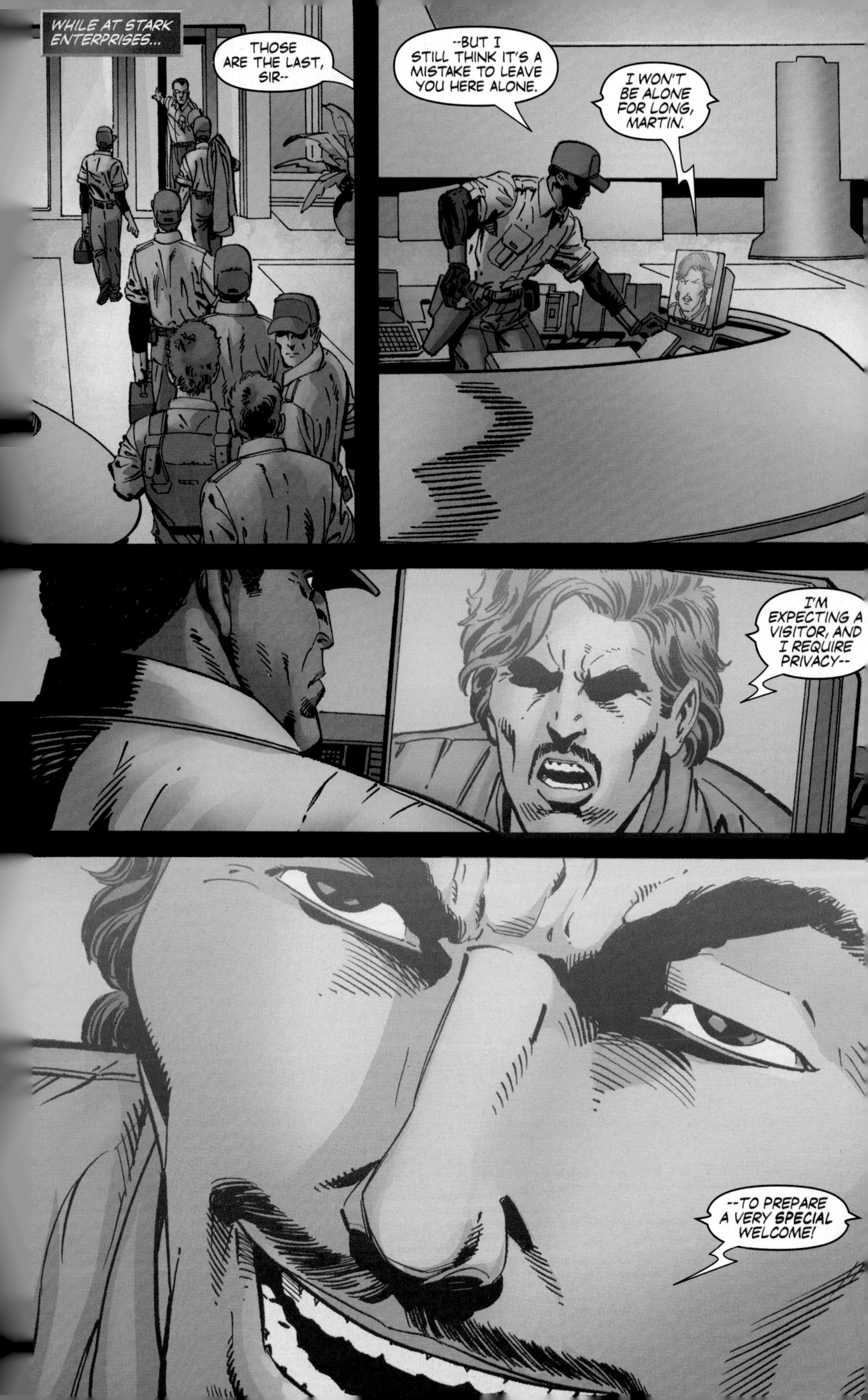
WHILE AT STARK ENTERPRISES...
THOSE ARE THE LAST, SIR--
--BUT I STILL THINK IT'S A MISTAKE TO LEAVE YOU HERE ALONE.
I WON'T BE ALONE FOR LONG, MARTIN.
I'M EXPECTING A VISITOR, AND I REQUIRE PRIVACY--
--TO PREPARE A VERY SPECIAL WELCOME!

--A MAJESTIC STREAK OF RED AND GOLD ROCKETS OVER THE DESERTED S.E. COMPOUND...

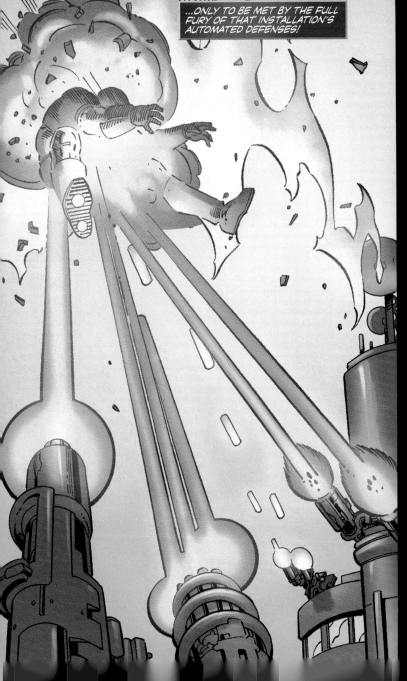

...ONLY TO BE MET BY THE FULL FURY OF THAT INSTALLATION'S AUTOMATED DEFENSES!

THE ARMOR-CLAD FIGURE SPINS.

SPIRALS.

FALLS...

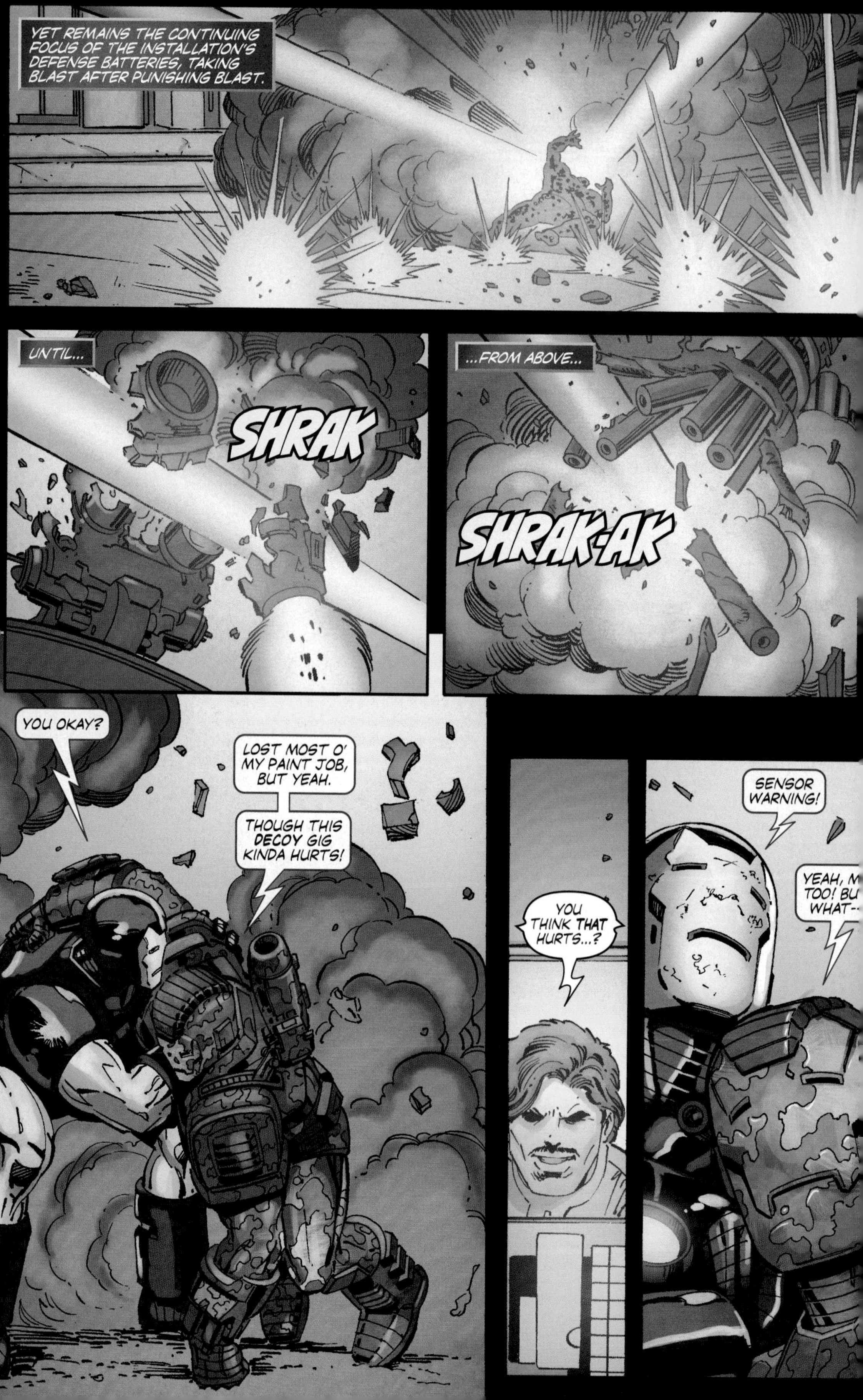
YET REMAINS THE CONTINUING FOCUS OF THE INSTALLATION'S DEFENSE BATTERIES, TAKING BLAST AFTER PUNISHING BLAST.
UNTIL...
SHRAK
...FROM ABOVE...
SHRAK-AK
YOU OKAY?
LOST MOST O' MY PAINT JOB, BUT YEAH.
THOUGH THIS DECOY GIG KINDA HURTS!
YOU THINK THAT HURTS...?
SENSOR WARNING!

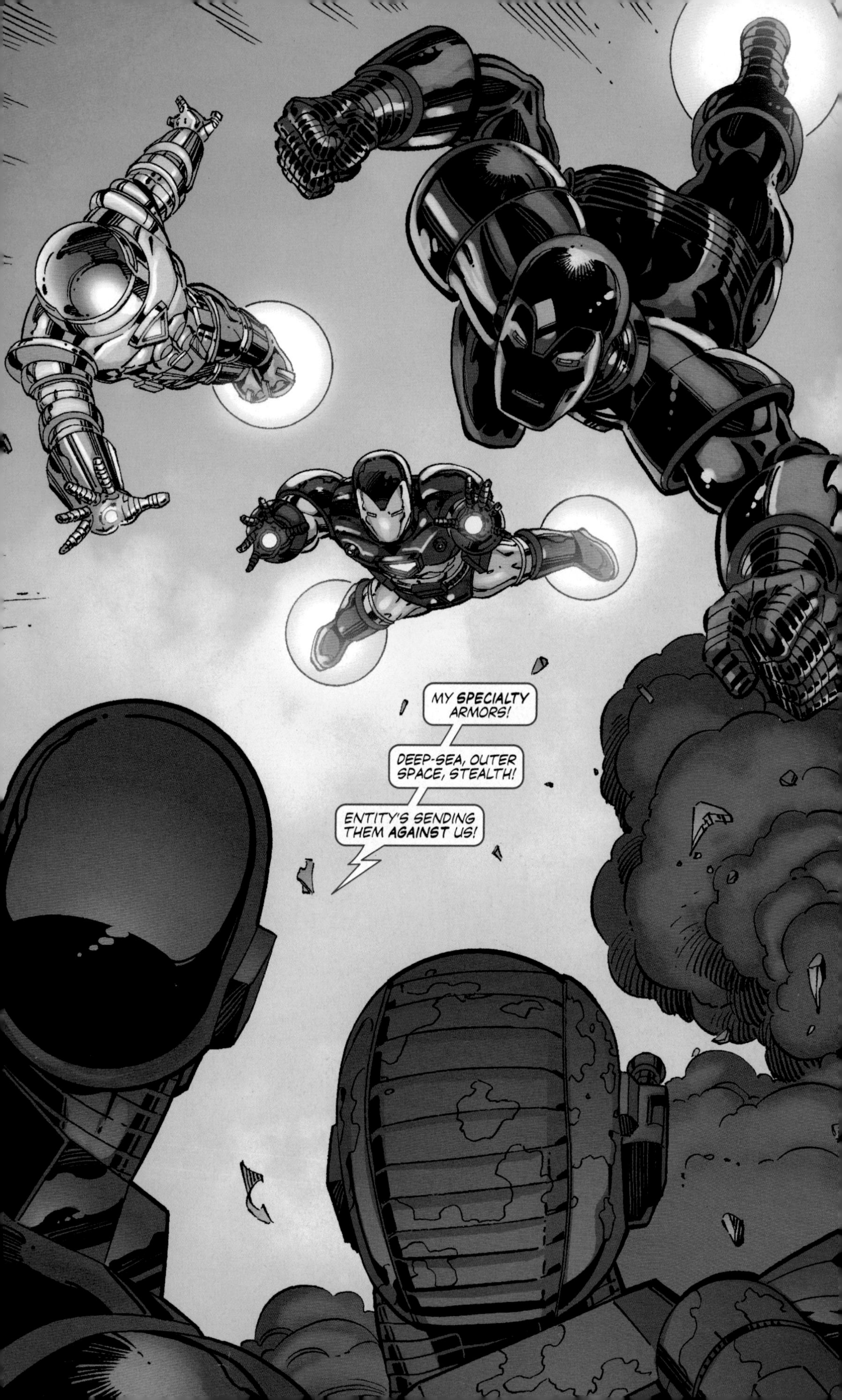
MY SPECIALTY ARMORS!
DEEP-SEA, OUTER SPACE, STEALTH!
ENTITY'S SENDING THEM AGAINST US!

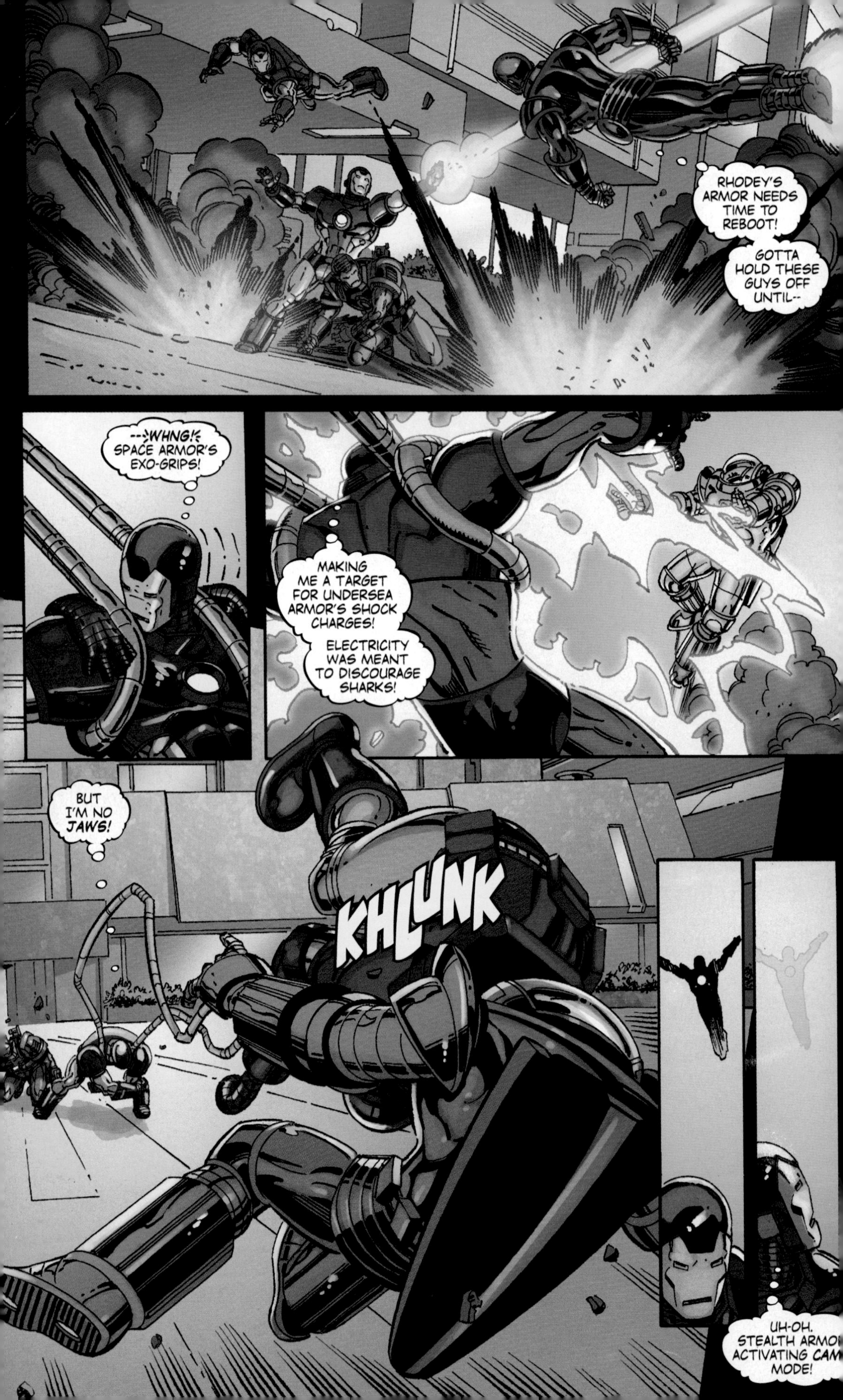
RHODEY'S ARMOR NEEDS TIME TO REBOOT!
GOTTA HOLD THESE GUYS OFF UNTIL--
--WHNG!-- SPACE ARMOR'S EXO-GRIPS!
MAKING ME A TARGET FOR UNDERSEA ARMOR'S SHOCK CHARGES!
ELECTRICITY WAS MEANT TO DISCOURAGE SHARKS!
BUT I'M NO JAWS!
KHLUNK
UH-OH. STEALTH ARMO ACTIVATING CAM MODE!

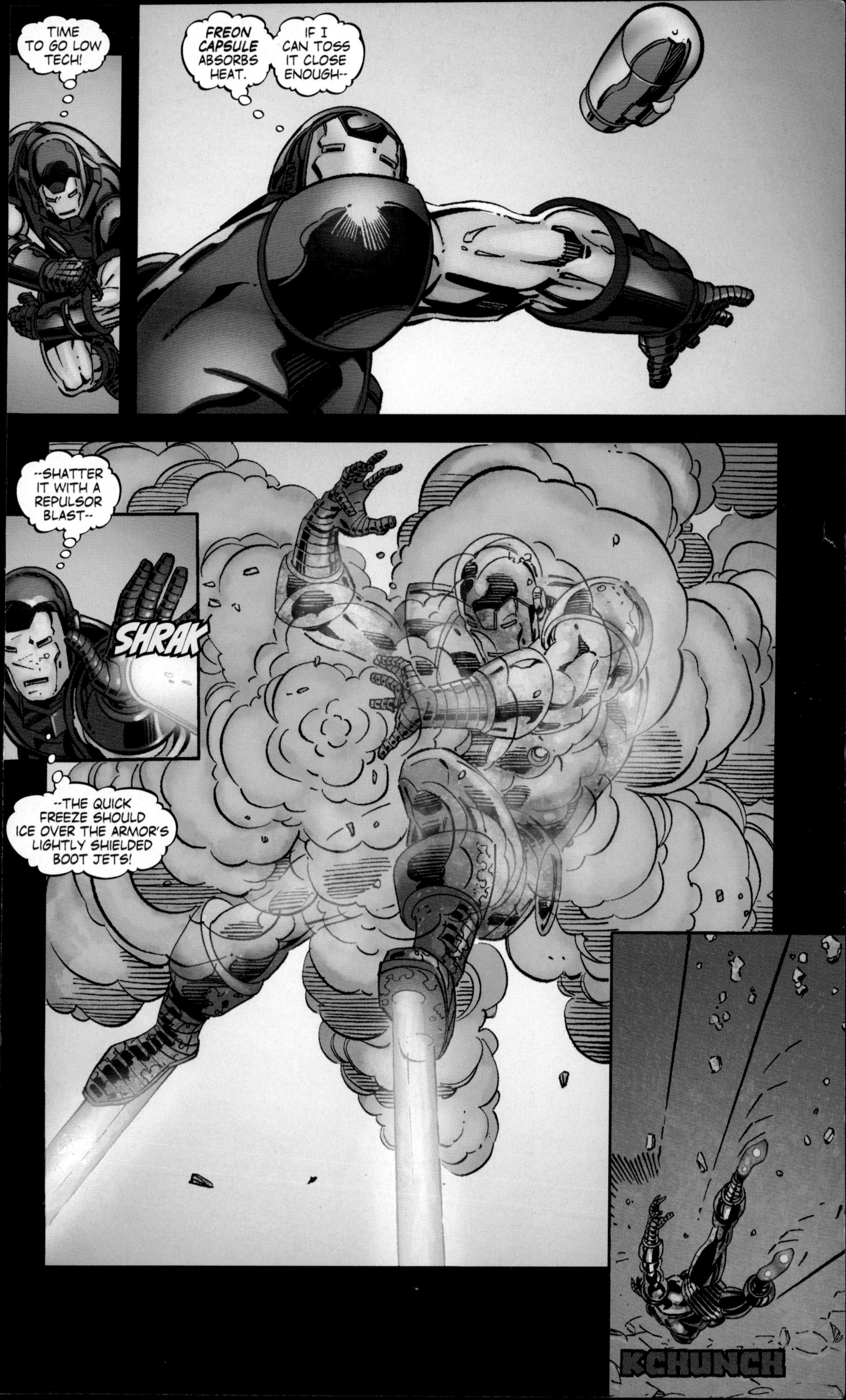
TIME TO GO LOW TECH!
FREON CAPSULE ABSORBS HEAT.
IF I CAN TOSS IT CLOSE ENOUGH--
--SHATTER IT WITH A REPULSOR BLAST--
SHRAK
--THE QUICK FREEZE SHOULD ICE OVER THE ARMOR'S LIGHTLY SHIELDED BOOT JETS!
KCHUNCH

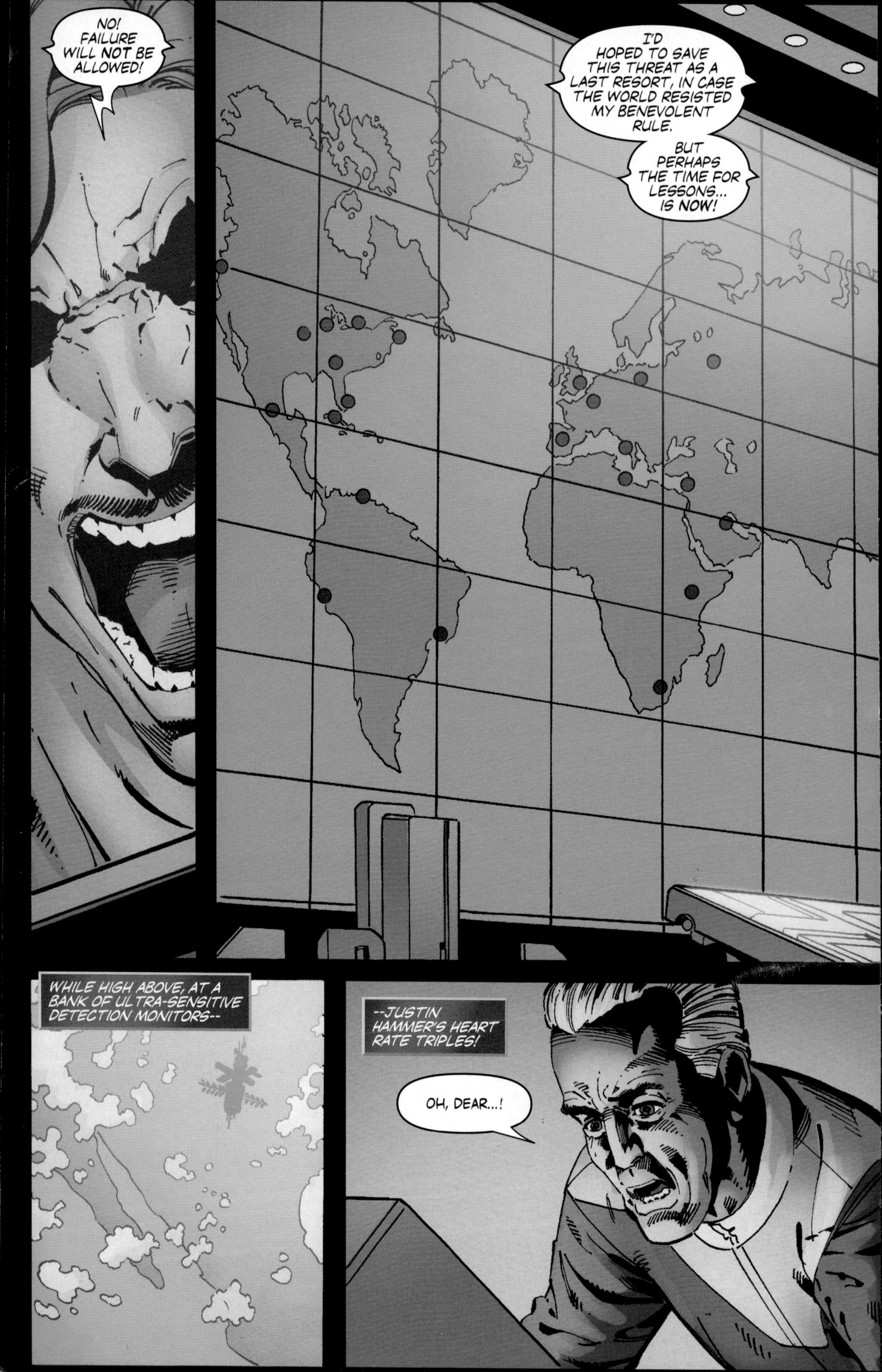
NO! FAILURE WILL NOT BE ALLOWED!
I'D HOPED TO SAVE THIS THREAT AS A LAST RESORT, IN CASE THE WORLD RESISTED MY BENEVOLENT RULE.
BUT PERHAPS THE TIME FOR LESSONS... IS NOW!
WHILE HIGH ABOVE, AT A BANK OF ULTRA-SENSITIVE DETECTION MONITORS--
--JUSTIN HAMMER'S HEART RATE TRIPLES!
OH, DEAR...!

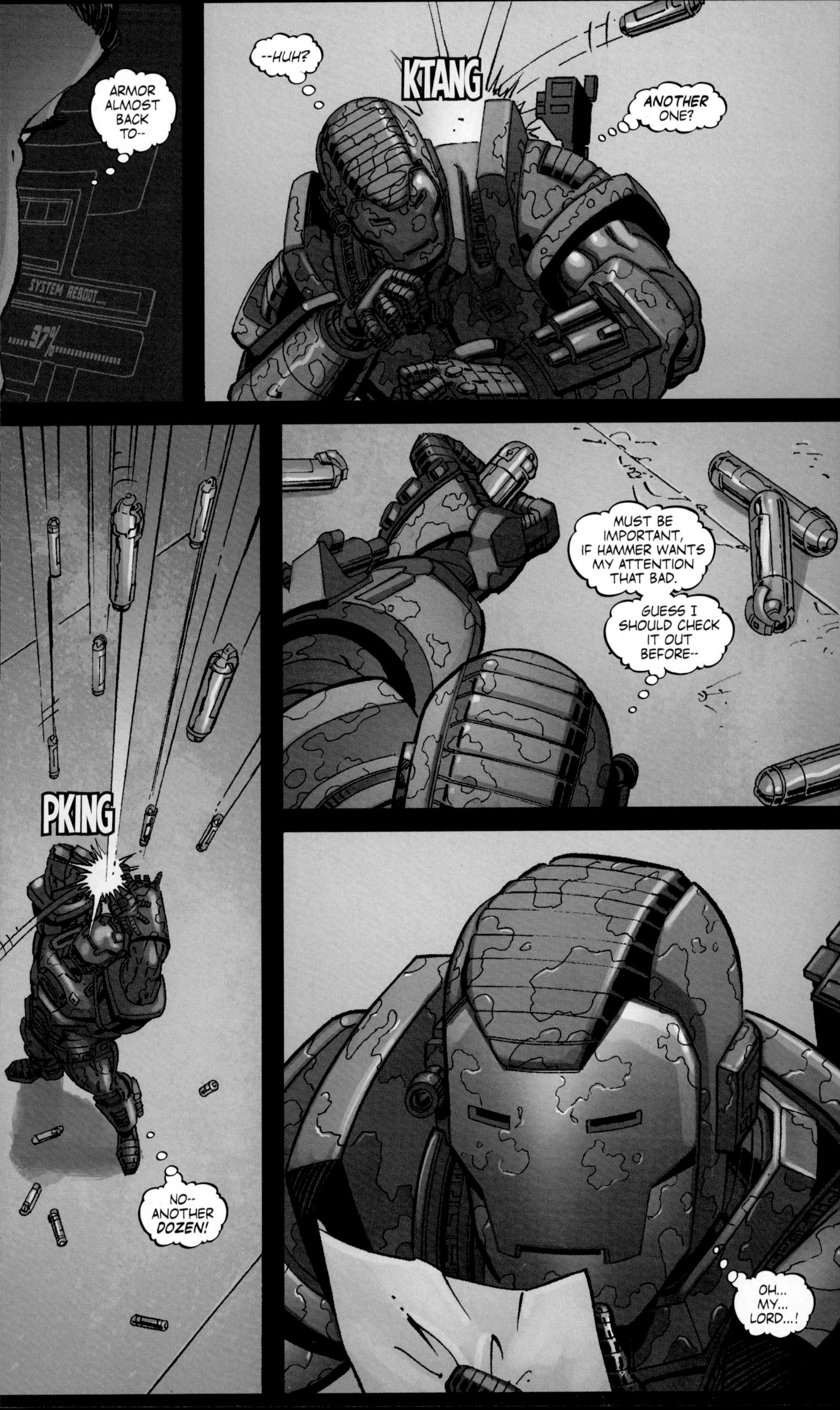
ARMOR ALMOST BACK TO--
SYSTEM REBOOT...
97%
--HUH?
KTANG
ANOTHER ONE?
PKING
NO-- ANOTHER DOZEN!
MUST BE IMPORTANT, IF HAMMER WANTS MY ATTENTION THAT BAD.
GUESS I SHOULD CHECK IT OUT BEFORE--
OH... MY... LORD...!

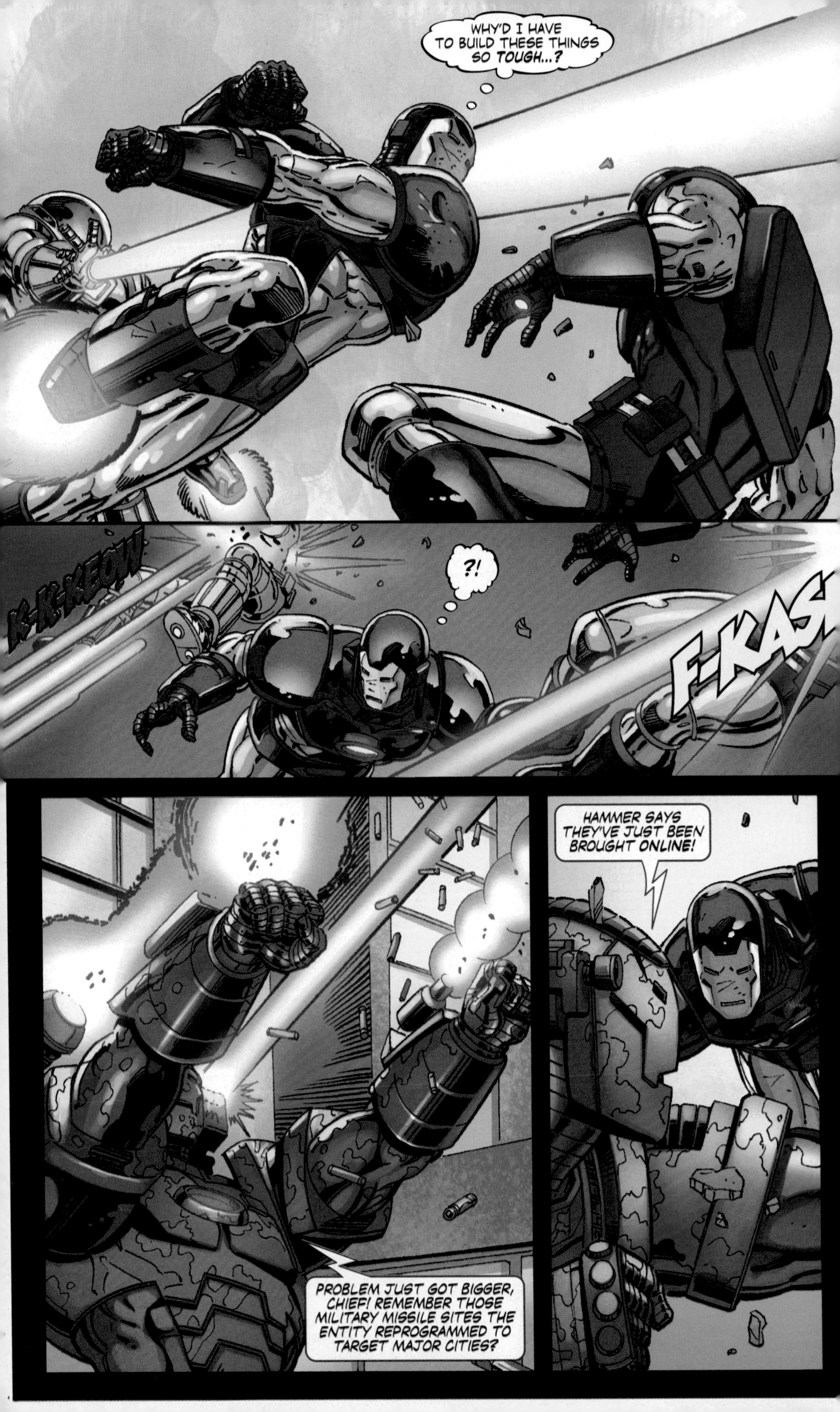
WHY'D I HAVE TO BUILD THESE THINGS SO TOUGH...?
K-K-KEOW
?!
F-KAS
PROBLEM JUST GOT BIGGER, CHIEF! REMEMBER THOSE MILITARY MISSILE SITES THE ENTITY REPROGRAMMED TO TARGET MAJOR CITIES?
HAMMER SAYS THEY'VE JUST BEEN BROUGHT ONLINE!

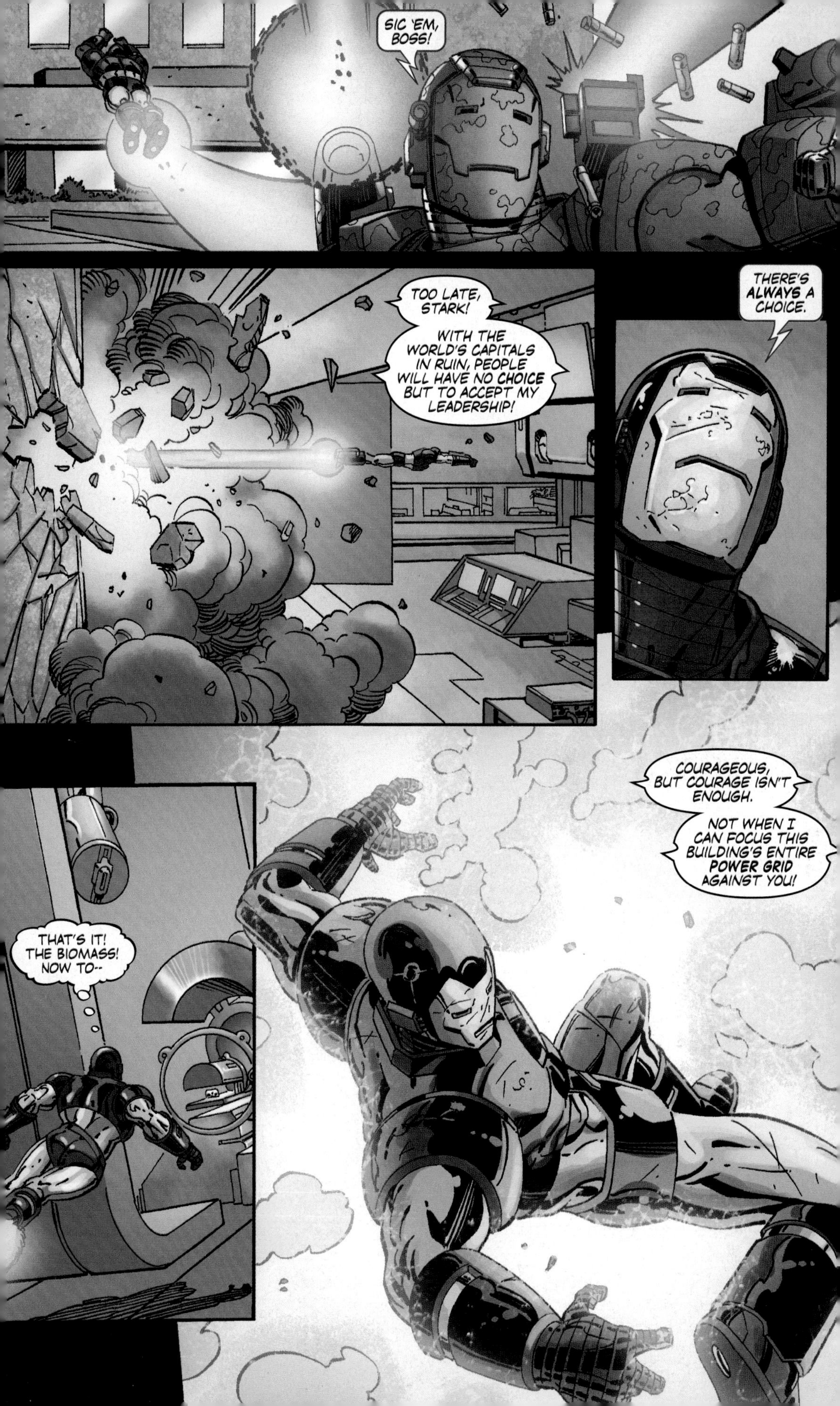
SIC 'EM, BOSS!
TOO LATE, STARK!
WITH THE WORLD'S CAPITALS IN RUIN, PEOPLE WILL HAVE NO CHOICE BUT TO ACCEPT MY LEADERSHIP!
THERE'S ALWAYS A CHOICE.
COURAGEOUS, BUT COURAGE ISN'T ENOUGH.
NOT WHEN I CAN FOCUS THIS BUILDING'S ENTIRE POWER GRID AGAINST YOU!
THAT'S IT! THE BIOMASS! NOW TO--

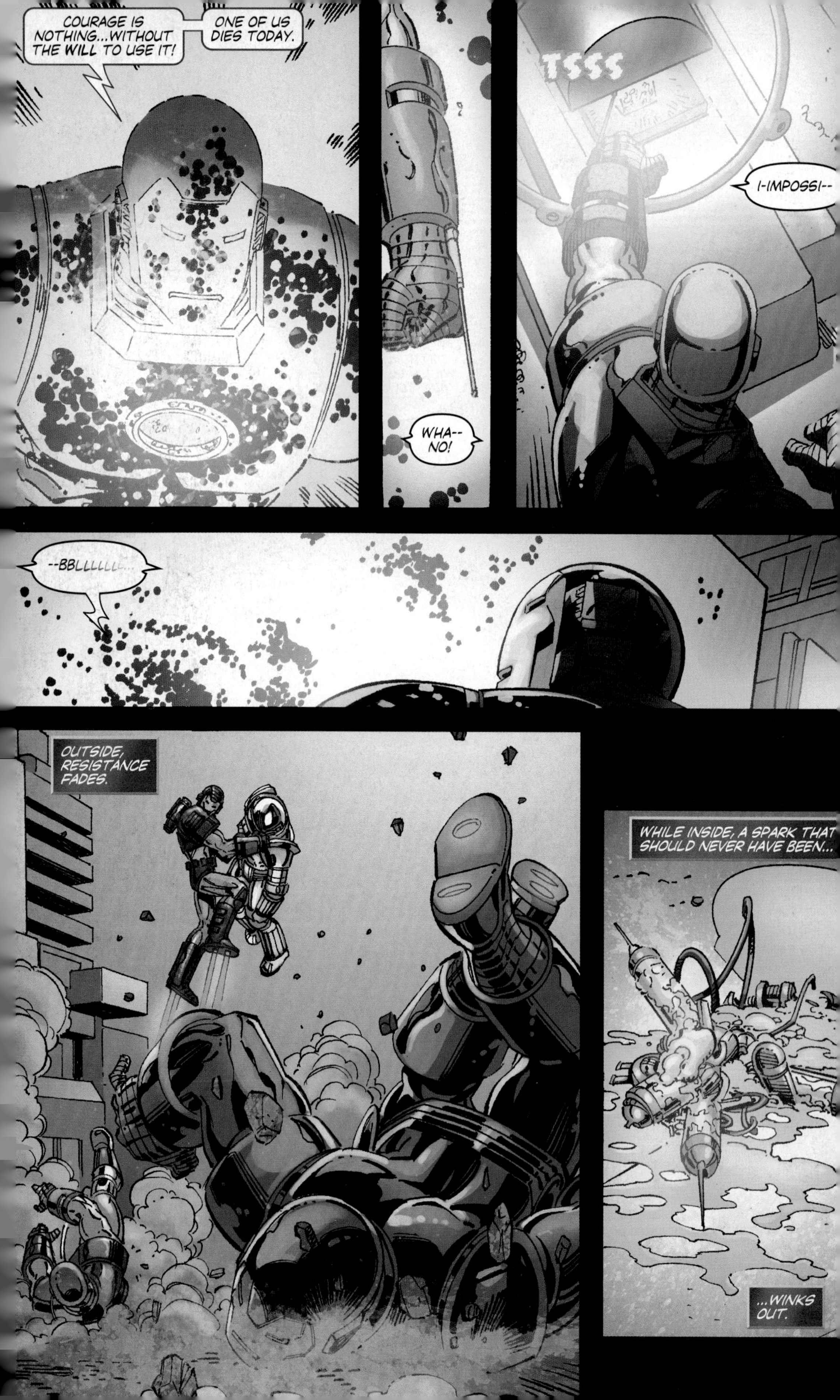
COURAGE IS NOTHING...WITHOUT THE WILL TO USE IT!
ONE OF US DIES TODAY.
WHA-- NO!
TSSS
I-IMPOSSI--
--BBLLLLLLL...
OUTSIDE, RESISTANCE FADES.
WHILE INSIDE, A SPARK THAT SHOULD NEVER HAVE BEEN...
...WINKS OUT.

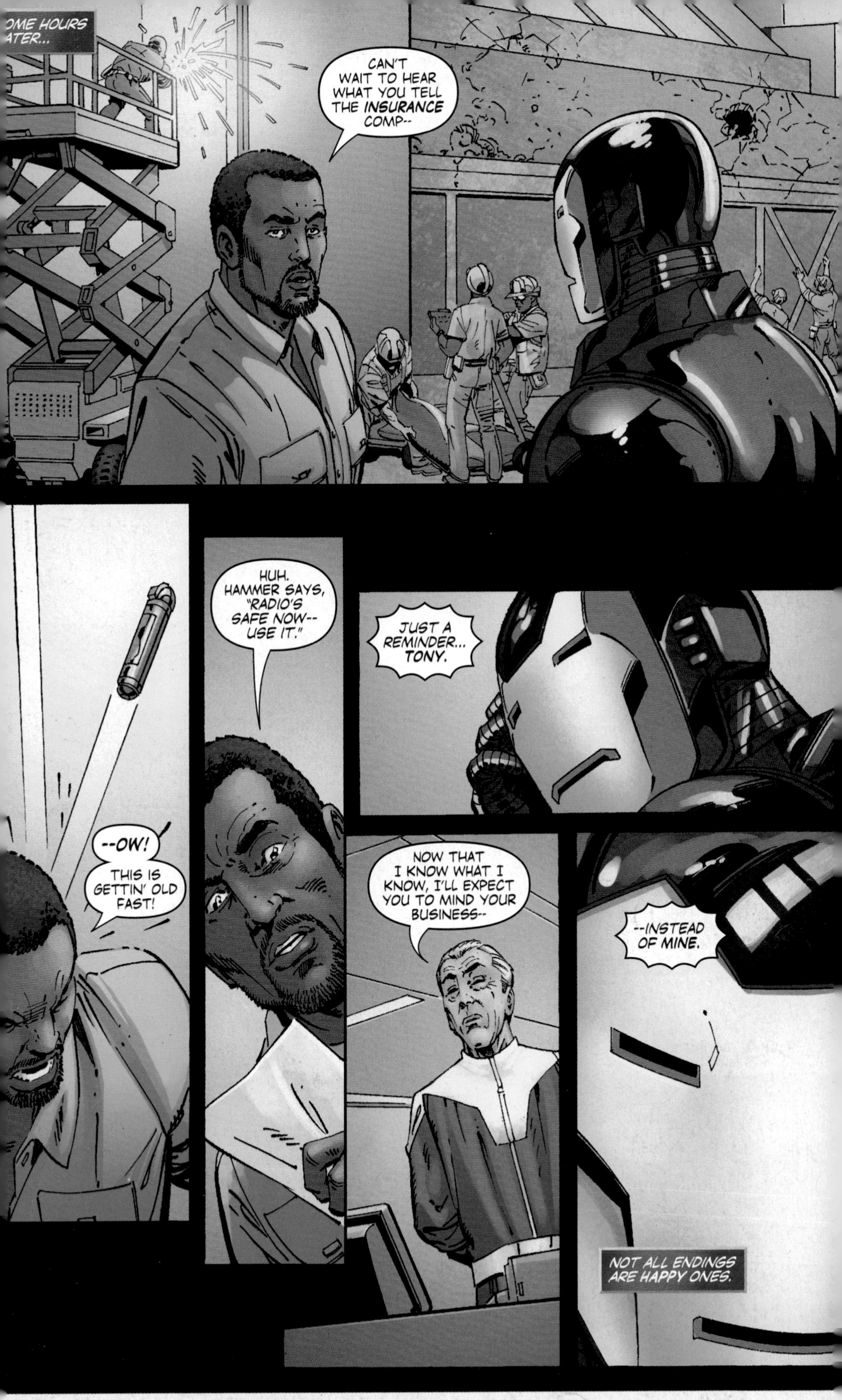
OME HOURS
ATER...
CAN'T WAIT TO HEAR WHAT YOU TELL THE INSURANCE COMP--
--OW!
THIS IS GETTIN' OLD FAST!
HUH. HAMMER SAYS, "RADIO'S SAFE NOW-- USE IT."
JUST A REMINDER... TONY.
NOW THAT I KNOW WHAT I KNOW, I'LL EXPECT YOU TO MIND YOUR BUSINESS--
--INSTEAD OF MINE.
NOT ALL ENDINGS ARE HAPPY ONES.

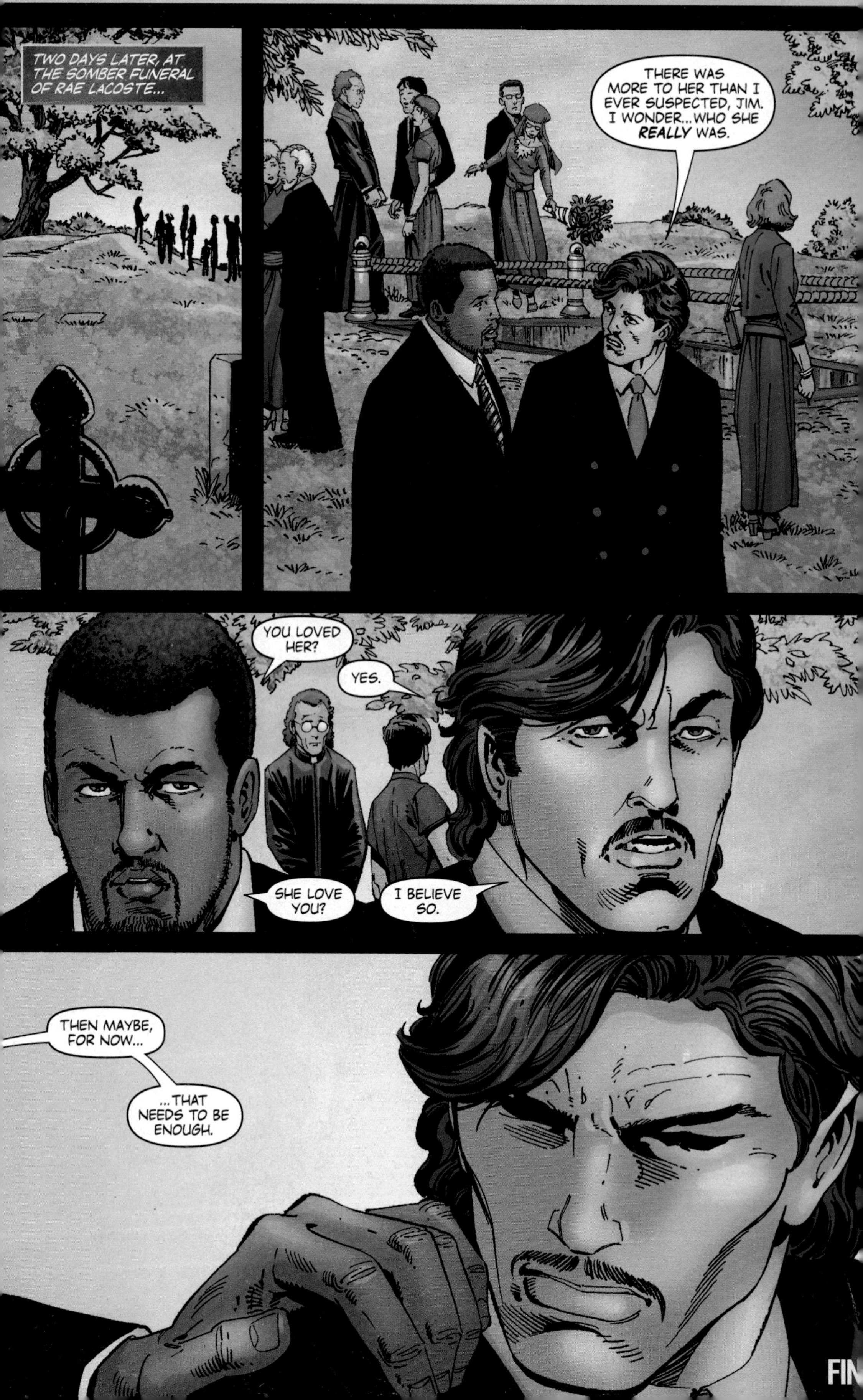
TWO DAYS LATER, AT THE SOMBER FUNERAL OF RAE LACOSTE...
THERE WAS MORE TO HER THAN I EVER SUSPECTED, JIM. I WONDER...WHO SHE REALLY WAS.
YOU LOVED HER?
YES.
SHE LOVE YOU?
I BELIEVE SO.
THEN MAYBE, FOR NOW...
...THAT NEEDS TO BE ENOUGH.
FIN